T0083531

Tereza Topolovská

The Country House Revisited
Variations on a Theme
from Forster to Hollinghurst

KAROLINUM PRESS
PRAGUE, 2017

KAROLINUM PRESS
Karolinum Press is a publishing department of Charles University
Ovocný trh 560/5, 116 36 Prague 1, Czech Republic
www.karolinum.cz
© Karolinum Press, 2017
© Tereza Topolovská, 2017
Layout by Jan Šerých
Set and printed in the Czech Republic by Karolinum Press
First edition

A catalogue record for this book is available from the National Library of the Czech
Republic.

ISBN 978-80-246-3672-6
ISBN 978-80-246-3696-2 (pdf)

The original manuscript was reviewed by Associate Professor Ladislav Nagy
(University of South Bohemia, České Budějovice) and Professor Milada Franková
(Masaryk University, Brno).

Contents

In memory of Anna Grmelová

Cue-Titles

HE   Forster, Edward Morgan. *Howards End*. 1910. With an Introduction and Notes by David Lodge, London: Penguin Books, 2000.

LS   Waters, Sarah. *The Little Stranger*. 2009. London: Virago Press, 2010.

SC   Hollinghurst, Alan. *The Stranger's Child*. London: Picador, 2011.

TS   Murdoch, Iris. *The Sea, The Sea*. 1978. With an Introduction by John Burnside, London: Vintage, 1999.

UG   Jones, Sadie. *The Uninvited Guests*. 2012. London: Vintage, 2013.

1. Introduction: The Country House Revisited

And suddenly a new and secret landscape opened before us.
(Waugh, *Brideshead Revisited*, 39)

More than the work of the great architects, I loved buildings that grew silently with the centuries, catching and keeping the best of each generation, while time curbed the artist's pride and the Philistine's vulgarity, and repaired the clumsiness of the dull workman. In such buildings England abounded, and in the last decade of their grandeur, Englishmen seemed for the first time to become conscious of what before was taken for granted, and to salute their achievements at the moment of their extinction.
(Waugh, *Brideshead Revisited*, 260–1)

The standing of the house as a literary symbol, setting, motif and subject reflects its vital role in human life. The focal point of this monograph is literary renditions of a typical English variant of this phenomenon, the country house, in twentieth and twenty-first century fiction. Both its contemporary standing and previous development are studied in the wider historical, cultural, philosophical and literary contexts. The diversity of the literary portrayals, which feature stately homes as well smaller, less ostentatious forms such as ancient converted farms, reflects the resonance of the country house in English culture. Whereas the opening of this work traces various theoretical approaches to the house in general, be it through architecture, philosophy, spatial poetics, history or literature, the following sections evolve exclusively around the country house. First, it is interpreted from the perspective of attempts at authentic dwelling in the countryside performed in two different novels, namely E. M. Forster's *Howards End* (1910) and Iris Murdoch's *The Sea, The Sea* (1978). Although these works herald current, post-millennial ecological anxieties, it is the following part of the book that revolves around contemporary variations on the theme, such as Sarah Waters' *The Little Stranger* (2009), Alan Hollinghurst's *The Stranger's Child* (2011), and Sadie Jones's *Uninvited Guests* (2012), stressing predominantly the various types of decline and transformation of the country house as well as their firm, intertextual ties with their literary predecessors.

A number of publications and monographs concerning various aspects of country houses, predominantly their cultural, historical or artistic significance, is published every year. Nevertheless, works dealing specifically with country house fiction and the relationship between the country house and English literature are relatively scarce. No systematic theoretical study has been published since Malcom Kelsall's 1993 contribution, *The Great Good Place: The Country House and English Literature*. However, both the country house and country house fiction have been discussed by prominent authors, such as Raymond Williams in his seminal work on the conception of rural and urban existence within the English tradition, *The Country and the City* (1973). There he marked the country house as an exclusive, temporary answer to the conundrum of human existence, the choice which needs to be made between "necessary materialism and necessary humanity" (Williams, 293–4). This dilemma tends to materialise in many ways: as the difference between the working week and the weekend, between work and leisure, or between the city and the technological processes associated with it and the countryside and its natural way of life. Despite the fact that some country houses originally were purely functional regional, feudal centres, the majority of them have offered a solution to the existential struggle between isolation and society, nature and technology, or, last but certainly not least, the country and the city. This conception elucidates the massive popularity of these places amongst the aristocracy and, later, nineteenth-century capitalists who either bought the residences from the impoverished gentry or built their own versions of stately homes.

Moreover, this type of settlement partly echoes Williams's insistence on the necessity of perceiving the country and the city as complementary parts, whose permanent division inflicted a wide range of negative effects on both of them. Hence, the country house, merging the advantages of both rural and urban existence, has inspired a number of imitations: from country cottages and semi-detached or detached suburban villas inspired by the aestheticism of the great country houses, to the emergence of Metroland, built on the premise of mobility and allowing an easy fusion of idealised countryside and fast-paced city centres. Despite

Williams's rather reductive description of the country house as a settlement attempting to solve the existential struggle, in all its possible permutations the country house stands out as a unique phenomenon, which has inspired, besides a wealth of literary creation, a considerable amount of all kinds of artistic endeavours over the centuries, ranging from architecture and interior and landscape design, to painting and sculpture.

This monograph delineates the manifold results of the transformation of the conception of the country house and its twentieth and twenty-first literary representation, country house fiction. At the beginning of the twentieth century, the idealised, mythical form, which symbolised orderly relations between the aristocracy and their tenants, was replaced by an understanding of the country house that highlights its abstract meaning as the embodiment of history as well as its role in the formation of national identity. Nevertheless, the contemporary stately home is a symbol under siege, struggling to find a place in the modern world, no longer satisfied with its publicly ascribed role as pure relic from the past or imitation of a socially and economically superior lifestyle.

In the wider social context of contemporary architectural theory introduced in the first chapter, the country house is primarily understood as a house, with all the twentieth-century implications of its necessity in human life, its integrating, centring properties, and its complex historical and cultural dimensions, as well as its treatment and position within contemporary architectural theory and practice. Seen from this perspective, the country house reflects the universal artistic and practical effort to move from residing to dwelling, understood as "existing in a human manner" (Heidegger, *Poetry*, 154) and therefore serves as a perfect vehicle for the analysis and interpretation of the various possible forms such an effort might take. This endeavour has inspired numerous literary portrayals but it first required the redefinition of the phenomenon of the country house. No longer restricted to stately homes and manor houses, the country house has embraced all kinds of countryside dwellings ranging from old, converted farms and cottages to sea-side villas. The country house has become the subject of detailed architectural scrutiny, practically, theoretically, popularly and literarily. In fiction, the houses are renovated, redecorated and sometimes even built, and the amount of suspicion towards modernist tendencies may only be explained with reference to the surviving vestiges of the old country house ideology which promoted orderly, hierarchical relations between the house and its surroundings, the house and its tenants, and particularly the tenants and their master. Any sign of abandonment of the remnants of this traditional approach is seen as potentially disruptive and unorderly, or even ungodly; there is no place for novelties which would mean a discontinuity with the past and the best of its heritage. Some of the descriptions of country houses, e.g. that one which McEwan presents in *Atonement*, even emphasise the ugliness of the Victorian houses in question, as if to echo the popular interpretation of their aesthetic as fraudulent and vulgar and to accentuate their "newness" as compared to the ancient, historical sites they often replaced. On the contrary, other works, such as Waugh's *A Handful of Dust* (1934) or Hollinghurst's *The Stranger's Child* reflect the effort of some theoreticians and historians to refute such a stance and an appreciation of Victorian architecture is consequently presented as implying emotionality and sensitivity, or even traditionalism, not necessarily bad taste.

The traditional, historical form of literary creation connected with the country house, the country house poem of the seventeenth and eighteenth centuries, with its tendency to idealise and mythicise the relationship between the house, its master and the tenants, has influenced modern country house fiction in a number of ways. For example, there is an inclination to situate the plot in summer, a typically pastoral setting partly reviving the idyll, with its eternal days of summer, or "days of peculiar splendour" (Waugh, *Brideshead Revisited*, 23) to quote Evelyn Waugh, a vocal admirer of these places. The guests tend to abound in country house fiction and this may also be seen as an echo of the country house poem in which guests and visitors come to the house as if to highlight its welcoming, gracious character. What is more, both types of literary portrayals are frequently written from the perspective of a guest and the outsider perspective highlights the exclusivity of the experience of living comfortably in the countryside. The perception of guests, who know that the duration of their stay is restricted, both intensifies the experience and points to the fact that not many people are entitled to such a privilege for a longer period of time. Nevertheless, this alien observer is, notwithstanding their unbecoming origin, often a central protagonist of the plot, mirroring the historical position of a poet guest visiting his patron.

The twentieth and twenty-first century depiction of the country house in fiction reflects shifts of social, cultural and economic paradigms. Great country houses of the past had been tied to the aristocracy, which, especially from the period after the end of the Second World War until the 1970s, lost most of its political and economic power and therefore a great deal of public hostility. No longer the subject of possible public criticism and resentment of the nature of their living arrangements, the aristocracy began to systematically exploit its possessions – many houses were sold, transformed, or opened to the public. Seeking new employment for spaces which, stripped of their original significance and function, became suddenly unsustainable and thus could only survive through a transformation into public spectacle: "Growing numbers of owners declared 'open house' and sought to profit from a gentle resurgence of popular interest in history of all kinds" (Mandler, 5).

Thus, the aristocracy's estates acquired a new role in society and became emblems of a new social and economic order, no longer serving only as idealised representations of their owners and their social class. The nature and the relative standing of country houses within English culture have transposed them into the domain of public interest. Country houses are often imagined as symbolising the country values of "old England" (Lucas, 71), which is boosted further by the booming success of various TV series such as ITV's well-known adaptation of Evelyn Waugh's *Brideshead Revisited* or the recent sweeping success of the idealising period drama, *Downton Abbey*.[1] The former was broadcast for the first time in the gloomy years of economic recession in the 1980s and the latter, with its first episode airing in the autumn of 2010, once again coincided with the aftermath of an economic crisis. There is a multitude of possible explanations for their immense popularity. The first, most obvious one might be that they present a retreat from depressing reality. However, these pretty pictures of an orderly social hierarchy might also serve is as an ideological glamorising of subservience.

In general, country houses in the original sense of "stately home" have not ceased to fascinate the public and guarantee the existence of the National Trust.[2] This idealised perception may elucidate the enormous popularity of stately homes both as sights and as subjects of various artistic renditions, ranging from a multitude of fictional, as well as non-fictional accounts of its existence to TV series. Non-fiction on the subject tends to take a historiographic approach and present life in country

---

1   Richard Vine laments the end of *Downton Abbey* and the gaping hole it left in the Sunday schedule in his article "Downton Abbey Review: The Glorious Fantasy of Britain Comes to an End" published in *The Guardian* on 26 December 2015. Besides praising the outstanding performances of some of the actors, he draws attention to the nature of the prevailing social contentment of the protagonists, who perform their duties without ever questioning their positions in the hierarchy.

2   In order to further promote local tourism in England, the year 2016 was named the "Year of the English Garden". Promoted by the *Visit England* website, it features guided visits of famous gardens on the occasion of the 300-year anniversary of Capability Brown, a famous garden and landscape designer, known as "the Shakespeare of the gardening world".

houses in all its complexity and variety. Individual places are approached from the point of view of their architectural properties, daily routines, the collection, analysis and classification of thousands of letters produced by their inhabitants and ubiquitous guests, poems and artworks, all of which map out the range of transformations they underwent, amplifying the grandeur of their artistic inventories, and pointing to the unknown or the dark sides of their history or to the personal histories of their owners.

The existence of the country house has been logically conditioned by its situation in the countryside. Literary production that authentically represents the countryside and does not limit it to the position of an inspiring backdrop, was rehabilitated by Raymond Williams's *The Country and the City*. He was nevertheless less optimistic as far as the viability of country house fiction was concerned. He described the middle-class detective story as the only possible and plausible future for the country house novel as these places tend to gather together a heterogeneous group, as does the plot of a typical detective story. The twentieth-century country house in fiction became a backdrop, an interchangeable setting for the complicated relations of its temporary inhabitants, with the focus shifting from the house and its symbolism to the untying of the knot of entangled relations. According to Williams, this literary development led to a reduction of the country house's importance and vitality, since it only provided a suitable space for events which had been prepared elsewhere and which would be resolved elsewhere: "It is not a sad end; it is a fitting end. The essential features were always there, and much of the history that changed them came out of them, in their original and continuing domination and alienation" (Williams, 250).[3] Its role, according to Williams, was reduced, both in reality and in fiction, to a purely instrumental one, which is reflected in its transition into an indifferent setting for a public school, museum, hotel, or secret police headquarters. At the same time, their status as symbols of power or success was maintained, with the real source of their funding situated conveniently elsewhere.

Another aspect which, from Williams's viewpoint, affected the importance of the future role of country houses was their exclusivity. Not

---

3   This persuasion concerning the concentration of decisive social powers, although only temporary, is echoed by Stevens, the embodiment of the perfect butler and the unreliable narrator of Kazuo Ishiguro's 1989 novel, *The Remains of the Day*: "... although we did not see a great deal of the country in the sense of touring the countryside and visiting picturesque sites, we did actually 'see' more of England than most, placed as we were in houses where the greatest ladies and gentlemen of the land gathered" (Ishiguro, 4).

only is the maintenance of these places economically demanding, but their position in the countryside requires the mobility of their inhabitants. If the countryside is to retain the qualities for which it is valued, it naturally indicates the absence of a larger number of commuters. The peaceful solitude of the countryside was threatened at the beginning of the twentieth century by the ever-expanding sprawl of suburbs, which represented a solution to the universal demand for the beneficial effects of life in the countryside. From the ecological point of view, if life in the countryside is to remain peaceful and harmonious and the natural environment unspoilt, it requires a sparsity of population and is therefore mutually exclusive with it becoming the living arrangement for the masses, which adds to its exclusivity. Romantic communing with nature seems to be destined to remain highly selective in terms of the intellectual and also economic disposition of those who embrace it. All these factors are projected with growing urgency into fiction, where they provide fertile soil for the depiction, questioning, re-valuation and re-definition of the various nuances of the pastoral of the country house, the delineation of which became, particularly in the post-war period, an increasingly demanding and delicate task. Post-war social and political changes, which gradually severed the ties binding the country house to its culture-specific and class-restricted reading as an emblem of national identity, opened it to a varied, more complex and consequently multi-layered interpretation and enabled its employment as a more universal, versatile metaphor of dwelling. Therefore, the precarious nature of stately homes and the considerable widening of the definition of the country house did not lead to the ultimate decline anticipated by Williams, it actually meant that country house fiction acquired a whole new dimension, spanning a range of unexplored topics. The country house ceased to be the embodiment of an ideal, and its definition broadened considerably to include many different types of permanent or temporary dwellings as well as a variety of approaches to the phenomenon, considerably expanding the spectrum of works suitable for analysis.

Accordingly, the chapter on E. M. Forster's novel, *Howards End*, and Iris Murdoch's novel, *The Sea, The Sea*, stresses the parallel focus on alternative, diminutive versions of the country house and it also provides an estimate of the actual degree of the physical, cultural and social change heralded by the alteration of the portrayal of the country house in fiction. As living in a country house typically presupposes living in the countryside, it offers the opportunity to challenge the stereotypical qualities typically associated with the rural mode of living, such as automatic communion with nature and authenticity of existence. At the same time, it elaborates on the theme of the growing subtlety involved in the exploitation of one class by another, which does not necessarily mean the strengthening of a traditional stratification.

The next part follows Alan Hollinghurst's subversive pastiche, *The Stranger's Child*, as it accentuates the spatial and textual affinities between its literary forerunners, such as E. M. Forster or Evelyn Waugh, and contemporary examples of country house fiction of the beginning of the twenty-first century, including Sarah Waters' *The Little Stranger*, or Sadie Jones's *Uninvited Guests* (2012), revisiting its original seat, the stately home. Their thematic intersection is the crumbling microcosm of the house, whose attempts at dignified survival or noble decline they explore and question. Its imminent material decline and gradual slide into the impersonal spaces of hotel or school institution provide both physical metaphors of the historic state of the country house and an acutely decadent poetics of decline. The painfully striking physical distortion of the house, which stands in sharp contrast to the aspirations of its builders and owners, evokes ruminations upon the nature of time and its passing. With events revolving around the house as a dying star at the centre of the novel, alternately threatening implosion, imprisoning the tenants gravitating towards the centre, or explosion, scattering them eternally into the great unknown, leaving a treacherous void behind, the struggle to maintain a fragile equilibrium acquires the existential dimension of the perpetual human fight for authentic existence.

2. (Country) House since 1900

2.1 Building, Writing, Thinking

Architecture will no longer be the social, the collective, the dominant art. The great poem, the great building, the great work of mankind will no longer be built, it will be printed.
(Victor Hugo, qtd. in *Unpacking my Library: Architects and Their Books*)

The role houses assume in literature is patterned on their role in the lives of humans. From the point of view of human existence, a house embodies an archetype. Its vitality is projected into the depth and width of the spectrum of its influences. The study of the house stipulates the need for an interdisciplinary approach in order to embrace its complex role in human life. Despite the number of possible perspectives of study this phenomenon enables, three have been determined as pivotal: architectural, philosophical and, naturally, literary. The twentieth century has acknowledged and accentuated the interconnectedness of these three disciplines, especially owing to the works of Martin Heidegger and Gaston Bachelard. The emphasis which philosophy, architecture and literature put on the dependence and mutual conditioning of houses and humans reflect the essentiality of this connection. The current practice can be seen as further developing their gradual merging. Contemporary architecture is preoccupied with a semantic approach to buildings, which are read and interpreted as signs. The growing level of abstraction and involvement of semantics in architecture imply its linguistic turn. At the same time, the frequency of employment of building terms in literature indicates its architectural turn.

The literary perspective generally mirrors respect for houses and their role in human life. Given its flexibility, it endows the fictional houses with a spectacular array of qualities and interpretations. Despite their variety, some of the properties might be designated as predominant. First and foremost quality of the house, given its place and importance in human life, is the ability to integrate. Gaston Bachelard, a French philosopher and literary critic, the author of the seminal study of intimate spaces as they are reflected in and by literature, *The Poetics of Space* (1958), highlights the integrating properties of a house: "in the life of a man, the house thrusts aside contingencies, its councils of continuity are unceasing. Without it, man would be a dispersed being" (Bachelard, 7). Apart from that, the house shelters and, to a certain extent, even conditions existence, producing a body of images which provide human life with the notion of stability, as it is a "human being's first world" (Bachelard, 7).

Bachelard's emphasis on the binding properties of the house, of the vital importance of the spaces which allow for daydreaming, such as nooks or corners, and his insistence on the metaphysical dimension of a house, which represents a microcosm of the world, is echoed in several essential texts by the German philosopher, Martin Heidegger. He, via the example of the Black Forrest Farm, introduced another principal function of houses as having the ability to preserve "the fourfold, to save the earth, to receive the sky, to await divinities, to escort mortals – this fourfold preserving is the simple nature, the "presencing", of dwelling. In this way, then, do genuine buildings give form to dwelling in its presence and the house this presence" (Heidegger, *Poetry*, 156). It is the house which allows for dwelling, both in the practical and existential sense. This fundamental role of the house in the lives of humans is in both cases tightly connected with literary production. From Bachelard's perspective, houses and their recollection allow for daydreaming. Heidegger insists on the poetic nature of measure-taking, building and dwelling, since: "[p]oetry is what first brings man onto the earth, making him belong to it, and thus brings him into dwelling" (Heidegger, *Poetry*, 216). Both approaches resonate with highly distinctive yet similar themes. Houses, or buildings, are seen as distinctive "letting dwells", conditioning and conditioned by human existence: "A house without people has no dimensions. An enclosed space, a box" (Mawer, *Glass Room*, 308); "A house that has been experienced is not an inert box. Inhabited space transcends geometrical space" (Bachelard, 47). The involvement of humans in all the processes and the absolute dependence of houses on their treatment and perception by humans are specified by highly influential and distinctive theoretical perspectives which strengthen the ties between the abstract, the poetic and the material, and determine the direction of contemporary architectural thinking.

As Adam Sharr points out in his interpretation of Heidegger's texts from an architectural point of view, few philosophers have spoken or written exclusively for an audience of architects. In Heidegger's case, the most marked occasion was the lecture "Building, Dwelling, Thinking" he gave on the occasion of *Darmstädter Gespräch*, a conference focused on the theme of "Man and Space," which was held in Darmstadt in August 1951. Besides the text of the lecture, there are others, which he wrote on the subject and which further accentuate its meaning, the 1950 essay "The Thing" and 1951 "... Poetically, Man dwells..." They are essential both from the perspective of the interpretation of Heidegger's conception of architecture and their influence on contemporary architectural theory and practice.[4] Sharr considers these texts, although they are the least quoted ones amongst philosophers, to be the most architectural of his writings, stressing the importance of immediate experience. With translations into a number of languages and continual reissues, these works have influenced, if not shaped, much of the architectural theory and practice in the second half of the twentieth century. At this point, however, Sharr stresses the degree of controversy surrounding the philosopher. Heidegger was a member of the Nazi party and his naming as a rector of Freiburg University in 1933 coincided with the rise of the fascists to power. Despite his resignation from that post the following year, his romanticising approach to the rural and his resolute rejection of technology before, during and after Nazism, made him and his thoughts "skat[e] dangerously close to fascist rhetoric of 'blood and soil'" (Sharr, *Heidegger for Architects*, 2). Nevertheless, Heidegger's influence on Western architecture remains an irrefutable fact. Sharr metaphorically compares the impact to an infection. The effect of a mild infection might be irritation, with the possibility of both positive and negative outcomes. Generations of architects and architectural thinkers, such as Steven Holl, Juhani Pallasmaa, Peter Zumthor, Alvar Aalto, or Dalibor Vesely, Rowan Moore and Karsten Harries, have projected Heidegger's ideas in their works, more or less prominently. Directly or indirectly, they have been forced to ponder human experience and environment from a different, humanist and immediate perspective. These echoes might be considered beneficial. However, the radical, unconditional application of his conception is analogous to a serious infection with its disastrous results. Both Heidegger's converts and his critics insist on the importance of

---

4   Sharr claims that while "The Origin of the Work of Art" (1935), *Being and Time* (1927) and "Art and Space" (1971) elaborate architectural thought more or less prominently, they do not equal the intensity and forthrightness of the three texts from the fifties.

considering context for the correct interpretation of his works. In particular, claims which state that his theories the only legitimate model of the world and deny the possibility of existence of others, should be ultimately resisted. Furthermore, the notion of the soil of place dangerously borders on illiberal politics, with the possibility of racism. According to Sharr, "[w]here Heidegger's romantic provincialism is absorbed uncritically, it can allow right-wing ideologies to flourish. Redneck Heideggerian infections must be challenged" (Sharr, *Heidegger for Architects*, 114).

The context of Heidegger's thoughts concerning architecture elucidates both their popularity and persistence and prevents their reduction into a set of primitive, treacherous dicta. At the time of their formulation, post-war Europe relied with growing urgency on the technocratic outcomes of technological progress and economic conceptions. Heidegger refuted these dehumanising tendencies by emphasising the immediate human experience and the universal vitality of human perception. Humans tend to model their perception of the world, and their emotional response to it, according to their first experience of inhabitation. According to Heidegger, it is only later, that the experience is classified and quantified according to the rationalist concepts of economics and technology. The essential role of the architect in the development of human experience relies on designing spaces which adequately fill their important part in this process. Philosophy, according to Heidegger, should acknowledge the role of a building in the developmental process of humans. A building is therefore capable to reveal how its builders and/or its inhabitants conceived the space and measured their place in the world. Building could be understood as reflecting the ethos of both builder and dweller. Architecture, in its purest and most beneficial form, could be viewed as helping to navigate people, or pointing them directly, towards their centre in the world. Heidegger noticed the ability of traditional, historical buildings to provide people with places from which they may question and grow. He therefore stressed the necessity of lessening the influence of technology on building and returning to its fundamental conception.

The major task of an architect, a builder, and subsequently an inhabitant is to elevate the activities above mere construction and residing. His mission, similarly to a philosopher's, is to reintegrate building with dwelling. This tendency equalised the status of vernacular architecture with aestheticized, expert, official architecture and insisted that the produced space harmonize with the nature of its inhabitation and its typical manifestations. Architecture has thus been taken from the pedestal of untouchable perfection and become more than a formalist quest for perfection of proportions, colours and materials. Instead it is more identified with the everyday activities performed in the spaces. A building, as Heidegger illustrates with the example of a bridge, whose usage and function dictate its aestheticism and its position of human life, "shouldn't be understood just as an object to be admired or the product of a construction management process. Rather, it is primarily part of an ongoing human experience of building and dwelling" (Sharr, *Heidegger for Architects*, 46). Heidegger's insistence on the morality of architecture and the vital importance of human presence, experience, perception and inhabitation recur in different variations and decisively shape contemporary architectural practice. Sharr adds mysticism, nostalgia and the tendency to stress the limits of science and technology as further qualities of Heideggerian rhetoric. This, consequently, celebrates provincials, who are reductively glorified as romantic incarnations of individuals who are able to commune with nature, past, their ancestors as well as being able to interconnect their bodies and minds. The perilous potential of such a frame of mind can be successfully reduced by consistent critical assessment and by interpreting it within the context of its creation.

The mutual conditioning of houses and humans is reflected in numerous contemporary works of architectural theory, which tirelessly elaborate on the ideas of the two great crusaders of the metaphysical character of houses, Heidegger and Bachelard. Karsten Harries is the most influential contemporary theoretician of architecture. He founds his 1997 opus magnum, *The Ethical Function of Architecture*, on the affirmation or redefinition of Heidegger's premises.[5] Harries insists that architecture's major function should not be purely aesthetic, but ethical, stemming from the humanist preoccupation which replaces general disorder and formal chaos. In his work, Harries employs the Biblical metaphor of the Fall of Man, which he infuses with a Promethean reading suggesting its Romantic interpretation and conceives it as a possible optimistic start:

> I would like to suggest that such a leave-taking from God for the sake of a genuinely human community is the foundation of any genuinely human dwelling. It is this leave-taking, this fall, this expulsion into insecurity and uncertainty that alone lets us develop into responsible individuals. Every human being has to repeat it for him – or herself. But human beings

---

5   Harries mainly develops ideas which appeared in "Building, Dwelling, Thinking" and … "Poetically Man Dwells…"

are not self-sufficient: having lost their place in paradise, they have to find their place in a genuinely human order; they have to know and join themselves to one another (Harries, 365).

An ethical conception of architecture therefore presupposes a tight connection between building, dwelling and community. Another influential architectural critic, Rowan Moore, in his study of human emotions and desires projected into buildings, *Why We Built* (2012), labels buildings as perpetually incomplete, "completed only by the lives for which they are setting. From this paradox comes much of the fascination and misunderstanding of architecture" (Moore, 91). Alain De Botton is a practical thinker and a great promoter of the practical implications of philosophy, which makes him an object of constant ridicule from the side of experts and great admiration from the side of the mass reading public. He develops his by far most successful work, *The Architecture of Happiness* (2006), on the premise that: "As we write, so we build: to keep a record of what matters to us" (De Botton, 123). Both Christopher Day and David Holl are practicing architects, the first being the author of *Spirit&Place* (2002), the latter of *Parallax* (2000), who accentuate an ecological approach to building, respecting the natural structures and cycles. Both insist on purely human dimensioning where man is the principal, fundamental measure of architectural works, as far as the size, character, quality and functioning are concerned.

The house is an entity endowed with an undisputable degree of integrating properties in terms of the dynamics of dichotomies it creates, such as the inside and the outside, the upstairs and the downstairs (or "the attic" and "the cellar" in Bachelard's terminology), the masculine and the feminine, the past and the future, the material and thought, the mind and matter, the microcosm and the macrocosm. Yet, its power of integration does not cease there, but extends even to the realm of possible approaches to the phenomenon of the house, both as a physical object and a literary representation. The interdisciplinary nature of studies of the house in literature involves historical, social, cultural, gender, architectural, psychological, and philosophical perspectives, with all these frequently layered, interconnected and multiplied.

Karsten Harries juxtaposes the spatial and temporal properties by claiming that "… just as buildings establish regions, wrestling place from space, so they establish temporal situations, placing the individual in time – but not just in time, but in a communally shared time, in history" (Harries, 264). This ability to integrate social, cultural and technological history within the space of a house inspired another popularising historian of the everyday, Bill Bryson, to dedicate the volume he entitled *At Home: A Short History of Private Life* (2010), which dissected the intimate space of the house he inhabits, an old Church of England rectory situated in Norfolk, to the colourful and enjoyable tracing of the roots of individual spaces and their furnishings. The private and the public, the contemporary and the historical, the artistic and the everyday thus meet, intersect and coexist in a joyful union. Bryson's experiment proves this while providing a vast audience with a pleasantly entertaining reading experience of easily digestible historical data: "Houses are amazingly complex repositories. ... So the history of household life isn't just a history of beds and sofas and kitchen stoves, as I had vaguely supposed it would be, but of scurvy and guano and the Eiffel Tower and bedbugs and body-snatching and just about everything else that has ever happened. Houses aren't refuges from history. They are where history ends up" (Bryson, 22).

The integrative potential of the house extends well beyond the ability to interconnect social and individual history. Its integrative nature of an enormously powerful archetype binds the past, present and future together: "This house, as I see it, is a sort of airy structure that moves about on the breath of time. It really is open to the wind of another time" (Bachelard, 54). What also needs to be acknowledged is the tight connection between language, dwelling and literature, where one phenomenon presupposes the presence and existence of the other. According to Martin Heidegger, "[l]anguage is the house of Being. In its home man dwells. Those who think and those who create with words are the guardians of this home" (Heidegger, "Letter on Humanism", *Basic Writings*, 147). Exactly this type of universality and general applicability, as well as the archetypal nature of the house and its enormous integrating force, which implies, inspires and invites a rich, multi-layered interdisciplinary interpretation, are all factors which have contributed to the transformation of the house, both as a physical presence and as a versatile literary symbol, setting, subject, or motif, into a popular field of scrutiny. As Francesca Saggini and Anna Enrichetta Soccio, the editors of the wide-ranging monograph, *The House of Fiction as the House of Life: Representations of the House from Richardson to Woolf* (2012), claim in the preface, entitled "The Paper Houses of English Literature":

> In more recent years, the interest for the house has grown irresistibly, to the point that in many ways houses seem to be situated at the very core of

the creative, artistic and cultural domains of contemporaneity. Their presence sprawls across the media, from magazines to TV programmes, and across the globe, possibly because as repositories of the human, houses have a long-standing and profound connection not only with human beings but, at a deeper level, with the ways of representing — imagining, ostending, articulating — man's world, across its declinations of gender, class, and race. (Saginni, 2)

A house, a fundamental type of building and architectural archetype, endowed with a powerful, universal symbolic meaning, is often compared and contrasted with the utmost form of human expression – language. Approaches to these two types of man-made structures, one material and the other abstract, vary, with some authors highlighting the difference between the two: "A building is not a sentence, which in principle has the ability to match and express closely. It is not linear, like language. Compared to the fluidity of words, a building is atrociously clumsy, but it can be lived and inhabited as books cannot be" (Moore, 91–2). Nevertheless, contemporary architectural theory and, quite surprisingly, even architectural practice have witnessed a steep rise in abstraction permeating through a field which has been traditionally associated with materiality. This upsurge in abstraction has been facilitated by the penetration of high-tech technologies involving virtual models and calculations into the design process. It also enabled the rise and fame of such architectural conceptions as Poststructuralism and Deconstructivism infused Free-form architecture, thereby almost entirely replacing the process of model making and any physical connection of architects with the body of their work.

The loosening, if not complete severing, of the ties of physical connection between the architect and the building is implicated in the same process of disintegrating relations between inhabitants and their houses, cities, even countries. The relation to place and space is thus severely damaged and endangered leading to what is referred to as the contemporary crisis of dwelling, which has been labelled and amplified by the group of previously mentioned architects and theoreticians. Another aspect which contributes to this development, which contemporary architects and theoreticians, such as Juhani Pallasmaa, the author of the monograph *The Eyes of the Skin: Architecture and the Senses* (2012), warn against, is a loss of tactile properties and the complete rejection of the material dimension of architecture triggered by computer design:

Computer imaging tends to flatten our magnificent, multi-sensory, simultaneous and synchronic capacities of imagination by turning the design process into a passive visual manipulation, a retinal journey. The computer creates a distance between the maker and the object, whereas drawing by hand as well as working with models put the designer in a haptic contact with the object, or space. In our imagination, the object is simultaneously held in the hand and inside the head, and the imagined and projected physical image is modelled by our embodied imagination. (Pallasmaa, 13)

Urs Peter Flueckiger, a practising architect and a teacher at Texas Tech University, whose monograph, *How Much House? Thoreau, Le Corbusier and the Sustainable Cabin* (2016), explores three minimal housing solutions and their design approaches: Thoreau's house at Walden Pond, Massatchusets, Le Corbusier's le Cabanon in Roquebrune-Cap-Martin, France and Texas Tech's Sustainable Cabin on the High Plains of West Texas, inspired by the two previous designs and executed with the help of students themselves. He echoes Pallasmaa's concern and stresses the vitality of this hands-on experience, which makes the students embrace a more haptic nature of architecture and perceive it as less abstract and more real. According to him, both professional and academic architectural studios have changed because of the implementation of the computerized design process. To use a pen or pencil sketch on paper is no longer necessary and its employment is restricted to the conceptual stage. The experiment described in his monograph clearly proves that students long for a tactile experience and should definitely be exposed to the difficulties which arise from the resistance of a material and the amount of labour necessary for elementary construction work. This is so that: "when they interact on the building site with contractors and workers, give them a closer understanding of what their side of métier is. In the end that will lead to a greater understanding of the whole design/ build process which will then make a better architectural creation altogether" (Flueckiger, 84).

The processes of computerisation and digitalisation of architecture together with the everlasting influence of Modernism have resulted in the growing appetite for inert materials such as steel, glass and polished stone. From the perspective of the interpretation of architecture, these materials have proved to be an extremely fruitful field of study. In her enlightening monograph, *Glass State: The Technology of Spectacle, Paris, 1918–1998* (2003), Anette Fierro analyses and interprets the phenomenological foundations, metaphorical impressions, material execution and ideological platform behind the enormous glass buildings of François Mitterand's "Grand Projects" situated in Paris. She studies these buildings, whose inert, cool, gigantic facades provide various degrees of translucency and transparency, and reflect the outside world, thus enabling a view of the inside. Mitterand eventually discerns "three fundamental tensions undermining the implementation of contemporary symbol of transparency in Paris" (Fierro, 41). First of all, transparency is, as Fierro proves, typically associated with the Revolution, which is tainted by its inextricable connection with the Terror.

Secondly, transparency is linked to mechanisms of control as can be observed in the famous example of Jeremy Bentham's design of Panopticon, a special type of institutional building, a prison, which, in the words of Michel Foucault "reverses the principle of dungeon; or rather of its three functions – to enclose, to deprive of light and to hide – it preserves only the first and eliminates the other two. Full lighting and the eye of a supervisor capture better than darkness, which ultimately protected. Visibility is a trap" (Foucault, *Discipline and Punish* 200).

The third cause of tension is concerned with the failed attempts of modernist architects, who, glorifying transparency as the ultimate summit of desired, beneficial qualities, naïvely aspired to infect the rest of the world with their conception of aesthetic and moralism. According to Anthony Vidler, the author of *Warped Space: Art, Architecture, and Anxiety in Modern Architecture* (2000), a study of the mutual effects of the phenomena delineated in the title, modernists, having revived the eighteenth myth of transparency, and, inspired by the treatises of Jean Jacques Rousseau, Jeremy Bentham and numerous others, aspired to a complete social and spatial transparency. Their desire to reshape the very basis of urban space was evoked by pictures of a "glass city, its buildings invisible and society open", with the "resulting 'space'" being "open, infinitely extended, and thereby cleansed of all mental disturbance: the site of healthy and presumably aerobically perfect bodies" (Vidler, 51). Their major preoccupation with new conception of public space stemmed from this idea combined with the belief that agoraphobia and claustrophobia were products of unhealthy urban environments "and that their cure was dependent on the erasure of the old city in its entirety, to a natural state, within which the dispersed institutions of the new society would be scattered like pavilions in a landscape garden" (Vidler, 51). Le Corbusier, one of the leading figures of the Modern movement in architecture, believed transparency, with its sensation of "ineffable space", where buildings are subjected to space, in which they get absorbed and dissolved, "penetrated from all sides by light and air, undercut by greenery, roofs planted as gardens in the sky" (Vidler, 62), is able to single-handedly heal neurosis, psychoses and phobias associated and triggered by traditional metropolitan environment. In Fierro's view, these efforts frequently overestimated the role of technological rationalization and rendered the resulting buildings physically inhabitable, overlooking elementary human needs of shelter, privacy or comfort.

As is apparent from the range of fields Fierro covers and the formulations she employs, the interdisciplinary character of her study proves to be more than just the description of the physical sensations gained by empirical observation of the tactile properties of the surface, which might be quite monotonous in the case of glass. She clearly proves that although such extensive employment of glass might be problematic, it nevertheless invites critics, both professional and lay, to a wide-ranging discussion concerning a multitude of new impressions and possible interpretations. The nature of the mental processes involved in this interpretation, their structure, their outcome as well as their wording resembles those connected with reading. Thus, disembodied architecture, the result of the continual process of abstraction of its physical properties, has inspired its own interpretation from the point of view of language, often resulting in a thorough linguistic scrutiny.

This linguistic turn has strongly influenced the development of recent architectural theory and practice. Terms which are typically associated with linguistic study, such as semantics, syntax or morphology have been fully absorbed by architectural discourse. Heinrich Klotz, the author of *The History of Postmodern Architecture* (1988), traces the roots of linguistic involvement as provision of tools employed in order to "'liberate architecture from muteness of pure forms ... in order that the building might once again become an occasion for creative effort, attend not only to facts and utilization programs but also to poetic ideals and the handling of subject matter on an epic scale" (qtd. in Harries, 84).

Where architecture indicates a textual turn, literary theory displays a spatial turn with a wide array of works dealing with the spatial practices behind the poetics of a literary text. As Michel Foucault predicted in his 1967 lecture entitled "Of Other Spaces", "[t]he present epoch will perhaps be above all the epoch of space" (Foucault, "Of Other Spaces", 22). Architecture is interpreted as the art of imposing boundaries on space which is, even prior to the constitution of regions, never inert or devoid of meaning. Human beings are perceived as the measure of all things. To underline the humanist turn, Karsten Harries calls for the development of the "semantics of the natural language of space" (Harries, 180), which would reflect human dimension and involvement within the question of space and spatial relations. The crude, material distinction between the two spheres remains unchallenged as "the human world is literally structured as the built environment, and symbolically structured as language. The art of the built environment is architecture; that of language is literature" (Spurr, 49). Nevertheless, the abstract, symbolic level reflecting the ubiquitous, irreplaceable presence and the prominence of space and architecture in human experience surpasses the physical forms and encompasses other rich sources such as "paintings, poems, novels and fairy tales" (Harries, 180). What is more, from the point of view of contemporary architectural criticism, architecture and language are, each in their respective ways, instruments of representation:

> Works of architecture speak to us as all buildings do, and yet there is the difference insisted on by Ruskin and Pevsner: architecture must be thought of both in relation to and also in opposition to all merely functional building. The same goes for 'language' – but how then is that language to be understood? Eco points out that buildings denote the building type they exemplify. Works of architecture, I want to propose – very tentatively, only as a kind of trial balloon and quite aware of how preposterous such a proposal is likely to seem – do not just denote the kind of building they are: they do so by representing buildings. *Architecture is an art of representation.* (Harries 96, emphasis in original)

Whereas contemporary architecture has only quite recently acknowledged the possibility of literary aspects of its interpretation and creation, literature has successfully implemented its archetypal model of the house into its morphology. The twentieth century intensified the interest in the house as a symbol, setting, subject and motif of literary works, it was Henry James in the preface to his 1881 novel, *The Portrait of a Lady*, who approached his work from an architectural perspective: the proportioning of his novel as a "house of fiction" (James, 7) elevated it to the architectural structure of a "large building of *The Portrait of a Lady* (James, 8), which turned out to be a "square and spacious house" (James, 9). Similarly, contemporary English novelist Ian McEwan acknowledges thinking of novels in architectural terms: "You have to enter at the gate, and this way must be constructed in such a way that the reader has immediate confidence in the strength of the building" (Ian McEwan, *The Guardian*). Also, his contemporary, Alan Hollinghurst, claimed: "'Normally I do have a brief but acute sort of depression when I finish a book, which is to do with saying goodbye to this place you've been inhabiting'" (Moss).[6]

The continuous rapprochement is supported by a number of works of critical theory, which employ the house as a multifaceted symbol while investigating its representations from the point of view of various disciplines. For example, the sixteenth volume of *European Journal of English Studies, Housing Fiction: The House in Writing and Culture, 1950 to Present*, published in 2012 and edited by Janet Larson, Francesca Saggini and Anna Enrichetta Soccio, addressed numerous approaches to the study of the house in Anglophone literature, such as the cultural architecture of the house, the discourses of the house, gendered and classed houses, or the house and the visual. The two latter editors entitled the introductory chapter of their monograph, *The House of Fiction as the House of Life: Representations of the House from Richardson to Woolf,* "The Paper Houses of English Literature". Lorna Sage named her 1992 study of feminine perspective in *Women in the House of Fiction: Post-war Women Novelists* (1992), and Lynette Carpenter and Wendy K. Kolmar edited *Haunting the House of Fiction: Feminist Perspectives on Ghost Stories by American Women* in 1991.

The Faculty of English Language and Literature of University of Oxford organised an interdisciplinary conference on the subject of the mutual conditioning of architecture and literature, *Spatial Perspectives: Literature and Architecture, 1850 – Present* in 2012. The conference fostered the dialogue between these two disciplines by amplifying their interaction and engagement. One of the mottos of the conference was the statement by French sociologist and urbanist Philippe Haman, who declared: "'Perhaps because literature and architecture are the two most 'visible' arts, since they organize both the everyday practices of reading and the everyday necessities of shelter, the crises and tensions that affect them seem strikingly parallel'" (Haman as quoted on the official website of

---

6   John Vanbrugh (1664–1726), the English playwright, the author of Restoration comedies such as *The Provoked Wife* (1697), and also the famous landscape designer and the English Baroque architect of Blenheim Palace (1705–1722), the birthplace of Winston Churchill. Whereas the mutual influence of his dramatic production and architectural designs is indisputable and both can be considered as the epitomes of bold and daring qualities, the degree of their influence and the effect of Vanbrugh's political activism (he was imprisoned in Bastille and his stay in France left a profound impression on him as far as the sophistication and ostentation of local building was concerned) has been embraced relatively recently, in works such as Frank McCormick's 1991 monograph, *Sir John Vanbrugh: The Playwright as Architect*, or Vaughan Hart's 2008 publication *Sir John Vanbrugh: Storyteller in Stone*. The former of the authors claims that both Vanbrugh's dramatic and architectural vocabulary is heavily marked by the employment of imagery connected with combat and siege, possibly connected with his experience as a hostage in France.

the conference). David Spurr develops the argument further and states that the encounter of literature with the built environment defines modernity, "meaning the set of material and symbolic forms that constitute the modern world and our experience of that world" (Spurr, 1). One of the speakers at the conference was the famous contemporary architect Steven Holl, the author of gigantic building complexes, enormous art galleries (e.g. Kiasma, Museum of Contemporary Art in Helsinki) and influential publications on the theory of architecture, who develops the principle of immediate architectural sensations, frequently employing watercolours to evoke various dynamisms and subtleties of space, light and mass. On the occasion of the conference, Holl was interviewed on the subject of the ability of books to express more than architecture, limited by its material substance. Holl's answer, printed earlier as a part of an essay in the 2009 publication tracing the libraries of famous architects, *Unpacking my Library: Architects and Their Books*, once again acknowledged the proximity of design, building and the printed word:

> I've felt that a book is like a building, and a building is like a book. Instilling either with intensity is an exciting challenge, which continues in the printed work. I once attempted to make a building out of Julio Cortázar's *Hopscotch*, a book that can be read straight through or according to formula, skipping several chapters, reading it another way with a different meaning. Unfortunately, my attempt failed. (Holl qtd. in Steffens, 97)

The anthology entitled *Home Sweet Home* (2004) echoes the practice but approaches the phenomena of house, home and dwelling from the point of view of fine arts, such as painting, photography, conceptual art. The volume even involves a CD with contemporary classical music composed on the subject. It is also where Max Henry, an art critic and poet, discusses the work of Jay Davis, whose paintings merge archetypical house/home imagery with futuristic or dystopian elements. He points to the capacity of architecture as featured in these paintings to incarnate a source of phenomenological experience that is capable of overcoming the obstacles imposed by various temporal constellations so that "[f]iltered through the eye of the postmodern pastiche, new interpretations of architecture that embody age-old ideas and references are threading the lessons of philosophers and artists from various epochs into a non-linear time" (Troy, 84). As the paintings of Jay Davis demonstrate, the historical, social and cultural developments of modern civilisation have disrupted the existence of the traditional "myth" of dwelling.

David Spurr dedicated his *Architecture and Modern Literature*, to the inquiry into the nature and degree of the mutual influence of modern literature and architecture. Over the years, the connection has become gradually tighter, with the literary portrayal becoming more accurate and far-from-idealising. Literature and architecture have become "alternate discourses of modernity itself, as constructions of modern thought through their respective conceptual and material forms" (Spurr, 48). Since the nineteenth century, with the development of first industrial, then informational society, the idealised tight connection between human and place has been challenged and dissolved with the majority of the attempts to restore the original state ending in disaster. If the traditional myth of dwelling cannot be successfully revived, it becomes the task of art, predominantly of literature and architecture, to redefine the notion of dwelling and develop a new relationship towards it. Thus, modern forms of meaning in architecture and literature stem from the discourses of being, dwelling, and homelessness:

> To be genuinely at home in this world, we have to affirm our essential homelessness, a homelessness illuminated by shifting ideals of genuine dwelling, figures of home, and precarious conjectures about what it might mean to dwell near the centre. Temples have functioned as such figures. But every attempt to step into the true centre, to come home in this sense, more especially to make house into such home, denies the essential eccentricity of human dwelling – an 'eccentricity' that needs to be thought in relation to a centre, but a centre that withdraws whenever we seek to seize it. (Harries, 200)

In an era which is plagued by a crisis of the traditional relationship between man and place and which therefore defies the traditional character of dwelling, it is the task of literature and poetic expression in general to define a new relation to dwelling as a type of being. If dwelling in its traditional sense requires continuity and a relation between human beings and their environment, and modern existence deprives people of this essential experience of appropriation of place, of the sense of belonging, then dwelling always has to be learned or invented anew. This is where the tasks of both contemporary literature and architectural theory and practice intersect.

2.2 "Houses are alive. No?"
Houses from the Viewpoint of Modernist Sensibility

It's the houses that are mesmerising me, I've no control over the saucy things.
Houses are alive. No?[7]

Twentieth century English fiction contributed to the discussion of the role of houses in literature by its insistence on their personified properties. This is observable in particular in the works of literary Modernists, such as E. M. Forster's *Howards End*, which stresses both the animate character of the houses in question. He also amplifies their binding influence, which imposes their integrating properties on the life of people. Virginia Woolf's 1921 short story "A Haunted House", or her insight into the realm of country house fiction, *Orlando: A Biography* (1928), develop the same principle. The pattern is repeated and particularly accentuated in the works of a celebrated Anglo-Irish author Elizabeth Bowen. Her novels, such as *The Hotel* (1927), *The Last September* (1929), *To the North* (1932), *The House in Paris* (1935), *The Death of the Heart* (1938), or the autobiographical account of her relationship with her family's home, *Bowen Court* (1946), are all echoes of the emblematic (and highly symbolic) Anglo-Irish house which "hovers before her characters, yet repeatedly fails them" (Kreilkamp, 142). According to Vera Kreilkamp, the author of *The Anglo-Irish Novel and the Big House* (1998), Bowen's fiction reflects her own tense and discordant Anglo-Irish experience which she transforms into a subject of her art. The reason behind such a specific choice of leitmotif is the result of her complicated identification with Bowen's Court, her family home, a domestic space which both naturally established and limited her personal and cultural identity. As she shows repeatedly through the example of the more or less temporary retreats of her fiction, these places influence and almost haunt their characters, but are unable to sustain them with the adequate amount of stimuli and sense of belonging. In accordance with the historical experience which laid the foundations for the literary development of Big House Literature, the houses described by Bowen fail to provide a sense of safety and thus the possibility for the full identification of their inhabitants with the spaces they inhabit.

---

7   Forster, Edward Morgan. *Howards End*. 1910. With an Introduction and Notes by David Lodge, London: Penguin Books, 2000, p. 132. [Subsequent page references preceded *HE* are given in parentheses in the text].

The treatment of the house as a body of stability-inducing images reflects, on a larger scale, the standing of a secluded, private space, which the Modernists filled with subjective meaning as a symbol of the retreat toward interiority. The house thus seems to stand as a counterpoint to the prevailing aesthetic of ruin and fragmentation so typical of the first third of the twentieth century. What it also reflects is the new kind of attention to the human body, which is seen as the ideal of proportioning, and whose healthy development is conditioned and replicated by the new forms of architecture. Pioneered by Le Corbusier's implementation of "the Modulor", much in the spirit of Leonardo da Vinci's and Vitruvius's "Vitruvian man", the ideal of a human body is regarded as a basic unit of building and designing measurement. Le Corbusier described his further insistence in his manifesto *Towards a New Architecture*, which, first published in England in 1927, "has had as great [an] influence on English architectural thought as any one publication of the last fifty years". According to its 1946 preface, the elimination of dead concepts of style "from our hearts and minds ... and look[ing] at the question from a critical and objective point of view, we shall arrive at the 'House – Machine,' the mass-production house, healthy (and morally so too) and beautiful in the same way that the working tools and instruments which accompany our existence are beautiful" (Le Corbusier, 13). The fellow Modernist architect of Austrian origin, Richard Neutra, who designed the majority of his exquisite living spaces after he moved to the United States, imposed similar principles on his work:

> Within the pantheon of great Modernist, memorable form-making is a requisite. Neutra certainly reconceived the human within the remarkable spaces as well as the technologies used to create those spaces. But what made Neutra unique was not an endless search for form but the endless search for the human being. The wellspring of that search was his belief, quite simply, that good architecture – that which reconciles humanity with nature in an "exultant dance of interconnectedness" – heals and that bad architecture – that which alienates the human from nature and from his or her essential naturalness – harms. (Lamprecht, 7)

François de Singly, a French sociologist and well-known theoretician of family, distinguishes two phases of modernity, the first coinciding with the period of literary Modernism, with the second phase reaching its peak in the 1970s. His understanding of modernity is purely sociological and is marked by the gradual severing of the ties placed on individuals by society. He defines the history of family on the grounds of the appropriation of domestic space. The first phase of modernity is distinguished by the emphasis it puts on the dissociation of a family from the rest of the society. This separation is mirrored by a family's living arrangement; and the second phase finalises the process of a complete emancipation of an individual from the rest of society. Unlike in the first phase of modernity, which prescribed only one social role a person could embrace at a time, the growing insistence on autonomy lead to the multiplicity of roles a person may acquire. At this point, de Singly points to two vital facts: walls and secluded spaces allowing personal intimacy represent an irreplaceable factor in the development of personal autonomy, and hence contribute to the development of a fully-fledged identity. Regarding the first stage of modernity, he underlines the fact that in order to limit the process of individualization, society prescribed each person an official role. An individual was allowed to realise only a single one at a time. It was in this context that brought about Virginia Woolf's famous and often quoted non-fiction books comprising several essays, *A Room of One's Own* (1929), loosely concluded by *Three Guineas*, conceived as early as in 1929, published as late as in 1938. Their message summarises Woolf's preoccupation with the unequal demands placed on both sexes. Starting with the ability to possess a private, secluded space, which would enable the performance of a different role than that typically ascribed according to sex, age and the position in family and society in that period, she concludes with the well-known dictum "it is necessary to have five hundred a year and a room with a lock on the door if you are to write fiction or poetry" (Woolf, *A Room*, 103). By this she rejects the typical role ascribed to contemporary women, the role of wife and mother in the centre of domestic chores, who did not need a special room to perform other activities. Although Virginia Woolf lived in the first phase of modernity, she heralded the demand of the second modernity – the existence of a room which would allow women to free themselves from the constraints of domestic demands and enable them to perform different roles, e.g. the fulfilment of their artistic potential. The importance of the existence of this different role, different occupation is manifested by the example of Susan Rowlins, a former successful professional, later a devoted wife and mother of four children, as found in the poignant short story "To Room Nineteen" by Doris Lessing. Just like the character of Laura Brown from Michael Cunningham's 1999 Pulitzer-prize winning *The Hours*, she desires a private space of her own and rents a hotel room.

What did she do in the room? Why, nothing at all. From the chair, when it had rested her, she went to the window, stretching her arms, smiling, treasuring her anonymity, to look out. She was no longer Susan Rawlings, mother of four, wife of Matthew, employer of Mrs. Parkers and of Sophie Traub, with these and those relations with friends, school-teachers, tradesmen. She no longer was mistress of the big white house and garden, owning clothes suitable for this activity and occasion. She was Mrs. Jones, and she was alone, and she had no past, no future. (Lessing, 895)

Unable to redefine and replace her role as housewife and fill the desolate feeling of pure void with any meaningful activity, she faces the absolute loss of identity and finally commits suicide.

The penchant of the Modernists towards the depiction of secluded spaces such as cities, houses, or, most frequently, rooms, stems from their preoccupation with walls, especially their paradoxical nature and irreplaceable role within the process of building one's own individuality. The walls which separate and seclude also protect, shield and enable the process of individualization – of becoming oneself. These walls may be built or torn down, they may be restructured, but they remain of crucial importance as far as the individual is concerned, which is acknowledged by the position ascribed to them during Modernism. When Michael Walzer pondered on Liberalism, more in the sense of individualism than the political conception, as the art of separation in his volume entitled *The Resources of American Liberalism* (1984), he drew attention to the original organic nature of society and the theoretical and practical insistence of liberals on the necessity and great benefits of neat structuring and separation: "They drew lines, marked off different realms, and created the socio-political map with which we are still familiar. The most famous line is the 'wall' between church and state but there are many others. Liberalism is the world of walls, and each one creates a new liberty" (Walzer, 315).

Modernists such as E. M. Forster, Virginia Woolf, Elizabeth Bowen or Vita Sackville-West did not merely content themselves with the vital importance of the wall, they even blurred the line between animate and inanimate by endowing the houses they incorporated in their writing with living properties. Virginia Woolf embraces this attitude in *Orlando: A Biography*, inspired by her infatuation with Vita Sackville-West and the country house she resurrected from ashes, working incessantly on clearing of the rubble of decades from what was to become the famous garden of Sissinghurst. In *Orlando,* Woolf demonstrated the persuasion she echoed a year later in *A Room of One's Own*: a great mind is of an androgynous nature. It is also Orlando's country house which becomes his/her utmost poetic creation, the fruition of his/her artistic endeavours and life aspirations. Unsurprisingly, the house in question displays palpable signs of having a life of its own, with rooms changing their moods and minds, brightening and blinking their eyes as she comes in, observing her knowingly, being at ease with her, since they have known her for centuries:

> She had hidden nothing from them; had come to them as boy and woman, crying and dancing, brooding and gay. ... Ah, but she knew where the heart of the house still beat. Gently opening a door, she stood on the threshold so that (as she fancied) the room could not see her and watched the tapestry rising and falling on the eternal faint breeze which never failed to move it. Still the hunter rode; still Daphne flew. The heart still beat, she thought, however faintly, however far withdrawn; the frail indomitable heart of the immense building. (Woolf, *Orlando*, 224)

Similarly, the house described in her short story "A Haunted House" is wide awake, its heart beating.[8]

Sissinghurst also proved to be highly inspiring with respect to Vita Sackville-West's own literary production. Having always been "a person for whom places were at least as important as people, and with this new passion for Sissinghurst dominating her daily life, it is not surprising that a house plays such a large part" (Glendinning, 7) in her highly-esteemed novel *All Passion Spent* from 1931.[9] Retreating to a tiny house in the Hampstead Heath, Lady Slane, or "Queen Lear", the eighty-eight-year-old protagonist of the novel, is to retire from her former life as the wife of the first Earl of Slane to observe her life and marriage from a triple vantage point, her widowhood, her age and her red-brick house in the God-forsaken wilderness of the Heath. The house is an intimate place of "familiar geography", which provides her with a unique perspective

---

8   "'Safe, safe, safe,' the pulse of the house beat softly. ... 'Safe, safe, safe,' the pulse of the house beat gladly. 'The treasure yours.' ... The doors go shutting far in the distance, gently knocking like the pulse of a heart. ... 'Safe, safe, safe,' the pulse of the house beat proudly. 'Long years –' he sighs. Again you found me.' 'Here,' she murmurs, 'Sleeping; in the garden reading; laughing; rolling apples in the loft. Here we left our treasure –' Stooping, their light lifts the lids upon the eyes. 'Safe! Safe! Safe!' the pulse of the house beats wildly. Waking, I cry 'Oh, is *this* your buried treasure! The light in the heart.'" (Woolf, *A Haunted House: The Complete Shorter Fiction*, 117)

9   Leonard Woolf, Sackville-West's publisher, considered it to be her finest one.

and unforeseen space in which to ponder her life. The work is infused with a highly complex character and personal history of the author, such as her vast travel experience and her views on feminism, marriage, and feminine values. While Lady Slane is absolutely uncompromising and therefore true to herself, Vita Sackville-West was, despite a great deal of controversy surrounding her private and public life, "a complex person drawn to the great simplicities" (Glendinning, 17), torn between her contradictory desires until the end of her life. Lady Slane is no longer subject to these torments: 'those days were gone when feeling burst its bounds and poured hot from the foundry, when the heart seemed likely to split with complex and contradictory desires" (Sackville-West, 117). If indeed nothing is left for Lady Slane but "a landscape in monochrome, the features identical but all the colours gone from them" (Sackville-West, 118), and she has truly spent all her passion, then her relationship to the house is something utterly remarkable. The qualities with which she endows it are astonishing, given her reserved, rational approach to matters of her own life.

> Nor could one expect them to feel how strange a thing house was, especially an empty house; not merely a systematic piling-up of brick on brick, regulated in the building by plumb-line and spirit-level, pierced at intervals by doors and casements, but an entity with a life of its own, as though some unifying breath were blown into the air confined within this square brick box, there to remain until the prisoning walls should fall away, exposing it to general publicity. It was a very private thing, a house; private with a privacy irrespective of bolts and bars. And if this superstition seemed irrational, one might reply that man himself was but collection of bricks, yet man laid claim to soul, to a spirit, to a power of recording and of perception, which had no more to do with his restless atoms than had the house with its stationary bricks. (Sackville-West, 90)

The house's claim on her soul points to the lack of resignation on her part. This is almost to be unexpected, sadly at least by all her children, in the last days of her old age. It stresses the essential importance of the enclosed, secure, private space of the house. This importance gives credence to its primary function in the life of a man as illuminated by the works of Modernists.

2.3 The Evolution of Country House Fiction in Historical and Literary (Con)texts

Of all the great things that the English have invented and made a part of the credit of the national character, the most perfect, the most characteristic, the one they have mastered most completely in all its details, so that it has become a compendious illustration of their social genius and their manners, is the well-appointed, well-administered, well-filled country-house.
(James, *English Hours*, 154) [10]

The house, which conditions and shelters existence, is an irreplaceable entity in human life. Despite the ubiquitous presence of houses in literature and the universal importance ascribed to them, there are certain literary spheres where they dominate as settings, symbols, subjects or motifs. Such centring is never purely coincidental, but always reflects the specificity of the historical standing of their physical counterparts. In term of literature in English, we may speak about four realms which are thematically oriented almost exclusively towards the notion of a house. The English country house poem of the seventeenth and eighteenth century which has gone on to be replaced by country house fiction of the twentieth and twenty-first century, followed by Irish Big House Fiction and the position of the house in Caribbean fiction.

Irish Big House fiction is set in isolated, often desolate and shabby country estates. "The Big House was most often constructed of native limestone in alien architectural forms by representatives of a colonial power" (Kreilkamp, 7). Big House novels are one of the major genres of Irish fiction and they focus on the description of the tension between several social groups, stressing conflict rather than conciliation. The tradition emerged in the late eighteenth century with novels by Maria Edgeworth and continues until today marking the persistence of Irish historical memory Edgeworth, a contemporary of Jane Austen, felt the urge to write novels about Ireland, sensing the lack of definition of contemporary Irish identity. The extent of responsiveness to problems the Irish national identity had to face at the time distinguishes nineteenth – and

---

10   *English Hours* is the collection of essays by Henry James, inspired mainly by his over fifty-year long stay in England, collected over the course of thirty years and published in 1905 as a travel book. Despite their celebratory nature, James does not avert eyes from poverty and some of the perils of contemporary society. E.g. immediately after he describes the ambient hedonism provided by English country house, he ventures on to depict the charitable Christmas activities of the lady of the house in a workhouse.

twentieth-century Irish fiction from its English counterparts. According to Vera Kreilkamp, the author of the study *The Anglo-Irish Novel and the Big House,* the development of twentieth century Big House fiction reflects the rupture and turbulence typical for Irish history. During the struggle for independence from 1919 to 1921 and the subsequent civil war, "nearly two hundred Irish country houses were destroyed as symbols of colonizing force, sometimes without consideration for the politics of their owners" (Kreilkamp, 6). From the literary perspective "for the Anglo-Irish novelist, the gentry house becomes the most compelling symbol of ascendancy survival: on occasion the assertive economic, political , and social power centre of rural life, but more often the shabby derision and contempt" (Kreilkamp, 7). The nature of the term "Big" may be understood as slightly ironic, as it did not enter into the collective cultural consciousness until the late nineteen century, when the historical and political power of the truly existing estates was already in decline. Irish Big House fiction failed to produce an all-comprising novel, typical for the nineteenth century, which would both embrace and brace the national identity, whose homogeneity was severely disrupted by impositions of class, religion, language and national origin. Therefore, Ireland had to wait for Joyce's modernist revision of the novel, in order to provide an integrative literary work. In the meantime, works of smaller scale and ambition from the authors such as Charles Lever, Charles Maturin, Elizabeth Bowen, Molly Keane, William Trevor or John Banville, originated and provided original and eloquent testimonies of the traumatic effects of the colonial usurpation.

J. G. Farrell incorporated elements of Big House fiction into his 1970 novel *Troubles*, which, being the first part of the *Empire Trilogy* followed by *The Siege of Krishnapur* (1973) and *The Singapore Grip* (1978) revolves around the potent symbol of a formerly majestic hotel falling prey to gradual disintegration.

> Curiously, in spite of the corrosive effect of the sea air the charred remains of the enormous main building are still to be seen; for some reason – the poor quality of the soil or the proximity of the sea – vegetation has only made a token attempt to possess them. Here and there among the foundations might still find evidence of the Majestic's former splendour: the great number of cast-iron bathtubs, for instance, which had tumbled from one blazing floor to another until they hit the earth; twisted bed-frames also, some of them not yet altogether rusted away; and a simply prodigious number of basins and lavatory bowls. At interval along the outer

walls there is testimony to the stupendous heat of the fire: one can disinter small pools of crystal formed in layers like the drips of wax from a candle, which gathered there, of course, from the melting of the windows. Pick them up and they separate in your hand into the cloudy drops that formed them.

Another curious thing: one comes across a large number of tiny white skeletons scattered round about. The bones are very delicate and must have belonged, one would have thought, to small quadrupeds ... ("But no, not rabbits," says my grandfather with a smile.) (Farrell, 3–4)

Its gilded microcosm mirrors its formerly powerful, pompous coloniser, whose gradual decline culminates with a baroque image of the hotel on fire, with the overpopulation of cats it sheltered jumping ablaze from the windows. The equally atmospheric opening passage foreshadows the events with its brilliant evocation of the splendid dereliction of the deserted hotel in which the novel abounds.

In post-colonial Caribbean literature, marked by the traumatic experience of slavery, colonialism and fitful democratic development, the persistence of the historical memory places a sense of place at the very core of its literary production. According to Malcom Bradbury, Caribbean fiction is illuminated by "[t]he heady perfume of the islands, the light, the colour, the dramatic shot-silk sunsets which precede a darkness that comes with the suddenness of a door slamming, the brilliant hues of the hibiscus and bougainvillea, the burnished feathers of the humming-birds" (Bradbury, *The Atlas*, 281). In addition to this intoxicating exoticism, a large portion of Caribbean novels deals with the details of everyday life, minutia that retain an aura of freshness: "For black people, freedom from slavery meant the right to live in your own house, choose your own food, marry as you pleased: in other words all the things a free person, one who is not a prisoner or a slave, takes for granted" (Bradbury, *The Atlas*, 281). Thus, Mr Biswas' unfailing determination to own his own house, overcoming all the imposed obstacles, from the eponymous novel published in 1961 to a wide-world success and critical acclaim of its Trinidadian author, V. S. Naipaul, acquires the dimension of existential drama.

He thought of the house as his own, though for years it had been irretrievably mortgaged. And during these months of illness and despair he was struck again and again by the wonder of being in his own house, the audacity of it: to walk in through his own front gate, to bar entry to whoever he wished, to close his doors and windows every night, to hear no noises except those of his family, to wander freely from room to room and about his yard, instead of being condemned, as before, to retire the moment he got home to the crowded room in one or the other of Mrs Tulsi's houses, crowded with Shama's sisters, their husbands, their children. As a boy he had moved from one house of strangers to another; and since his marriage he felt he had lived nowhere but in the houses of the Tulsis, at Hanuman House in Arwacas, in the decaying wooden house at Shorthills, in the clumsy concrete house in Port of Spain. And now at the end he found himself in his own house, on his own half-lot of land, his own portion of the earth. That he should have been responsible for this seemed to him, in these last months, stupendous. (Naipaul, 8)

In the course of the novel, Mr Biswas's quest for his own house reflects and cements his individuality as well as his individualist approach to life, brushing aside both the communal way of life practiced by the Tulsis (his wife's branch of family) and the colonial frustration.

The literary production connected with the third prominent positioning of the house in English-written literature, English country house, is yet another example of the impossibility of a purely formalist interpretation of the issuing works. Although, to a certain extent, the interdisciplinary approach complicates the critical assessment of these works, it may be regarded as fulfilling the premise of the integrating nature of a house as a universal, archetypal symbol as well as the marker of symbiosis between history and fiction. This type of connection is advocated by Hayden White, who acknowledges the decisive role of metaphors in ordering of the world and compares historian to literary artist. The choice, in both instances, has the same result, a narrative consisting of terminologically determined forms "represented by the figures of speech without which discourse itself is impossible" (White, 134): "Readers of histories and novels can hardly fail to be struck by the similarities. There are many histories that could pass for novels, and many novels that could pass for histories, considered in purely formal (or I should say formalist) terms. Viewed simply as verbal artefacts, histories and novels are indistinguishable from one another" (White, 121). Stephen Greenblatt, a key figure of New Historicism, is persuaded about the artificial and, in a way, absurd separation of a literary text from its social context, of literary production from history itself. Louis Montrose, a fellow proponent of New Historicism has introduced the well-known formula which summarizes the nature of mutual involvement and conditioning of facts and fiction reflected in texts as "the textuality of history, the historicity of text" (Montrose, 8).

Therefore, the paper houses of English country fiction are to be "read" through the prism of their material counterparts and the actual historical experience they resulted from. The country house is a phenomenon endowed, often contrary to expectations, with a rich, colourful and highly varied history. Originally, country house used to be a term interchangeable with manor house, the seat of aristocracy, which stood at the centre of the manorial system and whose jurisdiction was among the most valuable feudal rights. Although the term "manor" (French manoir, a dwelling) was obviously a lexical borrowing from French brought by the Norman invaders, "the manorial system was in existence before Domesday. Something akin to it can even be said to have flourished in Roman Britain, where the organization of agriculture was based upon the "villa" or big country house with fields around it" (Cook, 9). The Middle Ages enriched the lexical field of the country house with yet another toponym – ahead hall. Houses from this period often feature it in their compound. The presence and prominence of these great halls, whose models were churches, can be seen as the architectural markers of the manor houses in the period before the arrival of the Renaissance. These halls played the part of legal, administrative, social centres of the manor and since the 14th century became the subject of a profound aesthetic re-evaluation. This process was not reserved to the space of increasingly loftier halls, but to the whole construction, which displayed a steadily decreasing amount of fortifying features which were completely abandoned in the end. Starting with the period of Henry VIII and, more importantly, his daughter, Elizabeth I, we may speak about an outburst of domestic building, which was provoked by several factors: firstly, the growing wealth of the proprietors, also, the tendency to counterbalance the precipitous materialism of society by creating artificial retreats replete with natural and magical imagery, and finally due to the demands of the Queen who, together with the whole court, moved incessantly between estates whose owners took great pains with their effort to impress her.

The seventeenth century witnessed the growing comfort, intimacy and quiet luxury of these places as well as the threat impressed by the Puritan government. This was just an overture to the eighteenth century, the Golden Age, where the main concern of the rich was art, and an ideal which was established and sustained by the wealthy. Contrastively, the nineteenth century might be regarded as a period of decline. Although a heroic effort was made in order to provide the houses with aesthetic properties, whose traditionalism would shield the dwellers, both metaphorically and literally, from the impeding sweep of technology and industry, those schemes often went awry. The ancient houses were bought and the newly constructed houses were often built by wealthy entrepreneurs from the money gained from what the houses tended to gaudily deny: industrialisation and the rule of technology: "It is as though the home, and especially the home of the wealthy magnate playing the part of a feudal lord, were a feverishly erected bulwark to guarantee the survival of the individual against the tide of technology and the industry which were sweeping inexorably on towards the impersonality of the modern world" (Cook, 215).

The Victorian period was the age of great ambiguities and contradictions, where the public attitude towards stately homes was no exception to this characterisation. In particular, the first part of the nineteenth century was marked by the growing hostility of the public towards the aristocratic abodes. This anger was founded on the exotic, often extravagant image of the houses which marked them with a great deal of exclusivity and foreignness. Despite widespread suspicion of these newly built places, the public appreciated older houses, with growing intensity, which according to them epitomised the ideals of the olden days. This interest inspired a massive rise in tourism and suggestions concerning the right of the public to visit the stately homes. As Peter Mandler points out in his 1997 monograph, *The Fall and Rise of the Stately Home*, by the 1880s the hostility towards the aristocracy grew to such a degree that to show interest or even appreciate any country house became politically, socially and intellectually treacherous. The next sixty years were characterised by the decline of the status of these former seats of power. Only after 1945, when the aristocracy was no longer considered a threat, was a gradual revival of the stately homes possible. After the 1970s, this revival acquired the dimension of a triumphal return to the spotlight of public interest, with the public seeing itself no longer as an observing intruder, but a rightful inheritor.

In terms of the reason for the unceasing attraction of stately homes and their potential to stage an overwhelming comeback, there are more possible explanations. Besides the public feeling somewhat responsible for the development and maintenance of these places, according to Olive Cook's eponymous guide to the history and present of the country house, *The English Country House*, published in 1974, the attraction cannot only derive from changes in society, from the shift of power from those who lived in these houses to an impersonal centre of authority and the consequent removal of former antagonism: it must also lie in the contrast between all the country house stood for and our own way of living, between our uprootedness and the continuity and stability of the life led in the great mansion, between our dislocation, diffusion and isolation and that image of community and intensity. (Cook, 1)

She sees the English country house in decline and emphasises the irony of the mounting public interest. What is more, Cook claims that the deeper into the history, the more the social significance of these houses is inscribed in the landscape. Despite the sweeping impact of the suburban and industrial sprawl, the historical feudal contours are still visible with the manorial house at their centre: "The older the house, the more clearly proclaimed are its associations with this pattern. They are announced by the very components of the structure which were originally dictated by practical needs and tradition rather than by high creative impulses" (Cook, 1).

Vera Kreilkamp scrutinises the field of the Big House, both from a literary as well as historical perspective. Comparing it to the English country house and other idealised conception of life in the countryside, she claims that the continuous, unflinching appreciation of these outdated phenomena, which she brands as a "conservative cultural form", marks our inability to break permanently with the past.

What is discarded recurs, stirring submerged needs and common longings – suggesting both the incompleteness of revolutionary narratives and an enduring fascination with hierarchical social and aesthetic formulations. Monarchist sentiments reemerge in a newly liberated eastern Europe; city dwellers decorate their condominiums with gentry country house furnishings sold by Ralph Lauren; record-breaking crowds of middle-class Americans visited *The Treasure Houses of Britain* exhibition at the National Gallery in Washington. (Kreilkamp, 1)

As far as literary studies are concerned, this middle-class reactionary conservativism is rejected by the "vigilant left" represented by cultural materialists in England and new historicists in America.

From this perspective, it arises that no discussion over the role, nature and position of the poetics of the space of the house within English literature would be possible or complete without the realm of country house inspired literary production. Initially, the country house influenced the development of a highly specific sub-genre of poetry, the so-called "country house poem", in the seventeenth century. With its idealising character, it composed an ode to the country house and its master, usually the poet's patron, such as in the case of Ben Jonson's "To Penshurst" (1616)[11] and Andrew Marvell's "Upon Appleton House" (1651). In time it contributed to the development of what David Spurr, in his *Architecture and Modern Literature* (2012), describes as "country house ideology", where the pastoral poems embodied the houses which were already "representations of a mythic past" (Spurr, 23). In accordance with Louis Althusser's conception of ideology, Spurr draws attention to the fact that a typical country house poem "is the representation of the imaginary relation between individuals and their real conditions of existence" (Spurr, 19). Later he observes the resemblance between Althusser's concept of ideology and Walter Benjamin's conception of mythology. Thus the English country house poem nurtures and also incarnates country house ideology since it portrays an imaginary structure of relations between the estate, the patron, the tenants, the landscape, the poet and the social and political spheres. These relations already existed but were transformed in order to fit into the artistic shape and the resulting ideology stipulated an orderly, hierarchical, centralised vision of the world. It should be noted that such a perception had already been challenged by contemporaries. This can be observed in one of Alexander Pope's lesser-known country house poems in which he mocks the "grandeur" of Blenheim Castle and thus points to its unwelcoming, pompous nature.[12] Consequently,

---

11   Now, Penshurst, they that will proportion thee
     With other edifices, when they see
     Those proud, ambitious heaps, and nothing else,
     May say their lords have built, but thy lord dwells. (Ben Jonson, "To Penshurst").

12   See, sir, here's the grand approach,
     This way is for his Grace's coach;
     There lies the bridge, and here's the clock,
     Observe the lion and the cock,
     The spacious court, the collonade,
     And mark how wide the hall is made!
     The chimneys are so well designed,
     They never smoke in any wind.
     This gallery's contrived for walking,
     The windows to retire and talk in,
     The council chamber for debate,
     And all the rest are rooms of state.

today's perception of country houses often either subverts or reverberates with a nostalgia-infused romantic longing for an orderly hierarchical division of the past, echoing certain aspects of "country house ideology". In his *A Country House Companion* (1987), an anthology dedicated to the presentation of various aspects of life in country houses across the centuries, Mark Girouard claims that in reality country-house life has never been even remotely reminiscent of its idealised representation:

> For although, in some moods and under some circumstances, they are magical places, country-house life was far from pure gold all the way through. There is a mythology of the English country house which runs something as follows. The English upper-classes, unlike their continental counterparts, have always been firmly rooted in their estates. They know the land, and enjoy its ways and sports. They look after their tenantry and their servants, and have an easy and natural relationship with working-class people. At the same time they have a sense of duty, which leads them to devote much of their lives to public service, with no thought of personal gain. (Girouard, 8)

In literature, this idealised perception of the orderly notion of the country house has managed to survive centuries of perils such as the treacherous attack of Alexander Pope or the treatment of the topic by Charles Dickens in *Bleak House* (1852–3). It has continued to represent settled relationships and mutual responsibility until the beginning of the twentieth century, as John Lucas observes in his study, The Sunlight on the Garden (1996), in which he explores the exclusive and elusive nature of pastoral England from the social and literary perspective of Modernism.

Beginning with the twentieth century, the definition of a country house was broadened considerably as the previous social exclusivity was gradually dissolved with the absorption of ostentatious, newly-built seats of the nineteenth and twentieth century capitalists' residences, ancient farmhouses, cottages and villas into the tradition. Besides the relatively rich variety of transformations of stately homes, which more or less radically challenge the remnants of the seventeenth-century "country house ideology", their diminutive versions, such as converted old farmhouses, cottages or inland and seaside villas, develop some traits of the

---

Thanks, sir, cried I, 'tis very fine,

But where d'ye sleep, or where d'ye dine?

I find by all you have been telling

That 'tis a house, but not a dwelling. (Alexander Pope (attributed), qtd. in Girouard, 24).

eighteenth-century "villa ideology". Through this, emphasis is put on "creating an architectural counterpart to enlightened human understanding" (Spurr, 24), so the houses in question reflect neoclassical principles of reason, clarity, and symmetry, rather than mirroring the position of their masters within the social hierarchy. One of the strongest motives which has shaped the understanding and conception of villas in general is the owner's claim to an almost absolute autonomy tightly connected with the sense of ownership (Dalibor Veselý qtd. in Machalová, 30).[13] However, the pivotal point of this ideology is the suburban setting of these villas, since it positions them in a neutral zone which is far from the town and court as well as detached from the rural idyll of the countryside. Consequently, the eighteenth-century villas and their depiction anticipate the conception of suburbia as a liminal region full of social, political and artistic potential on the one hand, yet providing its inhabitants with relative independence from the ancient dichotomy of the country versus the city on the other hand.

According to Williams's *The Country and the City*, the country and the city share a long history of mutual conditioning and defining, however, they present merely two types of settlement. Real social experiences largely extend the limitations of these two singular forms and reflect new, intermediate kinds of social and spatial organisation. Nevertheless, both these historically refined archetypes have become central parts of our experience and the perception of contemporary society. The images of country and city remain highly forceful and evocative. Their stable position in the general knowledge may be partly elucidated by the great flexibility with which they respond to individual historical, social and cultural changes while managing to maintain their places in general cognizance. By further process of simplification, reduction and abstraction, these images are transformed into symbols or archetypes, which persist even through the most tumultuous historical periods.

At this point Williams insists on and subsequently attempts the exploration of both the reasons of persistence and the individual historical variations of both concepts. In his study, he approaches the phenomena in their complexity, in the wider social, cultural, political and economic context of the period. Thus, he is able to delineate certain general observations, such as the sixteenth and seventeenth-century association of the

---

13 For a more detailed and enlightening introduction to the history and philosophy of the conception of a villa with the emphasis put on the original Roman and Italian embodiments, see Dalibor Veselý's foreword to Jana Máchalová's volume on famous Italian villas, *Příběhy slavných italských vil* (*The Stories of Famous Italian Villas*).

city with law and money, the eighteenth-and nineteenth-century vision of cities as centres of wealth and luxury and ever-growing masses of people, as well as the nineteenth and twentieth century identification of urban existence with isolation and impersonated mobility. Some ideas can be found in different periods with radically different interpretations, such as the view of the country as settlement, implying motionlessness, as well as its twentieth century interpretation as rural retreat, which implies mobility. Williams accentuates three main periods of rural complaint over the loss of the happier days of the past as the late sixteenth and early seventeenth centuries, the late eighteenth and the early nineteenth, and the late nineteenth and the early twentieth centuries. Each of these periods coincided with exceptional change in the rural economy. The external threat imposing changes followed by the refusal of the rural environment was replicated within the urban environment in the twentieth century. This demonstrated that, although urban and rural are different environments, seemingly contrastive, they "are forms of isolation and identification of more general processes" (Williams, 291). This is why the author insists on putting the generalised notions to the historical realities and ideas, which might be seen expressing a human agenda which at the moment lacks any other available form of expression.

Williams traces major processes and their numerous variations within the tradition of English literature and society, which, owing to its rapid industrial progress, heralded global development. Williams is inclined to see the city as capitalism, with its roots firmly embedded within the rural English economy. According to him, it is more important to see the similarities between the forms of settlement and the forms of exploitation within the rural and the urban condition e.g. the behaviour of landlords and mining companies, than it is to perceive the conventional contrast between agriculture and industry – with the former as the cooperation of country with nature and the latter as the industrial city crushing and transforming nature. As the author states, there are considerable similarities between the effect extensive farming has on the landscape and the effect of extensive mining. Capitalist production is the most effective tool for all kinds of transformations, either social or of the physical environment. Both the country and the city are prominent examples of these profound changes and prove that, together with people's intensity of attachment to seemingly unspoiled places and the belief in the high degree of cultivation of country, at least in the period around the finalising of *The Country and the City*, capitalism was in one of its most vivacious stages.

The approach towards technological progress, welcomed by some and abhorred by others, is an embodiment of conflicting needs and aspirations within human soul. This dichotomy, often described as the human condition, is illustrated by the effort to divide one sphere from the other: week and weekend, work and leisure, city and country, suburbs and garden cities, town houses and country cottages. Williams sees the country house as one of the first efforts of resolving the contrastive, if not contradictory pulls of materialism and humanity, of the city and the country. Despite his denigration of the viability of country house fiction, which stems from the precarious nature of the twentieth-century country house, the house's frequent employment further accentuates its quality as another kind of settlement, neither utterly rural, nor completely urban and illustrates his claim of its integrating properties. The country house is able, if perhaps only temporarily, to metaphorically reconcile two contradictory motivations typically associated with the country and the city.

From the urbanist perspective, the suburb, representing an intermediate type of settlement according to Williams, has become the prevailing mode of existence since the beginning of the twentieth century. The masses of commuters searching for the benefits of living in the countryside, but still close enough to the city centre, branded a new region, "Metro-land", which heavily promoted a set of commonly held beliefs in the beneficial effect of life in the countryside. Nevertheless, the major motivation for the development of Metro-land was largely economic. The Metropolitan Railway saw an opportunity and, by supplying the means of connection, enabled a massive expansion of London into the countryside, which defined a new style of living – the suburb. Its essence was that "it would provide the benefits of country living with the convenience of being close to the city, so that a man ... could travel by train to work in the noise and grime of the city but come home in the evening to his family and the healthy air of the countryside" (Dimbleby, 233). This building of suburbs on surplus railway land in the early twentieth century promoted the idea that the spiritual growth and the physical well-being of an individual were conditioned by proximity to nature. In reality it produced a lifestyle which, with "living in little rows of slate-roofed houses so lamentably similar that no man of individual taste could bear to see them" (Galsworthy, *Country House*, 10), inspired a great deal of disdain and contempt. The past was mythicized and romanticised as a period which enabled a direct, honest relationship between man and land, which was projected in the deliberately premodern design of the new houses.

Apart from the Metro-land, this style applied to the building of monumental, dreamy pre-war country houses of the rich capitalists. Issuing from the tradition of the Arts and Crafts movement and the Gothic Revival, based on the adoration of the "thorough and honest spirit of the good work of old days" (Gertrude Jekyll qtd. in Lucas, 72) and the refutation of novelty, as well as the acknowledged employment of pre-fabricated or industrialised items, these residences presented their owners as the holders and cherishers of the beauty and sweetness of the English countryside and as advocates of peace. Architects such as Edward Lutyens, Detmar Blow and Sydney Gimson were in truth building monuments to those "who were among those most directly responsible for bringing that peace to an end" (Lucas, 75). The majority of the big houses were being built on money either from armaments or enormous factories. Both these instruments of exploitation caused an enormous increase in pollution and slums in the cities, thus endangering, in their own way, the countryside: "For those who had made a fortune from such industries, to want to escape from the pollution, noise, and slum dwellings they had caused might be understandable. But for them to imagine themselves as rooted in country house values, identified with "old" England, was as inauthentic as the fake Tudor gables to be found on many of their houses" (Lucas, 75). The yearning for the easily achievable, false pastoral was projected in the peculiar style of houses of Metro-land, usually tiny semi-detached villas with a puny front-garden. Often they featured a garage, which was so small that when a car was driven inside neither the driver nor the passengers could get out. This serves as yet another proof of the aspiration of the investors and the owners of this housing development to disregard rationality and the rules of logic.

As a result, beginning with the twentieth century, the country house has become, both as a motif and setting, a rich object of continuous scrutiny, of questioning and rethinking and, consequently, has been reinvigorated. The bucolic pastoral of the seventeenth-century country house poem was renewed and transformed beyond recognition. The first decade of the twentieth century produced three exceptional novels from three exceptional Edwardian authors.[14] These novels attempted to

---

14 In comparison with the employment of the country house in the works of his contemporaries, Arnold Bennet, another extraordinary Edwardian author, oscillating between domesticity and exoticism, frequently depicts a hotel in his writing, either as a setting or as a part of the inventory, "that temporary wanderer's centre of a wanderer's life, that home-from-home that is never home" (Sanders, 494). Such as in the case of an early work, *Grand Babylon Hotel* (1902), or a later documentary novel, *Imperial Palace* (1930).

diagnose contemporary society with the help of a country house employed as a potent symbol of social and cultural development and as the incarnation of the relationship between identity and place. Examples of this are John Galsworthy's *The Country House* (1907) and *The Man of Property* (1906), the latter was originally a separate novel which was to become the first part of a trilogy embracing forty years of the Forsyte clan – *The Forsyte Saga,* H. G. Wells' semi-autobiographical *Tono-Bungay* (1909) and E. M. Forster's[15] 1910 novel, *Howards End.*

The Man of Property was published in 1906 by well-established writer and dramatist John Galsworthy. Its satirising features, apt descriptions and a bitter, disappointing ending contribute to its classification as a typical representative of novels criticizing the traits of the upper-middle classes during the late Victorian period. Galsworthy himself claimed "that in these pages he had pickled the upper-middle class, placed it "under glass for strollers in the wide and ill-ranged museum of letters to gaze at. Here it rests, preserved in its own juice; the sense of Property" (qtd. in Barker, 106). Galsworthy's background and his real-life experience display a close affinity with the events described in the novel, mainly the focus on criticism of the legal procedures of divorce and the loveless institution of Victorian marriage. Being himself an outcast, ostracized from the upper society for starting a shocking affair with a married woman whom he later married, Galsworthy's view in *The Man of Property* is sturdy and uncompromising: "Bosinney is beaten and killed by the Man of Property, and Irene is brought back to the slavery from which she revolted. ... Thus the curtain rings down on Irene Forsyte, crushed under the heel of prosperity, robbed of her love by a sudden awakening of the sense of property in the heart of the man she had thought clean of it" (Kaye-Smith, 62–63). However, the moment his personal situation changed, he felt the desire to pursue his wandering through the fields of upper-middle class society, inducing highly contrastive feelings: nostalgic admiration as well as contempt and loathing, sympathy as well as hostility. As both Irene and her real-life inspiration, Galsworthy's wife Ada, had been brought back into respectability, and the impeding war had obscured the public memory of his own scandal, "it was necessary for the original

---

15 In her 1924 critical study "Mr Bennett and Mrs Brown", Virginia Woolf separated her contemporaries into two groups: Edwardians: A. Bennett, H. G. Wells, J. Galsworthy and Georgians: T. S. Eliot, E. M. Forster, D. H. Lawrence and J. Joyce. This thesis adheres to a more conventional approach and counts E. M. Forster amongst the Edwardian authors, in compliance with the division proposed by Andrew Sanders in his *The Short Oxford Dictionary of English Literature.*

novel of protest to be hidden by the huge humanity – sometimes even sentimentality – of the saga of English prosperous family life" (Barker, 185). The bite of the criticism was lessened and *The Man of Property* was followed by the interlude of *The Indian Summer of a Forsyte*, which was just the overture for the remaining parts of the three-volume saga. His tone and the whole perspective have changed considerably: "*The Indian Summer of a Forsyte* ... made Galsworthy a quite different novelist from the man who wrote *The Man of Property*, and completely changed his whole Forsyte theme. ... He betrayed his own purpose but he made the Forsyte idea much more acceptable to the English reader" (Barker, 183).

Galsworthy was frequently accused of neglecting a more detailed and appropriate psychological portrayals of his characters. While reviewing his novel *Beyond* in August 1917, Virginia Woolf memorably described his creation with a complex apposite metaphor which implies the similarity between the effects of a day of open-air exercise on human mental processes and the ponderous psychology of Galsworthy's characters.

> Everyone, especially in August, especially in England, can bring to mind the peculiar mood which follows a long day of exercise in the open air. The body is tired out; the mind washed smooth by countless gallons of fresh air, and for some reason everything seems dangerously simple, and the most complex and difficult decisions obvious and inevitable. There is something truly or falsely spiritual about this state, and it is one which if prolonged may easily lead to disaster. In Mr Galsworthy's new novel the people fill us with alarm, because they appear all more or less under the influence of the great narcotic and therefore not quite responsible for their actions. They have been out hunting all day for so many generations that they are now perpetually in this evening condition of physical well-being and spiritual simplicity. With minds one of field and lane, hounds and foxes, they make sudden and tremendous decisions marked by the peculiar lightness and boldness of those who are drugged out of self-consciousness by the open air. Just before they drop off to sleep, they decide that they must get married tomorrow, or elope with a housemaid, or challenge someone to fight a duel. (Woolf, *Contemporary Writers*, 63)

It is true indeed that Galsworthy did not truly strive to create plausible, detailed outlines of the development of the human psyche, and his description of the inner life of animals seems much more persuasive than his insight into the psyche of human characters. However, what he aims at is the detailed description of a social type, rather than a fully-fledged, thoroughly delineated individual. From this perspective, *The Forsyte Saga* is a closely observed and well-crafted description of the world of the Forsytes with the occasional excursion into their individual psyches. The procedure Galsworthy applies is the observation of their exterior, the wider and the immediate one. In the books, Galsworthy provides observations of their exterior, starting with the region, town, houses, rooms, clothes and bodies, he ventures on to the unknown realm of the soul. As a species the Forsytes are conditioned by their environment which often seems to outweigh their importance as individual human beings. Woolf added to her warning against the relative flatness and psychological implausibility of Galsworthy's characters: "This is not a clear way of distinguishing character. ... If you collected and multiplied traits of the kind Galsworthy has here given, you might in the end at some slight discrimination of character" (qtd. in Liddel, 125–6). With the exception of Soames and Old Jolyon, *The Forsyte Saga* almost entirely avoids any potential identification with the characters, instead supplying the readers with copious details of the environment. What is the decisive factor from the point of view of this study is the role Galsworthy, due to the method of description he employs, attributes to the "habitat". The first three volumes of *The Forsyte Saga*, *The Man of Property*, *In Chancery*, *To Let* orbit around the doomed house in Robin Hill. Soames, "the pioneer leader of the great Forsyte army advancing to the civilization of this wilderness" (Galsworthy, *The Man of Property*, 66), invests in the construction of an unusual, "odd" house in the countryside, or, better said, in the future suburbs yet unperturbed by massive housing developments: "The times were good for building, money had not been so dear for years; and the site he had seen in Robin Hill ... – what could be better! Within twelve miles of Hyde Park Corner, the value of the land certain to go up, would always fetch more than he gave for it; so that the house, if built in really good style, was a first-class investment (Galsworthy, *The Man of Property*, 60–1). Nevertheless, the house which might be seen as a symbol of everything that eludes Soames – authenticity, style, beauty, loftiness – defies and rejects him, as well as his wife, Irene: "He might wish and wish and never get it – the beauty and the loving in the world!" (Galsworthy, *To Let*, 906).

The same paradigm is observed in the 1907 novel *The Country House*, where it is no longer a Forsyte who is contemplated, monitored and dissected, but a Pendyce, and the habitat in question is not an extravagantly costly suburban villa, but a country house. The country classes are described as backwards and ruled by their "meat-fed instincts" (Galsworthy, *The Country House*, 181). Again, Galsworthy paints a fresco of an extramarital affair doomed to failure, with the only difference that this time it is not a heartfelt romance but a whim with a highly destructive potential. A Pendyce is typically a representative of country gentry. With the air, the woods and the fields having passed into their blood, they are dominated by their love for their homes and the homes of their fathers while keeping firmly to their false dignity, status and resolutions at the expense of reason, practicality and the destructive side-effects. The Pendyces and those alike are self-righteous to the point of being persuaded about the absolute legitimacy of their conduct and lifestyle:

> What, indeed, could be more delightful than this country-house life of Mr Pendyce; its perfect cleanliness, its busy leisure, its combination of fresh air and scented warmth, its complete intellectual repose, its essential and professional aloofness from suffering of any kind, and its soup – emblematically and above all, its soup – made from the rich remains of pampered beasts? (Galsworthy, *The Country House*, 9)

Quite unexpectedly, it is Mrs Pendyce who temporarily rebels against this rigid, ossified comfort, willing to free herself as well as her good-for-nothing son from the constraints imposed upon them by "pendycites". She is one of hundreds of women "sitting waiting for their hair to turn white, who, long before, at the altar of a fashionable church, had parted with their imaginations and all the little changes and chances of this mortal life" (Galsworthy, *The Country House*, 54), waiting for everything and nothing. Just as Irene in The Man of Property, if less explicitly and crushingly, is defeated and lured back by the traditional, comforting embrace of "Home", the instinct of which is, according to Galsworthy, older and more important "than the fever of change" (Galsworthy, *To Let*, 906).[16]

---

16 P. G. Wodehouse's tone while depicting a similar preoccupation with a piece of property in *The Girl on the Boat* (1921) is naturally slightly more sardonic:
"More than anything else in the world she loved her charming home, Windles, in the county of Hampshire, for so many years the seat of the Hignett family. Windles was as the breath of life to her. Its shady walks, its silver lake, its noble elms, the old grey stone of its walls--these were bound up with her very being. She felt that she belonged to Windles, and Windles to her. Unfortunately, as a matter of cold, legal accuracy, it did not. She did but hold it in trust for her son, Eustace, until such time as he should marry and take possession of it himself. There were times when the thought of Eustace marrying and bringing a strange woman to Windles chilled Mrs. Hignett to her very marrow. Happily, her firm policy of keeping her son permanently under her eye at home and never permitting him to have speech with a female below the age of fifty, had averted the peril up till now." (7)

Home! The long narrow lane without a turning, the mists and stillness, the driving rain and hot bright afternoons; the scents of wood smoke and hay and the scent of her flowers; the Squire's voice, the dry rattle of grass-cutters, the barking of dogs, and distant hum of threshing; and Sunday sounds – church bells and rooks, and Mr. Barter's preaching; the tastes, too, of the very dishes! And all these scents and sounds and tastes, and the feel of the air to her cheeks, seemed to have been for ever in the past, and to be going on for ever in the time to come." (Galsworthy, *The Country House*, 290)

If the plot and the characters are flat and negligible, there are elements in Galsworthy's descriptions, and particularly those of their environment, which reveal a close connection between an individual and the surroundings. At the same time, he highlights the landmarks in the architectural and urbanist development in England, the lessening of power of the country houses and the country gentry, and the expansion of the urbanites into the countryside on the outskirts of the cities with the suburban commuters becoming the life's blood of London. He also portrays the ferocity of housing development and the housing market and the building of grand Edwardian villas in the countryside. These houses merged and defied the remnants of the Gothic Revival and the Arts and Crafts movement with "Wrenaissance" (Frampton, 50), which was the newly discovered passion for the turn of the century Neo-Palladianism. The mastermind behind this development was the famous architect Lutyens, whose contribution together with the first large scale war and the gradual crumbling of the Empire, buried the Gothic Revival and paved the way to Modernism. Despite multiple attempts, architectural Modernism proved unable to conquer Britain. Due to its overtly revolutionary and revolutionising access to living, its costly building methods and the overall conception of building as severing ties with tradition and the past doomed it to failure within a British context.

Another Edwardian novelist, H. G. Wells, pays close attention to the description of houses in his rags-to-riches, semi-autobiographical novel *Tono-Bungay*, where he employs them as symbols of social and economic progress and aspiration as well as a potent illustration of the different strata of English society. A well-versed author of sci-fi prophecies, Wells combined his thorough knowledge of contemporary science and scientific methods with his belief in the beneficial outcome of scientifically and socialistically planned future in order to emphasise the intrinsically anti-human aspect of scientific progress and planning. He even wove some of his leitmotifs into to his social fiction, and seen from this perspective, *Tono-Bungay* involves a vivid portrayal of the quest for success of the main protagonists as well as science as an irreplaceable source of their economic and social progress. It depicts the narrator's transitions between three spheres, three different environments, incarnated by three different domestic spaces. Firstly, George Ponderevo admires an old country house which, falling into decline, stands for a defunct society in a desperate need of refashioning. George observes this development with a great deal of nostalgia, since it deprives him of any sort of organized, schematic vision of society like he used to have as a child:

> There came a time when I realised that Bladesover House was not all it seemed, but when I was a little boy I took the place with the entirest faith as a complete authentic microcosm. I believed that the Bladesover system was a little working-model—and not so very little either—of the whole world. ... The great house, the church, the village, and the labourers and the servants in their stations and degrees, seemed to me, I say, to be a closed and complete social system. About us were other villages and great estates, and from house to house, interlacing, correlated, the Gentry, the fine Olympians, came and went. The country towns seemed mere collections of ships, marketing places for the tenantry, centres for such education as they needed, as entirely dependent on the gentry as the village and scarcely less directly so. I thought this was the order of the whole world. I thought London was only a greater country town where the gentle-folk kept town-houses and did their greater shopping under the magnificent shadow of the greatest of all fine gentlewomen, the Queen. It seemed to be in the divine order. (Wells, 13–14)

Yet the system is failing to function, falling apart. "It is like an early day in a fine October. The hand of change rests on it all, unfelt, unseen; resting for awhile, as it were half reluctantly, before it grips and ends the thing for ever. One frost and the whole face of things will be bare, links snap, patience end, our fine foliage of pretences lie glowing in the mire" (Wells, 15). In the new English countryside, both in the literal and metaphorical senses, human beings are no longer tied to a place, which would be theirs, which would belong to them intrinsically, inextricably "from your birth like the colour of your eyes" (Wells, 16). The defunct country house is replaced by the restricted, reductive perspective of small-scale business only to give way to a profligate, pompous, unscrupulous world of patent medicine and its quick, heady progress in the field of market capitalism. The success of Edward Pondervo, George's uncle, is to be crowned by the building of a luxurious, extravagant house, "irrelevant unmeaning palace" (Wells, 272), whose construction disturbs the economic balance of the whole countryside and signals the inability of the economic system to comply with such a gigantic expenditure. Building is depicted as a swan song of many lucrative business careers of modern financiers: "Sooner or later they all seem to bring their luck to the test of realisation, try to make their fluid opulence coagulate out as bricks and mortar, bring moonshine into relations with a weekly wages-sheet. Then the whole fabric of confidence and imagination totters — and down they come ..." (Wells, 272).

Houses treated by the third Edwardian novelist, Edward Morgan Forster, are of decisively smaller scale, as in the case of his 1910 novel, *Howards End*: "Howards End is not a great country house. It is scaled down to a far more modest size than those houses that had been celebrated by Jonson, Carew, Marvell, Pope and others; but its naturalness echoes theirs, the implication that it was built with no man's ruin, no man's groan" (Lucas, 69). They are nonetheless not less significant and potent in the revelation of the contemporary social and cultural struggle of pretentious middle-class Edwardian society. Slightly more insistently domestic and provincial than his previous works, such as *Where Angels Fear to Tread* (1905), *The Longest Journey* (1907), or *A Room with a View* (1908), *Howards End* again mixes sharp-witted observation of the liberal guilt of English upper-classes with reflections upon the possibility of the connection of business and intellect, as well as the nature of the future holders of the British isle. The social as well as the environmental appeal which he makes at the final pages of the novel do not bode well for the undisturbed, peaceful, isolated countryside, paving the future direction of works on a similar subject.

With the countryside losing its traditional significance, the Empire falling apart and the inclusion of numerous new themes and motifs identifying the relationship between man and place, the country house novel fell into decline. There were attempts to restore the former dignity and grandeur of the English country house, for example in the novels of Evelyn Waugh, and in his nostalgic novel *Brideshead Revisited* (1944) in particular. The novel frequently revives the period before "the arrival of barbarians" (Stone, "Forster, the Environmentalist", 183), but also depicts the desolation of the transformation of these former seats of power, elegance and balance into lunatic asylums and military camps, as well as their inevitable absorption by the insatiable industrial and suburban sprawl:

And that people should go on existing by the million in the towns, prey-ing on each other, and getting continually out of work, with all those other depressing concomitants of an awkward state, distressed him. While suburban life, that living in little rows of slate-roofed houses so lamen-tably similar that no man of individual taste could bear to see them, he much disliked. Yet, in spite of his strong prejudice in favour of country-house life, he was not a rich man, his income barely exceeding ten thou-sand a year. (Galsworthy, *The Country House*, 10)

Nina looked down and saw inclined at an odd angle a horizon of strag-gling red suburb; arterial roads dotted with little cars; factories, some of them working others empty and decaying; a disused canal; some distant hills sown with bungalows; wireless masts and overhead power cables; men and women were indiscernible except as tiny spots; they were marry-ing and shopping and making money and having children. (Waugh, *Vile Bodies*, 219)

Suburban sprawl is the result of the unscrupulous exploitation of the pastoral vision which would traditionally identify the unspoilt landscape with national identity. However, its existence only further jeopardised the belief in the uncorrupted, unspoilt countryside. The questioning and challenging of the relevance and authenticity is a natural process which follows the creation of any kind of idealised state. The more thorough and complex this questioning becomes, the more varied an interpreta-tion of the problem it produces. As Dominic Head argues, the course of the twentieth century brought numerous changes to the connection be-tween identity and place. The overall urbanist development which start-ed with the growing urbanisation of the population in the nineteenth century challenged "the Wordsworthian notion of finding a home in the landscape, a place of belonging" (Head, 190), and finally made it un-convincing if not irrelevant. Further development, which includes the rise of the suburb as the new style of living, the gradual crumbling of Empire and the massive migration of whole populations, even increased the pressure on the relevance and authenticity of the connection between identity and place. The post-war writers fervently employ the idea of the pastoral, redefining, refashioning it according to the contemporary para-digm, questioning, challenging, examining, even refuting it ceaselessly: "even if the effort of re-evaluating pastoral may seem a more delicate and complicated operation than it had in the past" (Head, 191). The process of redefining and re-evaluating the pastoral vision is hindered by several factors which verge on undermining the whole concept. Terry Gifford, the author of the monograph *Pastoral* (1999), claims that the term "pastoral" is used in three distinctive ways: as a historical form with a long pedigree starting with poetry, later on adding drama and currently even novels, which started with the description of life in the countryside, especially that of shepherds, a version of pastoral Leo Marx summarised as "[n]o shepherd, no pastoral" (Gifford, 1); the second meaning is broader as it stands for any literature which implicitly or explicitly contrasts life in the countryside, whose beneficial effect it highlights, with the urban experience; the third meaning is a pejorative one, stressing the delusional simplification of life in the countryside in its literary renditions. The manifold definition of the term does not represent the greatest threat to its validity. The possibility of pastoral escapism is severely endangered since, by the end of the nineteenth century, it has been impossible to distinguish clearly between the country and the city which merged together by means of ongoing suburbanization.[17] At this point Gifford cites John Barrell and John Bull, the authors of *The Penguin Book of the Pastoral Verse* (1974), "[t]he separation of life in the town and in the country that the Pastoral demands is now almost devoid of any meaning. It is difficult to pretend that the English countryside is now anything more than an extension of the town" (as cited in Gifford, 3).

The process of questioning and challenging the obsolete, conservative meaning and form of pastoral brings Gifford to the introduction of two outgrowths – namely the well-established anti-pastoral, which undermines the whole tradition, and post-pastoral. The latter is the outcome of the combination of the creative and critical perspectives, where both these approaches may be defined on the basis of their resentment and rejection of the traditional model of pastoral and their adherence to six principles stipulated by Gifford: the natural world is a source of marvel and delight, but also a highly productive as well as destructive force; human nature may be enlightened by its relationship to the natural world, culture's construction of nature and the understanding of nature as culture, the insistence on the impossibility of separating human conscience from ecological consciousness; and lastly, the awareness of the fact that environmental exploitation resides on the same principles

---

17   At this point the view of the author seemingly clashes with the opinion of Raymond Williams who called for the dissolution of boundaries between the concept of the country and the city. It is necessary to note that what Williams had in mind was the rejection of the separation of their mental concepts, which might be potentially dangerous for the development of both spheres. Gifford on the other hand calls for a clearer separation between the city and the country predominantly because of the growing agglomerations, urbanisation and industrialisation.

as social exploitation. Albeit the conception of post-pastoral seemingly fulfils the demands of and agrees with the principles of ecocriticism, Dominic Head brands it as "increasingly fraught, haunted by the sense of its own impossibility" (Head, 194). The growth of urbanized culture and the aftermath of the fall of Empire have hindered the sense of belonging as identity search conditioned by a place. "England (in particular) becomes the site for post-colonial contestation, as new identities are negotiated, and new grounds of 'belonging' are tentatively forged. The idea of pastoral of post-war writers, it seems, is stretched to a breaking point" (Head, 190).

The notion of the pastoral, subjugated to the growing scepticism and diversified approach of its creative and critical renditions and interpretation, is closely associated with the concept of the country house. Both these phenomena represent ideals which have never truly dominated any moment in literary history, although it might seem they have. The country house poem of the seventeenth and the eighteenth century provides a glorifying vision of the well-administered English country house, but, on closer inspection, Jonson's seminal ode to Penshurst "is rather at odds with the real circumstances under which it was written, and that the poem's congenial tone is marked by subtle misgivings" (Spurr, 22). Terry Gifford describes a similar rejection of the pastoral convention, where "the most serious accusation is the suggestion that pastoral in the seventeenth and eighteenth centuries created a false ideology that served to endorse a comfortable status quo for the landowning class who had been the reading public before the nineteenth century" (Gifford, 7). It seems that each generation will question and challenge the nature and standing of pastoral as its needs and demands continually evolve.

So does the country house fiction, which partly incarnates continuity with earlier periods, but whose re-evaluation, in accord with the pastoral tradition, becomes, due to the complicated social, cultural and economic circumstances, a slightly more complex and complicated process than in the past. Accordingly to the social and cultural development in England in the second half of the twentieth and the beginning of the twenty-first century, the fictional forms of country houses are bought and sold, often to foreigners whose buying power exceeds aristocratic exclusivity or expunges the crimes of the past, such as the case of Darlington Hall in Kazuo Ishiguro's *The Remains of the Day*, or transformed into schools, hotels, museums and monuments as in the case of Ishiguro's 2005 dystopia, *Never Let Me Go*, Alan Hollinghurst's 2011 novel, *The Stranger's Child*, or Ian McEwan's 2001 novel, *Atonement*. Some of the stately homes have become desolate, hollow shells kept for the sake of appearance as in the case of the Narborough estate described so memorably in Will Self's 2002 novel *Dorian, an Imitation*. Sometimes, readers may catch a glimpse of life in the past as seen through the prism of historical novels or novels which offer a playful twist on the depiction of a particular period, very often the period before or after the Great War, as in the case of the earlier mentioned *The Stranger's Child*, Sarah Waters' 2009 take on Gothic novel, *The Little Stranger*, or Sadie Jones's dreamlike 2012 novel, *The Uninvited Guests*.

3. In Search of a House with a View: Poetic Parallels between the Conception of Dwelling in E. M. Forster's *Howards End* and Iris Murdoch's *The Sea, The Sea*

The house was insignificant, but the prospects from it would be an eternal joy.
(*HE*, 185)

It's a great mistake ever to imagine one is home,' she said brokenly and sank onto the bottom stair.
(Jones, 47)

The house E. M. Forster presents in his novel, *Howards End*, opens a new chapter in the understanding of the roles houses may assume and anticipates the modernist preoccupation with secluded places and their strangely humanised properties. Bearing a striking resemblance to the Hertfordshire residence where the author and his mother spent ten years, Howards End plays the part of a datum which anchors his vision of England and the world. Forster's narration features and echoes a continuous calling for connection materialised by Margaret Schlegel's motto "Only connect!" The life in a spiritual continuum is opposed to the emerging civilization of flux, of constant erratic movements typical of culture in which the emptying of internal existence had been replaced by external accumulation.

Iris Murdoch's novel *The Sea, The Sea* revolves around the self-inflicted, hermit-like existence of Charles Arrowby, a formerly famous stage director, whose decision to become "good" (Franková, 37) entails his retreat to a secluded seaside villa, entitled fittingly Shruff End, on the north coast of England. Documenting his struggles in a fictitious "memoir/

diary/philosophical journal",[18] he is forced to abandon his meditation, as he is immediately immersed into an emotional tumult caused by the unexpected appearance of his former lovers and other visitors. His failed attempts at transforming himself into an authentic, good person, without any external intrusions, show the humanist preoccupation of Murdoch and serve as an inexhaustible source of comedy.

Both novels display a cyclical thematic composition which is highlighted by the employment of prevalently circular imagery and the chronological treatment of the plot as well as its positioning to the period of summer. Thus, "summer house fiction" comes to existence. Failed attempts at solving the existential struggle that verge on comedy, the ominous undertone of impending ecological disaster threatening the unspoilt view, and the degree and consequences of human involvement in nature, are all points of reference strengthening the thematic connections between Murdoch's *The Sea, the Sea* and Forster's *Howards End*. Howards End and Shruff End, the fictional houses at the centre of the novels, anchor the narration while incarnating a number of functions and meanings: they are emblems of the social classes to which their owners belong, they are attributed with highly humanised traits such as an eagerness to express their will, becoming slightly treacherous and ghastly in the process, they are spiritual sanctuaries reviving a sense of space in their owners, and they symbolise their owners' connection with the land. But the function which overshadows all the others is their ability to provide a view, both literal and metaphorical, and thus to provide their uprooted inhabitants with connection, with a sense of belonging to the world.

3.1 "Days of Peculiar Splendour": Summer in the Country House

The books on the low shelves were mostly summer reading you find in rented houses, books suited to the role, with faded jacket illustrations of other houses in other summers, or almanacs, or atlases, a sun stripe edging the tops of the taller books.
(DeLillo, 46)

And summer's lease hath all too short a date.
(Shakespeare, *Sonnet 18*)

---

18   Murdoch, Iris. *The Sea, The Sea*. 1978. With an Introduction by John Burnside, London: Vintage, 1999, p. 3. [Subsequent page references preceded *TS* are given in parentheses in the text].

Since the beginning of the twentieth century, the urge of urban dwellers to abandon life in the city for a few weeks in an unspoilt natural setting has been threatened by a commercialisation which has transformed all the truly beneficial outcomes of the change of scenery into a wide range of clichés and stereotypes. [19] This temporary change of address has acquired the dimension of a socio-cultural phenomenon, deeply rooted within the defining characteristics of the middle class, and has given birth to a considerable amount of literary production rendering all the different forms of such a kind of dwelling.

Another aspect of country house fiction restricts its action to the period of summer, with the majority of country house fiction taking place during the lustrous days of that season, during "days of peculiar splendour" (Waugh, *Brideshead*, 23), which often reflects the actual situation of people residing temporarily in the countryside. The resulting poetics tends to define what may be identified as "summer-house fiction", a subgenre which is thematically relatively uniform, but whose popularity is fuelled by the possibility of readers identifying with the situation of a restricted period of time spent in a place quite remote from their everyday reality. Summer, with its languid days and morality, all its promises of retreat, renewal and respite on the one hand, and splendour, rapture and intensity on the other, has inspired many novels and novellas crafted around the element of the country house. This specific form of residence is not reserved for literature only and authors from nations with a coastline frequently choose to buy or rent summer houses by the sea and thus replenish their inspiration.

Thus, the poetics which Albert Camus ascribes to "the House above the World" from his novel *A Happy Death*, which he wrote in the 1930s but which was published posthumously in 1971, adumbrates the major elements of subsequent works by him and others. The house is situated in Algiers, on the top of a hill overlooking the sea, drowned in flowers, bathed in sun, intoxicating its inhabitants with air and light.

> ... the House above the World trained its huge bay windows on a carnival of colours and lights, day and night. But in the distance, a line of high purple mountains joined the bay and its extreme slope and contained this intoxication within its far contour. Here no one complained of the steep path or of exhaustion. Everyone had his joy to conquer, every day. Living

---

19   Parts of this chapter's text appeared in "Days of Peculiar Splendour: *Howards End* and *The Sea, The Sea* in the Context of Summer House Fiction." *English Language and Literature Studies* 5, no. 3, 2015, Toronto: Canadian Center of Science and Education, pp. 1–12.

above the world, each discovering his own weight, seeing his face brighten and darken with the day, the night, each of the four inhabitants of the house was aware of a presence that was at once a judge and a justification among them. The world, here, became a personage... (Camus, 33–34)

However, the purity of the air and the sheer openness of the space and scorching sunlight are achieved at the expense of human sacrifice. Patrice Mersault, the main protagonist, kills a dying rich man because he believes he is entitled to happiness. As a result, the idyllic seaside villa is stricken because of his absence of guilt and conspicuous lack of remorse. The beauty of the idyllic setting is poisoned by the price at which it was achieved and the sharp contrast between Patrice's vitality and ravenous grasp of opportunity and the putrid effect of his fatal illness (Patrice contracts tuberculosis and dies) emphasise the existential struggle at the heart of the story.

Many novels continue in a similar pattern and are far from being pastoral idylls as the summer retreats they depict reinterpret the idyll, or defy it, and the intensity of their rejections varies from parody and mock pastoral to the Gothic. Seen from this perspective, Murdoch's twentieth novel, *The Sea, The Sea*, her only novel to win the Booker Prize, adds unexpected twists to its otherwise traditional narrative of retreat.

The country house in its summer form, both as theme and setting, has been revisited by a number of contemporary novels in English. The American novelist Don DeLillo performs a dissection of an abnormal process of grieving in his 2001 novel *The Body Artist*, set in a rented house on the New England Coast. The year 2014 witnessed the emergence of numerous novels reviving interest in the complexity of a seemingly pastoral setting, such as the thriller *Summer House with Swimming Pool* by Herman Koch, *The Lemon Grove* by Helen Walsh, in which the beauties of nature unleash elemental desires, Emma Straub's *The Vacationers*, featuring a Mediterranean retreat in Mallorca, and *The Arsonist* by Sue Miller, set in New Hampshire. One aspect all these literary works share is a certain form of exclusivity arising from the economic superiority of the middle-class protagonists. Since the beginning of the twentieth century, summer houses, country houses, as well as the countryside itself have decisively become expressions of a yearning for the pastoral which is closely associated with, if not reserved to, the middle class. Its association with the countryside, its cultivation, its preservation and the issuing environmental policy is partly inspired by the rhetoric of the advertising campaign for Metroland. Besides this essential step taken by the Metropolitan Railway towards the development of the London suburbs between 1915 and 1932, there are powerful literary portrayals of the exclusive country aspirations of the middle classes: where John Galsworthy layers pastoral images describing an ordinary country house and its surroundings in *The Country House* (1907) and an extraordinary house and its surroundings in idyllic Robin Hill in the first volume of *The Forsyte Saga* (1906–1921), Forster offers a house with a view achieved at the expense of sacrifices of different types in his 1910 *Howards End*, Murdoch mocks a failed attempt at leading a nature-infused existence in her 1978 *The Sea, The Sea*, and Fay Weldon draws a realistic picture of an "idyllic" weekend spent in the cottage in the countryside in her brilliant short story, "Weekend" (1978).

The middle-class Arcadia certainly has its perils and frequently counters the expectations of the readers. The majority of fictional country houses are often depicted as inconvenient, high-maintenance and, at times, even treacherous places. Their impracticality often resides in the fact that they were designed for a different function in a different period and are therefore unable to fulfil satisfactorily the practical demands of modern dwellers. The weathered charm of the places is put to the test when the new inhabitants are forced to deal with a lacking or inadequate plumbing system, smoking fireplaces, huge rooms which are impossible to heat properly, a vast number of charming, but uninhabitable rooms, and masses of bric-a-brac accumulated over the centuries. In her short story, Weldon echoed Murdoch's preoccupations and pertinently responded to the growing popularity in the period of country-life aspirations by playfully underlining the paradoxical nature of a weekend spent in a cottage in the countryside. A supposedly idyllic gathering of family and friends is seen from the point of view of a housewife who, tired after a gruelling week juggling office work and the demands of her family, continues her struggle with renewed intensity during a "relaxing" weekend, slaving over the stove in an ill-equipped kitchen, washing copious amounts of dishes and waiting on guests who keep urging her to relax. The shortage of supplies, inadequacy of the kitchen equipment, the demands of her family members and their insistence that her feverish activity is spoiling the relaxing nature of the weekend, only highlight the paradoxical and inauthentic nature of the middle-class aspiration to the pastoral. Weekly country-house commuting is depicted as a contribution to the set of burdens a middle-class woman has to endure.

Similarly, the house presented in the first instalment of the Cazalet chronicles, The *Light Years*, published in 1990 and written by Elizabeth

Jane Howard,[20] shelters three generations of the Cazalets during two romantic, interwar summers in Sussex. The never-ending process of adding to the former farmhouse, together with the absence of proper planning, contribute to the lack of practicality, comfort and sustainability of the resulting house, "a rambling muddle built round a hall with a staircase that led to an open gallery from which the bedrooms could be reached" (Howard, 67). As in the case of Fay Weldon's "Weekend", a family spirit should have been induced by their concentration in one place. However, the maintenance of the household and preparation of lavish meals place high demands on those in charge and their experience is a far cry from the romantic, idealized, relaxing time they are supposed to be having there.

Charles Arrowby, the narrator and main character of Murdoch's novel *The Sea, The Sea*, intends to detach himself from the corrupting forces of the urban milieu. He hopes to achieve a spiritual cleansing and awakening provoked by a self-inflicted isolation in a seaside villa, Shruff End, which is, despite its unwelcoming, dreary character, advertised as a charming place. Reasonable demands for comfort, suitability and practicality are overshadowed by the house's "uniqueness" (*TS*, 11) and potential to become a perfect hermit's den, transforming its inhabitant into an enlightened creature elevated above everyday material concerns. Nevertheless, after numerous attempts it turns out that Shruff End does not accommodate to Charles, nor does Charles accommodate to the house. It repeatedly manifests its own will and its hallucinatory properties gradually erode the clear distinction between reality and fantasy, vision and dream. With its repeated visions of the sea monster, occasional ghosts, and objects falling from shelves and tables for no reason, *The Sea, The Sea* embraces elements typical for the Gothic novel, which adds yet another layer of interpretation to this ironic revisiting of the narrative of spiritual awakening in the realm of the unspoilt countryside.

Despite the considerable diversification the model country house underwent from the beginning of the twentieth century, which may be seen

---

20 After decades of moderate professional success, life in the shadows cast by her husbands and relatively tumultuous private life, the work of this extraordinary author, who died at the beginning of 2014, is finally attracting the degree of attention it deserves, with Hilary Mantel and Martin Amis, her stepson from her marriage to Kingsley Amis, highlighting the quality of her works. Amis, her stepson, called her "the most interesting woman writer of her generation' alongside Iris Murdoch". As Elizabeth Day noted in the article published in the Guardian, Howard herself "is mildly astonished by the resurgence of interest in her work. Any talk of how her reputation as a writer is undergoing a long overdue re-evaluation is greeted with a startled glare" (Day).

partly as a result of the growing democratic aspirations of the period, there is one aspect that did not suffer any radical transformation and that is the temporal arrangement in which these houses exist. Both real and fictional country houses have always been marked with some form of specific temporality, be it temporariness or a firm rootedness in the past that connects the resulting literary portrayal with pastoral aspirations firmly linked with timelessness. As David Spurr claims with regards to Ben Jonson's ode "To Penshurst", "the ideology of the country house is shown to consist of a double-layered representation: the poem represents the house, which is already a representation of a mythic past" (Spurr, 23). Linear, chronological time is thus either dissected by the temporariness of the residence (especially in the case of rented houses or houses with a restricted period of habitability) or invaded by the more or less subtle pull of the past. The extent of the timelessness depends on the level of absorption of the country house-associated ideology. A temporal linearity is also threatened when ecological worries indicate its possible interruption. It was Forster who, at the beginning of the twentieth century, voiced the concerns of both his predecessors and contemporaries, such as D. H. Lawrence, and highlighted the threat of a potential ecological catastrophe ensuing from the complete appropriation of the land by the "red rust" of technological civilisation.

The temporal character of summer house poetics further increases their idiosyncratic character. In the case of rented summer houses the time elapsed is delimited by the lease or period. Time and its specific treatment may be regarded as the chief constituents of the poetics of summer houses. Generally speaking, time seems to pass differently in these places, following its own patterns, e.g. a mourning wife stepping into a different atmosphere induced by the spirit of the dead husband: "She was happy in a way, in many ways, folded in hope, having the house to come back to after long mornings rambling in stands of jack pine and spruce … . knowing she would mount the stairs, touching the top of the newel at the landing, and walk down the hall into his time" (DeLillo, 121), or Margaret Schlegel recapturing the sense of space within the walls of Howards End: "She must have interviewed Charles in another world – where one did have interviews" (*HE*, 171), but the common denominator is its exaggerated circularity. Howards End, which acquires the character of permanent residence only at the end of the novel, opens and closes with a parallel image of Ruth Wilcox and later the Schlegel sisters revelling in the sight of cut grass, relishing its smell, with the rest of the Wilcox clan taking shelter inside the house to shield their hay-fever-prone selves from the effects of the grass. The degree of fatality involved in the novel, where "'it does seem curious that Mrs Wilcox should have left Margaret Howards End, and yet she get it, after all'" (*HE*, 292), only enhances the circular character of the work where time seems to follow a cyclical trajectory, connecting the present, the past and the future in a spherical continuum verging on the temporal arrangement of a myth: "All signs are against it now, but I can't help hoping, and very early in the morning in the garden I feel that our house is the future as well as the past" (*HE*, 290).

Similarly, the striking density of circular motifs and the circular nature of the majority of the leitmotifs concerning the house and the sea in Murdoch's *The Sea, the Sea* reinforce the final impression of firm interconnectedness. Thus the movements of the sea, Charles's preference for daily routines, be it swimming, eating or shopping, and the close attention the narration pays to minute descriptions of meals he prepares, all repeatedly refer to the cyclical effect of such actions and thus refer to the geometrical nature of a circle which, while completely separating the inside from the outside, is first and foremost a closed curve. Its unique properties, apart from having triggered a great deal of technological progress, inspired its adoption as an emblem of perfection and, consequently, of divinity. The *ensó*, mandala and halo are therefore expressions of various religions sharing a belief in the circle as the symbol of ultimate perfection and unity.

The Sea, The Sea brings the notion of circularity to an overwhelming new level of complexity. Besides the Buddhist agenda incarnated by James, Charles's cousin, and the depiction of the failed attempts of Charles to access wisdom and spiritual connection in any form, the novel also offers an intricate, yet highly overt intertextual commentary on Shakespeare's *The Tempest*. Both Prospero and Charles are men of the world, trapped and alienated in and by the natural world, and may be called magicians, directors of dramas which they stage through the sheer force of their manipulation. Reflecting the form of the island where Prospero performs his version of pandemonium, circularity penetrates all aspects, layers and interpretations of *The Sea, The Sea* and thus may be regarded as the key element of the overall poetics of the novel.

When it comes to Shruff End, its circular properties do not apply to its peculiar atmosphere only but also extend to its physical properties. The arrangement of the house features a striking number of windowless spaces, be it various oblong spaces on the landings of the stairs or two windowless inner rooms:

The chief peculiarity of the house, and one for which I can produce no rational explanation, is that on the ground floor and on the first floor there is an inner room. By this I mean that there is, between the front room and the back room, a room which has no external window, but is lit by an internal window giving onto the adjacent seaward room (the drawing room upstairs, the kitchen downstairs). These two funny inner rooms are extremely dark, and entirely empty, except for a large sagging sofa in the downstairs one, and a small table in the upstairs one, where there is also a remarkable decorative cast-iron lamp bracket, the only one in the house. (*TS*, 16)

In *The Poetics of Space*, Gaston Bachelard ascribes primal importance to the study of intimate places, scrutinising the spatial properties of houses and the nooks and corners within. He views all these as being reminiscent of nests and shells, which are understood "as primal images; images that bring out the primitiveness in us" (Bachelard, 91). These peculiar places may be perceived as the focal points of all the emotional involvement of humans in spatial practices: "I repeat images of full roundness help us to collect ourselves, permit us to confer an initial constitution on ourselves, and to confirm our being intimately, inside. For when it is experienced from the inside, devoid of all exterior features, being cannot be otherwise than round" (Bachelard, 234). Seen from this perspective, Charles's attempts to colonise Shruff End, as well as his peculiar fondness for the two inner rooms, may be understood as demonstrations of his willingness to compose himself, to retreat, to withdraw into himself, protected against the world: "... every corner in a house, every angle in a room, every inch of secluded space in which we like to hide, or withdraw into ourselves, is a symbol of solitude for the imagination; that is to say, it is the germ of a room, or of a house" (Bachelard, 136).

Besides these inner, nuclear rooms positioned in the centre of the house, there, amongst the scarce furnishings of Shruff End, a collection of puzzling objects is to be found, such as lamp brackets, vases, mirrors, stones of different sizes, all of them possessing a certain degree of circularity, being oval, round, elliptical or spherical, all of them further enhancing the haunting air of the house. Charles feels the house existing around him, with parts of it colonized and other remaining obscure and "alien" (*TS*, 19). Even the entrance hall, otherwise dim and "pointless" is embellished by a large oval mirror is dark and pointless, except for the presence of the large oval mirror, which seem to be glowing with its own light (*TS*, 19).

The elliptical is not restricted to the inside only, but spills into the arrangement of Charles's "rockery" with its various pools: "I also picked up a number of pretty stones and carried them to my other lawn. They are smooth, elliptical, lovely to handle" (*TS*, 7–8). Circularity extends from collecting, observing and marvelling at round objects of various sizes to the presence of the rocky hole which, viewed from the bridge, affords the curious pleasure of observing waves: "as they rushed into that deep and mysteriously smooth round hole, destroy themselves in a boiling fury of opposing waters and frenzied creaming foam" (*TS*, 261) and culminates in the inclusion of a "martello" tower in the repertoire.

The accumulation of circular imagery is reinforced by the gradual intensification of the circularity of the various activities Charles performs. The growing urgency, with which he clings to routines, defying both self-inflicted and visitor-induced disturbances, reaches its climax with his final gyration into the destructive spiral of obsession: "The next day I was like a madman. I rambled, almost ran, round the house, round the lawn, over the rocks, over the causeway, up to the tower. I ran about like a frenzied animal in a cage which batters itself painfully against the bars, executing the same pitiful leaps and turns again and again" (*TS*, 215).

Bachelard highlights the role of images of roundness, both marking their simplicity, verging on the primitive, and revelling in their completeness. The round or circular character of images is marked and valued as the source of hypnotic powers:

> These images blot out the world, and they have no past. They do not stem from any earlier experience. We can be quite sure that they are metapsychological. They give us a lesson in solitude. For a brief instant we must take them for ourselves alone. If we take them in their suddenness, we realize that we think of nothing else, that we are entirely in the being of this expression. If we submit to the hypnotic power of such expressions, suddenly we find ourselves entirely in the roundness of this being, we live in the roundness of life... (Bachelard, 233)

Seen from this perspective the actions and images accumulated in the depiction of Charles's endeavour to learn how to be good may be regarded as utterly beneficial, if not from Charles's point of view, then from the reader's.

Besides the temporal arrangement, circularity permeates numerous other aspects of the novels in question and hugely affects the prevalent imagery and even thematic preoccupation of the novels. Shruff End in

The Sea, The Sea accentuates an idiosyncratic passing of time: "It was not exactly a sinister or menacing effect, but as if the house were a sensitized plate which intermittently registered things which had happened in the past – or it now occurred to me for the first time, were going to happen in the future" (*TS*, 227). This temporal arrangement echoes the one presented in *Howards End* where it invokes Margaret Schlegel's dictum which treats the circularity as the existential principle.

3.2 Defining Dichotomies: Countryside and Class

To speak against London is no longer fashionable. The earth as an artistic cult has had its day, and the literature of the near future will probably ignore the country and seek inspiration from the town. One can understand the reaction. Of Pan and the elemental forces the public has heard a little too much – they seem Victorian, while London is Georgian – and those who care for the earth with sincerity may wait long ere the pendulum swings back to her again. Certainly London fascinates. One visualizes it as a tract of quivering gray; intelligent without purpose, and excitable without love; as a heart that certainly beats, but with no pulsation of humanity. It lies beyond everything: Nature, with all its cruelty, comes nearer to us than do these crowds of men.
(*HE*, 93)

… there is nothing to get up for in London.
(*HE*, 59)

In *Howards End* Forster establishes a basic dichotomy in the opposition of the Schlegel sisters, namely Margaret and Helen, and the Wilcox family. He later labelled the two groups they represent "Mollycoddles" (the Schlegels) and "Red-bloods" (the Wilcoxes) in his unfinished novel *Arctic Summer*. This elemental dualistic principle is slightly disrupted by Ruth Wilcox and her "sanctuary", Howards End, and by the Schlegels' all-comprising, and at times brutal and self-absorbed, principle of connection. Where one would expect a simple animosity between the two clans, the two households, Forster places adversaries at the very centre of the opposing side, be it Ruth Wilcox, the wife of Henry Wilcox, or, later, Margaret Schlegel connecting the two opposite poles through her own exogamic marriage to Henry Wilcox.

Charles Arrowby, the main character of *The Sea, the Sea*, nearly fails to complete his mission of learning to be good, which he wants to achieve through his reclusive existence in a seaside villa in the North of England. Ever distracted by inquisitive visitors, his effort is perpetually endangered by his twisted longings e.g. his lusting after his childhood sweetheart Hartley, or by disruptions imposed by the ghastly house, Shruff End, itself.

> It is not that I find Shruff End in any way 'creepy'. It is just that, as it now suddenly occurs to me, this is the first time in my life that I have been really alone at night. My childhood home, theatrical digs in the provinces, London flats, hotels, rented apartments in capital cities: I have always lived in hives, surrounded by human presence behind walls. ... This is the first house which I have owned and the first genuine solitude which I have inhabited. Is this not what I wanted? (*TS*, 20)

The sought-after solitude proves to be less desirable than he had imagined and the series of distractions thus fittingly fills the vexing void: it is not until he is tucked away safely in James's London flat that Charles finally approximates his original intention. The country proves to be "the least peaceful and private place to live. The most peaceful and secluded place in the world is a flat in Kensington" (*TS*, 111). It is paradoxically the anonymity of the city which enables "the scattering anonymous feeling of returning into oneself" (*TS*, 168).

Forster insisted on a specific way of reading his novels; they greatly resemble musical scores in which leitmotifs associated with certain characters and situations are of special importance. The alternation of these utterances creates a distinctive rhythm: "The book's rhythms are carried mainly by key phrases, and words within these phrases, which are stated and repeated in ever-widening circles of meaning." (Stone, "Howards End: Red-bloods and Mollycoddles", 268). Forster's creation was shaped by an alternation of such opposing motifs and country versus city dichotomy may be regarded as one of *Howards End*'s principal elements. Especially in the case of *Howards End*, the motifs of connection versus detachment, the masculinity versus the femininity of the Schlegel sisters, only anticipate another duality present in the novel and that is the country as opposed to the city. Forster's position in this duality is self-evident; he had already established himself as an author of organic imagery and his earlier stories and novels are yearnings for an unobstructed view, with *Howards End* representing a decisive nod in this direction. Motorcars[21]

---

21   Kenneth Grahame's 1908 pastoral account of Edwardian England, *The Wind in the Willows*, provides its readers with one of the most memorable descriptions of a car recklessly ravaging the countryside.

and hurrying men with their luggage bring flux and an inevitable impoverishment of the spiritual, aesthetic and ethical dimensions of human life. Cities are perceived as centres of the secular and the materialistic, as Wilfred Stone points out, echoing Lewis Mumford, "the city is a form of death" (Stone, "*Howards End:* Red-bloods and Mollycoddles", 260). The countryside, on the other hand, is idealised to the point of paean.

Raymond Williams's *The Country and the City* provides a commentary on the shifting attitudes towards the two traditional centres of life, the country and the city, and the changing associations they have inspired. It successfully rebuts their stereotypical conception and calls for the suppression of traditional division of both spheres. Despite the fact that their understanding is surprisingly changeable and prone to contrastive qualification, it still manages to further solidify their normative status. Therefore, the country has been associated with the pastoral, innocent rural, or innocent rural idiocy, both communal settlement and retreat (which obviously implies separation from community and mobility). There have been vast differences between approaches to country land, with one highlighting its cultivation and the other emphasising the wild, unspoiled countryside. What also tends to vary is the view of labour, whose presence and necessity is either accentuated or supressed. The city is on the one hand connected with corruptive forces typical of the pull of metropolitan, intrigue, politics, money and corruption. On the other hand it typically involves law, wealth, luxury civilisation and civilising properties. Urban dwellers are seen as a mob, as homogenous, unidentified masses as well as crowds of isolated individuals. The constant process of comparing the country and the city highlights the settled way of

---

"Glancing back, they saw a small cloud of dust, with a dark centre of energy, advancing on them at incredible speed, while from the dust a faint 'Poop-poop!' wailed like an uneasy animal in pain. Hardly regarding it, they turned to resume their conversation, when in an instant (as it seemed) the peaceful scene was changed, and with a blast of wind and a whirl of sound that made them jump for the nearest ditch, it was on them! The 'Poop-poop' rang with a brazen shout in their ears, they had a moment's glimpse of an interior of glittering plate-glass and rich morocco, and the magnificent motor-car, immense, breath-snatching, passionate, with its pilot tense and hugging his wheel, possessed all earth and air for the fraction of a second, flung an enveloping cloud of dust that blinded and enwrapped them utterly, and then dwindled to a speck in the far distance, changed back into a droning bee once more." (Grahame, 26)

Not only does Grahame's approach to motor-cars echo E. M. Forster's prejudice presented with a particular fervour in *Howards End*, but extolling undisturbed countryside and his criticism of fast moving, ravenous beast of a car, it becomes the chief source of Toad's, one of the iconic literary incarnations of upper-class joviality, conceit and fickleness, obsession resulting in downfall.

life characteristic of the former, which contrasts sharply with unwanted, constant changes typical of the city. At the same time, both the country and the city are alternately described as formerly idyllic zones threatened by destructive forces of economy. Williams underlines the necessity to view agricultural and industrial development as the opposite sides of the same coin and warns against simplifying interpretation of the country as closer connection with nature and the identification of the city with industry threatening to transform, or even destroy it.

The process of glamorising and fictionalising the dichotomy between the country and the city, and London in particular, has inspired a number of studies and has become one of the leading concerns of contemporary literary criticism and studies. Petr Chalupský, for example, examines literary portrayals of London and elaborates the diversity and versatility of the urban milieu. According to his numerous articles on the topic, contemporary British authors such as Penelope Lively and Peter Ackroyd depict London as a city defying definitiveness in all respects, since it exists in mutations of reality and various degrees of fictionality and, moreover, it utterly suspends chronological time: "The various forms of time coexist here – the city becomes a phenomenon beyond the chronological understanding of time where the past, present and future perpetually collide and mingle" (Chalupský, *The Postmodern City*, 15). Ackroyd's vision of London in particular becomes a highly specific form of Bakhtin's chronotope, a meticulously crafted whole in which, with time transforming into the fourth dimension of space, space and time merge into an inherently inseparable form.

> Thus in London, according to Ackroyd, "events and actions reduplicate, echo and reinforce one another in recurrent cyclical or spiral patterns, their occurrence to a large extent controlled by the energies of the places where they happen rather than merely by chronological successiveness". (Chalupský, "Like a Furnace Burning and Turning," 19)

Forster's and Murdoch's visions of the countryside and the particular spaces they depict – Howards End and Shruff End, bear traces of a similar spatiotemporal arrangement, although in a less exaggerated form. *The Sea, The Sea* does not provide the readers with any substantial information concerning the history of Shruff End, apart from references to the poltergeist and its haunted character. The cyclical temporal arrangement revolves mainly around Charles's adherence to daily routines and the employment of prevalently circular imagery. In the case of

Howards End, which also features appearances of a ghost, the source of the cyclical temporal patterning is, apart from the overall composition of the plot and the structural arrangement of repeating motifs, due to the close resemblance between Ruth Wilcox and Margaret Wilcox, née Schlegel:

> It is the starved imagination, not the well-nourished, that is afraid. Margaret flung open the door to the stairs. A noise as of drums seemed to deafen her. A woman, an old woman, was descending with figure erect, with face impassive, with lips that parted and said dryly:
> "Oh! Well, I took you for Ruth Wilcox."
> Margaret stammered: "I – Mrs Wilcox – I?"
> "In fancy, of course – in fancy. You fancy. You had her way of walking. Good day." (*HE*, 172)

Consequently, the defining dichotomy between the country and the city is employed in both cases, but both cases manifest its unforeseen aspects. *Howards End* emphasises the fragility of the undisturbed countryside while hinting at the possible ecological threat to it while *The Sea, The Sea* challenges the myth of spiritual awakening in nature.

All the houses in question display an array of various contradictory dualities, they scare and soothe, they inspire and exhaust, they shelter and expose, they attract and deter, they welcome and reject, they tie and provide various forms of release: "The house, the sea-planet outside it, and how the word alone referred to her and to the house and how the word sea reinforced the idea of solitude but suggested a vigorous release as well, a means of escape from the book-walled limit of the self" (De-Lillo, 49).

Both Howards End, which is the result of the refurbishment of an old farm, and Shruff End, which is a typical seaside villa, are repeatedly described as country houses, both by the authors of the novels as well as scholarly works on the subject. Nevertheless, they incarnate a specific vision originating in the myth of the country house and it is exactly this discrepancy and the subsequent tension between lavish, idealised palaces and their far more common counterparts such as villas, cottages and farms, which energises both works. The opening phrase of Helen Schlegel's letter to Margaret, which is also the opening of the whole novel, is an encapsulating commentary on the nature of the house and also its inhabitants and their social standing: "It isn't going to be what we expected. It is old and little, and altogether delightful – red brick"

(*HE*, 3). Helen's description abounds with implications, it involves a pre-
diction of the whole course of the novel, and it embodies all sorts of
prejudices towards nouveaux riches as well as the firm belief in tradition
in its positive sense. The last part of the statement is concerned with
bricks, a traditional building material, whose production and employment is associated with universally beneficial values such as authenticity,
order, balance, and skill.[22] "Red brick" signals a claim on soul and, possibly, spirituality or even connection, which are typically considered to
be outside the reach of the new rich.

Neither Howards End nor Shruff End are secluded aristocratic seats,
both are rather ordinary middle-class houses. Since *Howards End* is dominated by the question of class and, according to Daniel Born, it provides
"the most comprehensive picture of liberal guilt in this century" touching with striking precision "the sensitive spot in the consciousness, or
conscience, of the liberal literary intelligentsia" (Lodge, 8–9), the scale
of the house in question provides the narration with a greater innovative-
ness than in the case of an upscale town or country house.

Although the precise place on the social ladder may differ slightly
since the Schlegels' fortune probably surmounts that of Charles, both
Forster and Murdoch create universes which are decisively middle-
class. As Malcolm Bradbury points out, Murdoch peopled her novels
with a number of middle-class prototypes: "Though the forms were
various, there was indeed something called Murdochland, as distinctive as Greeneland" (Bradbury, 370). Although her novelistic legacy is
sometimes considered to be overblown and her novels overflowing with
numerous, seemingly flat, characters, burdened with over-crafted plots
abounding with references to the self-reflective properties of the novel,

---

22 Eric Lomax, is a Scottish author of a moving memoir of his experience as a POW in a Japanese
military prison in Burma during World War II, *The Railway Man; A POW's Searing Account of
War, Brutality and Forgiveness*. At the height of his torment, Lomax provides the reader with
a haunting image of beautiful British countryside. The sheer desperation of his anguish is
ironically reflected in the sweetness and delightfulness of the image, standing in dark contrast
to the rest of his unexpectedly matter-of-fact narration, is even accentuated by it being the first
and the last recorded daydream of the main protagonist:

"I had one vivid and frequent dream with a scene that seemed utterly perfect and
unattainable, a vision of impossible beauty. It was the image of an old English garden
in summer, near a cathedral, with banks of honeysuckle and roses under oak and willow
trees, the cathedral spire rising above them. It seemed so entirely real, and at the same time
a romantic painting of such a scene, as though I was looking at it from the side so that the
smooth lawn swept away from me in a great green triangle. There was an old brown-red
brick cottage hidden in the trees; it felt like order and wealth and safety." (Lomax, 116)

it is necessary to underline that her fiction is always merged with her philosophic preoccupations:

> She inhabits "the middle ground" – what she calls "ordinary human jumble", the realist territory of nineteenth century novel tradition – more authoritatively than any of her contemporaries. Indeed she swarms over it at the head of army of words: she has published twenty-three novels in thirty-six years of fiction writing, and the sheer bulk and variousness of her oeuvre have become a major part of her meaning. She stands for continuity and for belonging, for the circumstantial life crowded with personal relationships and personal "things". Her plots are those of moralist and a match-maker. (Sage, 72)

Having filled her novels with peculiar characters entangled in philosophical nets, religious beliefs or spiritual enchantments, Murdoch forces these characters to deal with the fundamental questions human beings face. In this way Murdoch's novels replicate the failures and imperfections of human existence in the realm of fiction through what may be regarded as structural flaws. Pushing her readers to the extreme of fictionality, her literary efforts acquire the position of "wise encounters with the density of experience and otherness", urging their readers to: "return to contact with the real" (Bradbury, 372).

From the point of view of subject matter, *Howards End* represented an extreme thematic expansion for Forster: "Its thematic problems arise in part because Forster tried to say and do too much. 'I think *Howards End* is all right,' he wrote on his eightieth birthday. 'But I sometimes get a little bored with it. There seems too much, too many social nuances, there'" (Stone, *The Cave*, 267). Forster, along with D. H. Lawrence, is the last great English novelist who tried to include all social classes in his work. Beside this, they both believed that the violation of aesthetic values committed by industrialisation might be the explanation of what was wrong in the society: "The real tragedy of England," writes Lawrence, "is the tragedy of ugliness. The country is so lovely: the man-made England is so vile" (qtd. in Stone, "Howards End: Red-bloods and Mollycoddles", 175). Forster agrees, but not without hesitation and difficulty, because he saw that beauty (conditioned by the presence of space) to be only another special privilege.

Unlike his previous novels, concerned predominantly with the purely private concerns of individual characters, *Howards End* focuses on the representatives of England's main economic power – the middle classes.

With this rich and inspiring ground to build upon, he continues his construction by means of joining, clashing and mingling contradictory elements such as the country and the city, the rich and the poor, the feminine and the masculine, the intellectual liberalism of the Schlegel sisters and the crude materialism of the Wilcoxes. In the very way in which the English countryside (in its mystical, idealized sense) clashes with "the hollow Suburbia" (*HE*, 13), the country opposes the city, meadows and forests defy motor-cars, and anchored, authentic existence counters the flux of civilisation with its hurrying men.

Howards End puts the possibility of the connection of these adversaries to the test. Margaret Schlegel's motto reverberates throughout the novel as her striving for connection acquires an almost heroic dimension and brings fatal consequences to most of those with whom she, or her sister Helen, tries to connect. The wide social scope of the novel enables the inclusion of Leonard Bast, an aspiring representative of a lower class, who is trying to reach the heights of the middle class, at least through his clumsy attempts to embrace a cultured life. Forster himself undermines the plausibility of this inclusion stating: "We are not concerned with the very poor. They are unthinkable, and only to be approached by the statistician or the poet. This story deals with gentlefolk, or with those who are obliged to pretend that they are gentlefolk" (*HE*, 38). Leonard's ambition to achieve an intellectual existence is continually ridiculed: "Oh, it was no good, this continual aspiration. Some are born cultured; the rest had better go in for whatever comes easy. To see life steadily and to see it whole was not for the likes of him" (*HE*, 47) and it is only through his connection with Helen that something fruitful is produced. It is a child, the inheritor of Howards End, whose origin may be seen as an attempt to reconcile or "connect" the two distant, if not opposing sides. Nevertheless, the disruptive potential of those connections proposed, or even extorted, by the Schlegel sisters is projected into the overall structural composition of the novel, which follows Margaret's dictum and twists the plot into a cyclical shape.

Howards End, besides other topics, vigorously examines the power and significance of money and its role in social stratification. Forster, along with other authors, reflected ethical concerns regarding the financial manipulation that had established England as the world's leading financial power: "Money acquired by manipulation rather than by manual labour inaugurated a morality so much larger and more exciting than a pitch-beck calculus of right and wrong that writers found themselves in possession of a new and vital theme" (Stone, *The Cave*,

250). The Schlegel sisters, the Cazalets, Miranda Grey and Charles Arrowby are all people who, at least formally, could be described as upper-middle-class, entitled to a pastoral life in the countryside, or at least possessing the possibility of choice between the country and the city. However, authors such as Forster and John Fowles also create powerful portrayals of representatives of lower classes, such as Leonard Bast or Frederick Clegg, who are deprived of "essential experience of nature and its beauty, which is so important for developing a sense of humanity" (Chalupský, *The Postmodern City*, 18):

> Then she shocked me. She went up to the fireplace where the wild duck were, there were three hung up, thirty-bob each and before you could say Jack Knife she had them off the hooks and bang crash on the hearth. In smithereens.
> Thank you very much, I said, very sarcastic.
> A house as old as this has a soul. And you can't do things like that to beautiful things like this old, old room so many people have lived in. Can't you feel that? (Fowles, 54)

Seen from this perspective, both *Howards End* and *The Sea, The Sea*, or even *The Collector*, which depict the experience of typical urban dwellers with country-life, associate culture, cultivation, sensitivity to nature and consequent aspiration to environmentalism almost exclusively with the middle classes and condition those attributes by their ability to embrace the life in the countryside. What is more, the country, in the ideal case, should only be sparsely populated in order to be tolerable: "To love space is to wish people elsewhere" (Stone, "Forster, the Environmentalist", 179). English fiction has provided a broad variety of responses, ranging from exclusive to inclusive approaches, with regard to the disturbance of the landscape by the presence of other people. Where Forster offers the house with a view achieved at the expense of sacrifices of different types in *Howards End*, Murdoch shows a solitude overrun with unwanted visitors in *The Sea, the Sea*, and Ian McEwan, in his 1998 novel, *Amsterdam*, presents a cautionary tale about what a deliberate ignoring of a possible crime scene, which threatened to disrupt the desired peaceful view of nature, may inflict.

In the summer of 2013, the debate over the exclusivity of the countryside in terms of population and class spurred a series of wide-ranging articles on the website of *The Guardian* newspaper. George Monbiot, an environmental writer and an ecological activist, declared his sincere love of nature and "nature writing" whereas journalist Steven Poole immediately described this love of nature as a form of "bourgeois escapism".[23] Where Monbiot argues for "rewilding", Poole remarks

> The idealisation of the natural world is as old as the city, to the corrupting influence of which a return to pastoral life is always presented as a cure. But the increasing modern appetite of metropolitan readers about walking around and discovering yourself in nature is the literary equivalent of the rise of the north London "farmers' market". Both feed on nostalgie de la boue – the French term for a kind of rustic-fancying inverted snobbery, which literally means "nostalgia for the mud"'. (Poole, I*s our love of nature writing bourgeois escapism?*)

Having scrutinized a vast amount of contemporary nature writing, such as George Monbiot's *Feral*, Rebecca Solnit's *The Faraway Nearby* and Sylvain Tesson's *Consolation of the Forest*, Poole expresses the fundamental paradox of all writing about nature, echoed in Forster's *Howards End*, Murdoch's *The Sea, The Sea*, and McEwan's *Amsterdam*: "Paradise, it seems, has no people in it" (Poole, "Is our love of nature writing bourgeois escapism?").

Monbiot's riposte lies, quite predictably, in identifying a love of nature with a love of art. He calls attention to capitalist-infused corporate thinking which defies the right of the natural world to exist: "So those of us whose love of the natural world is a source of constant joy and constant despair, ... find ourselves labelled – from *The Mail* to *The Guardian* – as romantics, escapists and fascists. That, I suppose, is the price of confronting the power of money" (Monbiot). Seen from Monbiot's perspective, Poole and those like him are marked as "philistines" for seeing no value in the wonders which enrapture others. Martin Robbins, a journalist and ardent blogger, concludes the debate by claiming that it is relatively unfair to force the public to embrace the artificial and eventually non-existing dichotomy of the country vs. the city, when both worlds might be favoured without any necessary class-conditioned preference. Deep interest in questions concerning the exclusion of human involvement in nature, which echoes the Romantic preoccupation with its solitary experience, is thus still clearly present in the sphere of mass

---

23 In *Heidegger's Hut*, the study of the influence of the simple, authentic, efficient hut situated in the Black Forrest Mountains on Heidegger's philosophy and writing, its author, Adam Sharr, hints at the possibility of Heidegger's identification with the hut being "the indulgence of bourgeois romance" (Sharr, *Hut*, 111).

culture, namely journalism, in Britain, indicating a persisting concern with the class and exclusivity connotations of country living.

When Forster inveighed against the suburban villas gobbling up the countryside, most explicitly in *A Room with a View* or *Howards End*, and later in his 1951 collection of essays, *Two Cheers for Democracy*, he opposed the irritating nature of so-called "Metro-land" which heavily promoted a set of commonly held beliefs in the beneficial effect of life in the country. This building of suburbs on surplus railway land in the early twentieth century promoted the idea that the spiritual growth and the physical well-being of an individual were conditioned by proximity to nature. Obviously, the past was romanticised as a period which enabled such a kind of life, which was reflected in the deliberately premodern design of the new houses. As far as the architectural properties of the sites in question are concerned, in his study on the ecological and economic backbone of Edwardian fiction, John Lucas clarifies the reason of the peculiar style of large Edwardian houses which are miming the ancient specimen rather than embracing any form of novelty. Unlike in the rest of Europe, where the attempts of Modernist architects extended to the field of planning of utopian social projects or created a new standard of luxury with peculiar domestic designs of extraordinary villas, in England, according to John Lucas, the houses are "deliberately premodern" (Lucas, 65). These houses seem to be devoid of any knowledge of new money. Although it is true that the big country houses bought during the Edwardian era were paid from the money acquired by capitalist exploitation, their owners did not stay "over the shop" any more. Situated in the countryside, these buildings were symbols of their owners' identification with English traditions, politics and social hierarchies "while in truth the real work of England – the hand-hardening, back-aching labour of millions – was done elsewhere, in factories, down mines, and in conditions that could in no sense be thought of as gardenlike" (Lucas, 65).

The Metroland's growing masses of commuters and wide spreading suburbs horrified Forster as they threatened to obstruct the view, robbing him of "the sense of space, which is the basis of all earthly beauty" (*HE*, 174). To yearn for an unspoilt view and empty spaces in a world becoming more and more densely crowded every day is a mark of a reclusive behaviour so typical for the Georgian admirers of the countryside. Its observers, such as Foster, came searching for its soothing atmosphere. Like so many of his contemporaries he felt tired, haunted and daunted by the strain of citified life and was inclined to contemplate the country as "a version of rural history ... The honest past, the pagan spirit"

(Williams, 256). Thus, long-term residents of the countryside were ig-
nored, silenced or viewed through the reductive lens of a pastoral vision. "The Georgian version used rural England as an image for its own
internal feelings and ideals" (Williams, 258). What is more, Forster and
others situated their vision to the parts of England that were spared from
the corruption by the effects of industrialisation, most frequently in the
shires or south of the country. This pastoral envisioning sets its roots
firmly into the soil of the ancient, unspoilt land and thus connects its
inhabitants with the past. Seen from this perspective, Forster's depiction
of the Schlegel sisters' quest for home may be viewed as "a search of
the kind of dwelling that could symbolize or even embody uncorrupted
Englishness" (Lucas, 62). And it is by means of connection, of putting
down roots, that the existence of England is revived: "She recaptured the
sense of space, … , and, starting from Howards End, she attempted to
realize England" (*HE*, 174).

There is a motif which emphasises the association with roots and that
is the presence of ancient trees. In the case of *Howards End*, it is "the finest wych-elm in Hertfordshire": "the place (Howards End) was English,
and the wych-elm that she saw from the window was an English tree. No
report had prepared her for its peculiar glory" (*HE*, 176). Forster even
stresses the universal "binding force" (*HE*, 222) a tree is able to exercise
on the character and warns against the perils of cosmopolitanism, which
he sees as loosening the ties with the earth, the countryside and consequently with a sense of belonging, geographically as well as spiritually:
"Under cosmopolitanism, if it comes, we shall receive no help from the
earth. Trees and meadows and mountains will only be a spectacle, and
the binding force they once exercised on character must be entrusted
to Love alone. May Love be equal to the task!" (*HE*, 176). There is yet
another Modernist work in which a tree is given a prominent place, symbolising the firm link between the present and the past: the Great Tree of
Groby whose cutting down might be perceived both as severing the ties
with tradition or as the last of all the imaginable blows and humiliations
Christopher Tietjens is willing to endure from his wife, Sylvia, in Ford
Madox Ford's opus magnum, *Parade's End* (1924–1928). The countryside, at least from the point of view of Edwardian, Georgian and Modernist fiction, is associated firmly with the past, with roots, with Englishn-
ness, while people in the cities, all the crowds of hurrying, uprooted
individuals, are portrayed as desperately failing to establish or even seek
connection. Seen from the highly ambiguous Modernist point of view,
the city is on the one hand "celebrated as a cosmopolitan intellectual

and cultural centre" and on the other hand condemned as "symbol of an overall spiritual and cultural decay, the ultimate manifestation of the impasse in which modern civilization found itself trapped" (Chalupský, *The Postmodern City*, 15).

Natural imagery is assigned a prominent place in both Forster's and Murdoch's works, although it does not play the principal part in the narration. It extends well beyond the motifs of trees (*Howards End*) and rocks (*The Sea, The Sea*) into the realm of nature, and more specifically, the sea. The fascination of the sea is, besides its unique aesthetic properties, caused by its ambiguous nature, which unites cyclical, periodical, predictable movements with vastness and caprice. Murdoch's *The Sea, The Sea* pays homage to this unique phenomenon since it is the sea alone which, though unpredictable and cruel, retains its ethereal beauty and grandeur from the opening lines until the end. Notwithstanding Howards End's position inland, Forster contrasts the richness of the sea and its unfailing nature with the flux of London which reflects the 'panta rhei' motions of rivers: "'I hate this continual flux of London. It is an epitome of us at our worst – eternal formlessness; all the qualities, good, bad, and an indifferent, streaming away – streaming, streaming forever. That's why I dread it so. I mistrust rivers, even in scenery. Now, the sea.'" (*HE*, 156). In his collection of essays, *Two Cheers for Democracy*, Forster saw the long-standing, unshakeable position of the sea and its artistic and poetic potential threatened by the ecological and political perils the twentieth century inflicted upon it:

> Yet the sea today certainly is in retreat. Occasionally it reasserts itself, as in the Kontiki expedition, and occasionally, through the fringe of oil and dead birds and the chonking and bobbing of metal objects, we catch a glimpse of it from the shore. But it is in retreat poetically. A poet is needed to arrest it, to restore Neptune his majesty, to wet Canute his fears, to float the Old Man in the Boat. (Forster, *Two Cheers for Democracy*, 271)

Dominic Head identifies the re-evaluation of pastoral, in terms of both its relevance and its conception, as a natural part of culture "[a]s human needs change, so does the function of the pastoral evolve" (Head, 190). The pastoral, as depicted in both *The Sea, The Sea* and in *Howards End*, is never a fully-fledged one, it is presented as a temporary equilibrium and is highly prone to corruption. Neither the trees nor the meadows nor the sea are spared the possible risks emerging from human involvement in the countryside. The effort to recapture a sense of space and, consequently, the land and the nation, is characterised as fruitless and corrupting if performed on a larger scale than by a few selected individuals and may be therefore labelled a highly exclusive activity.

In his famous lecture "Building Dwelling Thinking", Martin Heidegger addressed the architectural issues connected with the ability of buildings to provide their inhabitants with the sense of place and enable dwelling. This text and Heidegger's other writings on this topic were inspired by, if not directly written in, a hut situated in the Black Forest mountains where he spent a considerable amount of time writing and studying. Although it seemed unlikely to provide Heidegger and his family members with sufficient comfort, he absolutely insisted on minimal furnishings. Each simple item of its sparse equipment was charged with philosophical potential and was able to bring him closer to the essential elements of existence. *How Much House? Thoreau, Le Corbusier and the Sustainable Cabin* (2016), a monograph written by Urs Peter Flueckiger, analyses and interprets the minimal amount of space necessary for an ideally sized home. The author brands the desire for a simpler existence, which might even be only a temporary one, as a natural, universal need: "The cabin, the getaway home, represents not only a physical place to escape to, it represents an ideal, a metaphor in our minds where we imagine that things are clear and manageable (14). Compared with cluttered reality, a house comprising of a single room, which is typically the case for a hut or a cabin, appears manageable and simple. The contemporary trend of coffee-table books parading cabins, huts, holiday retreats demonstrates how much we long for simpler lives. An abode set in dreamy, impressive natural setting does not necessarily need to be inhabited physically to serve its purpose, as it often "represents an imaginary space, a location where things become clear and manageable again because the daily routines are no longer dominated by information overload" (Flueckiger, 15). At the end of his introduction to *Cabin Porn* (2016), a volume he initiated and edited, Zach Klein first describes his desire to build: "I needed a remote piece of land where anything was possible. I'd spent six years in the city building online communities and now I wanted to build one offline. ... I imagined a landscape nested with shelters we would make ourselves without any previous experience" (Klein, 3). He moves on to the Beaver Brook community, the material outcome of his effort and also the initial idea behind the Web page *Cabin Porn*, where he first intended to share pictures which had inspired the cabins he and his partners built in the forest situated in Upper Delaware Valley in upstate New York. The page attracted millions of visitors as well as fellow twelve thousand cabin enthusiast willing to share pictures of their abodes or their inspirations. In the end, the huge following of this cult website resulted in the publication of a hugely successful coffee-table book. Klein, however, urges his readers to make use of their abilities and provide themselves shelters and offer warm hospitality when building a simple construction of a hut. "We have a home" he says, "inside us ready to be built if we try" (Klein, 13).

The obvious inspiration behind the cabin cult, explored respectively by Flueckiger and Klein, is to be found in the seminal work on the subject of simple living and minimal housing solution, Henry David Thoreau's *Walden*. Thoreau, American author, poet, keen naturalist and one of the first environmentalists, was strongly affected by the industrial revolution, with "men becoming the tools of their tools" (25). He emphasised the absurdity of the economic strategies of his contemporaries: "spending of the best part of one's life earning money in order to enjoy a questionable liberty during the least valuable part of it" (36) and pointed out the lack of logic and common sense in the planning and decision-making processes. The reason why the majority of people are doomed to live in a self-inflicted misery, slaving in order to make ends meet is to be found in their own failures in judgement and overambitious demands on unnecessary, materialistic must-haves, such as the ownership of vast areas of land, or big houses covered in ornamental embellishments, packed with ostentatious furniture. Valuing his freedom above everything else, he certainly did not "wish to spend my time in earning rich carpets or other fine furniture, or delicate cookery, or a house in Grecian or Gothic style just yet" (47). In short, Thoreau claims that to live simply and wisely does not mean to forsake comfort, leisure or pleasures, quite the opposite, but to renounce the accumulation of redundant phenomena, such as things, spaces, whose false necessity is justified solely on the basis of universal social acknowledgement. Having spent two years, two months, and two days living in a tiny cabin, constructed from a repurposed shed, at Walden Pond in New England, Thoreau's account of his self-sufficient life together with his ecological building methods documented in *Walden* continue to inspire current environmentalists as well as designer, architects and planners.

The emphasis and the effort, contemporary architecture puts into minimalist appearance of its designs, which are nevertheless filled with complex technology, might be redirected towards conception maintaining minimal appearance, while being maximal in substance (Flueckiger, 17):

> I went to the woods because I wished to live deliberately, to front only the essential facts of life, and see if I could not learn what it had to teach, and not, when I came to die, discover that I had not lived. I did not wish to live what was not life, living it so dear; nor did I wish to practise resignation, unless it was quite necessary. I wanted to live deep and suck out all the marrow of life, to live so sturdily and Spartan-like as to put to rout all that was not life, to cut a broad swath and shave close, to drive life into a corner, and reduce it to its lowest terms, and if it proved to be mean, why then to get the whole and genuine meanness of it, and publish its meanness to the world; or if it were sublime, to know it by experience, and be able to give a true account of it in my next excursion. (Thoreau, 61)

Heidegger often stressed his hut's vital role in his philosophy, and yet, unlike Thoreau, he never moved there permanently and lived a relatively ordinary city life in a town house as the chair of the philosophy department at Freiburg University. In his monograph, *Heidegger's Hut*, Adam Sharr, an influential theoretician and successful practicing architect, claims that Heidegger's house in the city was actually modelled on the hut and that the windows of Heidegger's study faced the Black Forest mountains and a valley, so he had at least an unobstructed view of his treasured places. The town house as such did not suit the philosopher since all its comforts and the emphasis put on family life was "clouding rather than emphasizing questions of being" (Sharr, *Hut*, 103). What is more, Heidegger never mentioned the house in his writings, which is in notable contrast to his passionate embrace of the solitary existence in the mountains and his vocal, repeatedly expressed admiration for his hut with its strong philosophical resonance.

The hut and the house symbolize two opposing tendencies that considerably influenced Heidegger's life and creation: "provincialism" and "cosmopolitanism":

> These positions are often considered in opposition. Cosmopolitans dismiss the provincial as invidious: introvert, inbred, prone to exclusion, and reliant upon romantic myth. Provincials dismiss the cosmopolitan as deluded: bound to abstract systems and priorities, entranced by fickleness of fashion, setting itself and its self-appointed heroes of false pedestals. (Sharr, *Hut*, 107)

In order to understand his position within this opposition, it is necessary to interpret rightly his metaphorical texts: Heidegger does not urge his listeners or readers to literally live in the past, adopting outdated ways of living, such as farming, nor does he impose any kind of social restrictions or the exclusion of fellow human beings. His conception of dwelling is not restricted to place, the past or to social status, it resides in the ability to search for the centre and to find it repeatedly, always fresh and new: "The real dwelling plight lies in this, that mortals ever search anew for the nature of dwelling, that they must ever learn to dwell" (Heidegger, *Poetically*, 159). Karsten Harries, one of the most influential contemporary architectural theoreticians, emphasises the importance of the ethical aspect of architecture. His understanding of dwelling, therefore, is in tune with Heidegger's conception, as it underlines its humble, respectful and assiduous nature. According to him, to dwell authentically and near the centre, to be genuinely at home in the world, we have to acknowledge our primal homelessness.

In *Howards End*, Margaret Schlegel learns an identical lesson concerning the nature of dwelling. She and Helen are cast away from the centre, only to search for it with greater vigour: "The loss of Wickham Place had taught her more than its possession." (*HE*, 189). If Forster's novel portrays volatility as the main principle of dwelling, the lesson is repeated in *The Sea, the Sea* where Murdoch's approach to authentic existence coincides with Heidegger's conception of dwelling. Both novels might be consequently viewed as depictions of a quest for dwelling or a truthful, authentic existence. Although both "quests" relate partially to the exclusive social standing of the protagonists, their significance should not be diminished by any kind of material conditioning, including their social or spatial exclusivity. A similar approach applies to Heidegger's hut, a place which permeates his writing. Although it was an exceptional place whose position in the landscape enabled a complete and self-imposed seclusion, and was also furnished according to Heidegger's demands for Spartan simplicity, it should be understood in terms of opening new horizons and possibilities rather than as being the manifestation of middle-class eccentricity: "Arguably, the greatest potential of the hut lies in the hope that such centring power need not be invidious or exclusive" (Sharr, *Hut*, 112). Its close connection with the philosopher's existence: "The small building was the philosopher's datum, its particularities delineating the particularities of his life and work" (Sharr, *Hut*, 112), its ability to communicate philosophical dimensions of existence, its capacity to shelter and at the same time expose a human being, all these exceptional qualities transformed it into a powerful source of inspiration for the philosopher and also for generations of architects who tried to replicate its beneficial, inspiring effects. In spite of the fact that it is typically the life in the countryside that is romanticised and therefore associated with authenticity of existence and philosophical significance, the true challenge for architects, dwellers as well as the authors of literary depictions, is to achieve such "centering" regardless of the relative social standing of all those involved or of the urban setting of their work.

3.3 Staging a Retreat in the Countryside: Problems of Dwelling in *Howards End* and *The Sea, The Sea*

Now I shall abjure magic and become a hermit: put myself in a situation where
I can honestly say that I have nothing else to do but to learn to be good.
(*TS*, 2)

One of the main allures of temporary or permanent ownership of a country house is seclusion, with all its desirable implications, such as an uncorrupted view, uninterrupted solitude, retreat, spiritual and physical awakening or renewal, and finding long-lost connections in all possible senses.[24] Time and its habitual requirements and restraints seem suspended in the country: "I'm only saying. How does it happen that Thursday seems like Friday? We're out of the city. We're off the calendar. Friday shouldn't have an identity here" (DeLillo, 19). Indeed, it is the cyclical movements of the sea or seasons which replace the arbitrary division of time into hours, weeks and months.

Such a type of isolated, privileged existence has always inspired literary creation. From John Banville to Françoise Sagan or Keri Hulme,[25] it seems that cloistered within the walls of houses situated on the sea coast, creative potential blossoms and artists are eager to translate their

---

24 Parts of this chapter's text appeared in "In Search of a House with a View: The Conception of Dwelling in E. M. Forster's *Howards End* and Iris Murdoch's *The Sea, The Sea*." *International Journal of Applied Linguistics and English Literature* 5, no. 4, 2016. Melbourne: Australian International Academic Centre, pp. 189–199.

25 E.g. Keri Hulme, one of the most prominent New Zealand contemporary writers and author of the bone people writes in the main room of her sea coast house, overlooking the shore, and she has underlined the role of the coast in her writing and in a number of interviews. The same applies to Eleanor Catton, a fellow New Zealand author, whose novel *Luminaries*, which won the 2013 Man Booker Prize, reaffirms the importance of the New Zealand West Coast as both a source of inspiration and as remarkable literary setting.

experience into fictional narrative. Lauren, the grieving widow and body artist in *The Body Artist*, a novel by American author Don DeLillo set in a secluded house on the New England coast, at first relishes the separation which nourishes the artistic performance into which she translates her grief but, gradually, she feels stifled and needs to free herself: "She walked into the room and went to the window. She opened it. She threw the window open. She didn't know why she did this. Then she knew. She wanted to feel the sea tang on her face and the flow of time in her body, to tell her who she was" (DeLillo, 132).

Similarly, Charles is eager to translate his hermit's existence into artistic form at the beginning of his stay by the sea. He has two major sources of inspiration and thus two major themes he is willing to portray in his unspecified literary production – himself and the sea: "The sea. I could fill a volume simply with my word-pictures of it" (*TS*, 2). Charles's spiritual and ethical struggle is projected into the form of the novel, which is endowed with a great degree of intertextuality, the affinity to William Shakespeare's *The Tempest* is manifested by his close resemblance to another great stage director, Prospero, and an excessive employment of sea imagery. As a man of the world and as an artist, Charles feels entitled to stage the drama of his new existence as well as to accompany it with lengthy remarks concerning the nature of the theatre, the novel and the viability of their connection with the real world. Theatre, even at its utmost best, is portrayed as being profoundly scurrilous: "the theatre, even at its most 'realistic', is connected with the level at which, and the methods by which, we tell our everyday lies" (*TS*, 36). Its lying nature is ascribed to the fact that emotions either rule a personality or play an inconsequential part in its determination, and therefore mediocre feelings and ideas, those we express every day and those we perceive in others, are acted and that is why "all the world is a stage, and why the theatre is always popular and indeed why it exists: why it is like life, and it is like life even though it is also the most vulgar and outrageously factitious of all the arts" (*TS*, 36). Though the novel cannot boast the same degree of spectacularity as the theatre, according to Charles, it is, nevertheless, much closer to truth and is therefore chosen to reflect Charles's preoccupation: to be humble, to live well, to slow down, to replace the chaos of London with the stillness of the countryside with its routines and the circularity of its seasonal existence.

The proximity of natural elements, which is often achieved at great expense, both financial and in terms of sacrificing basic modern residential comforts (such as electricity, plumbing, and efficient heating systems) forces the human being to fully embrace the notion of living in a present that cannot be controlled by any sort of plan or design. Thus, life may seem to be comic or dreadful but it never acquires the quality of tragedy since tragedy, with its artificial pomp and grandeur, "belongs to the cunning of the stage" (*TS*, 39). Theatre is thus marked, and ironically so by a former stage director, as facetious. Charles intends to divide his time between walking, cooking, resting, reading and re-reading his books, and Shakespeare in particular, and, most importantly, swimming.[26] His stay by the sea, however, involves scarcely any of these activities and is filled with unexpected visitors and emotional turmoil, to the point that the whole plot resembles a badly staged melodrama.

Howards End lacks the theatrical preoccupation of *The Sea, The Sea*, but its overall form has often been compared to that of "a morality play" (Stone, *The Cave*, 255) in which the dichotomy between the Red-bloods, the Wilcoxes, and the Mollycoddles, the Schlegels, acquires an almost allegorical dimension. The close proximity of life and drama, their constant shifting, mingling and interchanging, may be delineated as one of the major motifs of *The Sea, The Sea*. *Howards End* may be seen as echoing, if less explicitly, this belief in a close connection between life and drama: "I inflict all this on you because once you said that life is sometimes life and sometimes only a drama, and one must learn to distinguish tother from which, and up to now I have always put that down as 'Meg's clever nonsense'. But this morning, it really does seem not life but a play" (*HE*, 4). What is more, the Schlegels feel a strong artistic inclination which manifests itself in their efforts to commune with the world and mediate this communion to others. Shruff End and Howards End thus provide a basis for the narration, enable the staging of the dramatic events, provide necessary inspiration, shelter their owners in their artistic endeavours and symbolise their visions of the world and authentic existence.

When Charles retires from the glamorous London life of a famous stage director, he chooses the concept of "simple but sumptuous" in terms of his life, a concept which had previously characterised his

---

26 As Urs Peter Flueckiger, the author of *How Much House? Thoreau, Le Corbusier and the Sustainable Cabin*, points out, neither Henry David Thoreau nor Le Corbusier, two famous pioneers of minimal house solutions, lived solitary lives. They both stayed in their respective abodes only for a limited time, Thoreau occupied his house at Walden Pond, Massachusetts for two years, two months and two days, and Le Corbusier's typically stayed a month in the summer from 1952 to 1965 in le Cabanon in Roquebrune-Cap – Martin, France. What is more, they enjoyed the company of others and also worked. Similarly to Charles Arrowby, they took long swims in the pond/sea. Sadly, Le Corbusier's body was found washed ashore after he took his final swim in August, 1965.

culinary efforts, fittingly described by a journalist in the novel as "*Wind in the Willows* food": "What is more delicious than fresh hot buttered toast, with or without the addition of bloater paste? Or plain boiled onions with a little corned beef if desired? And well-made porridge with brown sugar and cream is a dish fit for a king" (*TS*, 9–10). The meals Charles prepares play a crucial role in the process of consolidating the overall poetics of the work as they incarnate Charles's ostentatious preoc-cupation with "intelligent hedonism" and "felicitous gastronomic intel-ligence" (*TS*, 9). Charles deprives himself voluntarily of electricity, hot water, heating and sophisticated shopping facilities. All such luxuries, gimmicks, gadgets and appliances are associated with the corrupted life of citified existence. Charles wants to live a life of simple, if even more sophisticated, pleasures, such as contemplating the colour of the skies and the sea, filling his notebook with their images. Nevertheless, the elements he meant to admire and indulge in, reject, torture, mock and haunt him. The house is unbearably uncomfortable and creepy, probably even haunted. The neighbours and weather are hostile. What is more, it is almost impossible to go swimming because the cliffs by the house do not enable safe access in and out of the water. The intended life of simple pleasures turns rapidly into an elusive vision defying hopes, wishes and dreams, and crushing, both metaphorically and literally, those in vain quest of the pastoral ideal. Thus, Titus, the son of Charles's childhood sweetheart, Hartley, drowns when trying to merge with nature. It is as if the forces of nature as well as the house, decided to refuse to obey the interloper through a series of failures, disasters, diseases, nightmarish visions and mysterious appearances and disappearances. Charles fails to get a single refreshing night's sleep in the house, or write into his journal, he is subject to the vision of a sea-monster, he repeatedly falls ill and achieves peace only after he acknowledges the unattainability of his pastoral plan, leaves the place and embraces city life in London.

Besides their great vitality and their ability to subjugate the country-side, speeding through it in their motor-cars, buying country houses and land, some members of the Wilcox clan do not identify with, and are not even willing to comprehend, their mother's passion for their country house, Howards End: "She approached … trailing noiselessly over the lawn, and there was actually a wisp of hay in her hands. She seemed to belong not to the young people and their motor, but to the house, and to the tree that overshadowed it" (*HE*, 19). Ironically, though Ruth Wilcox takes immense pleasure from the wisp of hay she smells repeatedly, the rest of her family suffer from hay fever and are unable to leave the house or even open the window. All members of the Wilcox family, apart from Mrs Wilcox, stake their claim in the future, whereas everything their mother embodies – wisdom, aristocracy, tradition, superstition, "dwelling" in the sense underlined by Heidegger, is rooted in the past and thus stands in their way. The Wilcoxes are willing to build the future of the nation and trample on traditions, but, despite their immense vitality, cockiness and brute force, they are defeated by a wisp of hay, unable even to go bathing without strenuous preparations.[27]

The Wilcoxes take hold of the country and its future, symbolising economic progress, ruthlessness and power, which attracts the liberal minds of the Schlegel sisters with an unexpected and seemingly inexplicable allure: "To be all day with them in the open air, to sleep at night under their roof, had seemed the supreme joy of life, and had led to that abandonment of personality that is possible prelude to love" (*HE*, 20). This enchantment, however, fades away with the growing evidence of their inability to "connect" both in the physical as well as the metaphysical sense. Neither Charles Arrowby, nor the Wilcoxes are able to achieve any kind of authentic experience, which both novels emphasise through their absolute inability to commune with nature. Although Henry Wilcox makes an effort and decides to reside in Howards End, the inability remains unchanged, with him trapped inside and the rest of the clan at a safe distance from the house and all its connotations. Charles, on the other hand, ironically approximates authenticity when he abandons his far-fetched, theatrical efforts to achieve it. The realm he belongs to is the city, where he finds a peace protected against the unconstrained forces of nature and hordes of his friends, and the whimsical, malevolent nature of Shruff End, his house by the sea.

The way in which Ruth Wilcox, Margaret and Helen Schlegel deal with possession, and houses in particular, is diametrically different from that of the Wilcoxes: "'You see,' continued Helen to her cousin, 'Wilcoxes collect houses as your Victor collects tadpoles'"(*HE*, 145). Whereas they see houses purely as investments, Ruth, Margaret and Helen identify them as means of connection, sometimes even as sanctuaries. Howards End is thus elevated to a shrine to England, capable of linking some of its inhabitants with the English land and past. Houses in *Howards*

---

27   "If Margaret wanted to jump from the motor-car, she jumped; if Tibby thought paddling would benefit his ankles, he paddled; if a clerk desired adventure, he took a walk in the dark. But these athletes seemed paralysed. They could not bathe without their appliances, though the morning sun was calling and the last mists were rising from the dimpling stream. Had they found the life of the body after all?" (*HE*, 186)

End are undoubtedly laden with various symbolic properties. However, there is one which overshadows the rest, and that is the symbol of the feminine. Although men may hold the keys, the doors of the houses truly open, in the metaphorical sense of the word, to women only. Those who threaten to invade are crushed – Charles is imprisoned, Henry is broken and Leonard Bast killed. The Schlegels' attempts at connection, which might be summarised by Margaret's marriage and Helen's son, required a considerable number of sacrifices, heroic effort and at times the employment of the brute force of the Schlegels, as illustrated by Margaret's utterance "You shall see the connection if it kills you, Henry!" (*HE*, 263). Nevertheless, the novel concludes with a seemingly pastoral image of the two sisters sitting on the lawn overlooking the meadows.

The final acquisition of Howards End by the Schlegels, Henry's eventual submission, Helen's son, the beauty of the pastoral, the number of meadows dividing them from the red rust of civilization, all these elements point to the victory of the sisters. The nature of such a victory, achieved by means of exclusion, submission and the occasional annihilation of human beings, highlights the highly complex, knotty character of Forster's vision of human relationships.

Both *The Sea, The Sea* and *Howards End* question the demands of the metaphorical as well as the literal view, besides tackling the subjects of unrequited love, unfulfilled desires, twisted, dysfunctional relationships and doomed love stories. Both the reader and the characters are led to believe that what they witness is the Schlegels' good-hearted struggle for universal connection and the emotional turmoil of Charles who is fighting for his long-lost love, Hartley. Nevertheless, each emotional movement presented in the novels can be interpreted as delicate and yet rather ostentatious manipulation and what seems to be a full-blooded passion may be revealed as cold-blooded scheming.

Charles projects his desire for a lost world of purity and innocence into the resurrection of his childhood love for Hartley, which he conceives as "nearly an end in itself" (*TS*, 462) who, in the spirit of the Gothic, he captures, secludes and unsuccessfully tries to trick into submission. Charles's new life with Hartley would, he hopes, continue in the same idealistic vein as his life by the sea, which, since the beginning of his efforts, repeatedly proves to be the opposite of what he yearned for. Before walking out on him, Hartley was supposed to have become the instrument through which Charles could achieve ultimate peace and quiet in his artificial paradise: "And we would gently cherish each other and there would be a vast plain goodness and a sort of space and quiet, unspoilt and uncorrupted. And I would join the ordinary people and be an ordinary person, and rest..." (*TS*, 398).

Charles, however, does not seek a truthful, loving relationship, but continues in the arrogant spirit of the Schlegel sisters who attempt to connect heroically with the rest of the world despite the wishes or well-being of others: "... and there was an intelligence in her quiet negative reception of the kiss which was itself a communication" (*TS*, 229). In the case of Charles, no children are conceived, on the contrary, human life is sacrificed, when Titus, Hartley's adoptive son, drowns in the sea, close to Shruff End. Similarly, the Schlegel sisters' attempts at connection cause the death of Leonard Bast who is literally crushed and buried by a pile of books symbolising the knowledge and wisdom he did not seem worthy to embrace and the sphere to which he would not have been able to belong.

Forster fills his works with characters striving for connection as well as with pastoral images and he repeatedly refers to threats and violations of nature imposed by man's far-reaching involvement. An example of this is the "red rust" of civilisation invading the beauty of the meadows surrounding Howards End. His pleas and warnings against the perils of industrialisation is the "voicing of a personal fear and grief – the heartbreak and outrage of one who sees his private estate invaded by the barbarians – and only incidentally a moral argument for the health and welfare of the planet" (Stone, "Forster, the Environmentalist", 183). Although throughout his work Forster expresses an inclination towards the natural world, his enthusiastic embrace, which highlights its liberating properties, is gradually replaced by a scepticism concerning its future and also by a far more selective choice as far as the stability of the objects of his admiration is concerned. In the majority of his fiction, longer or shorter, he enthusiastically endows "the outside" with liberating properties reminiscent of pagan identification with the land or with Romantic preoccupations with solitude. Ranging from earlier short stories,[28]

---

28 In "Other Kingdom" (1909) Forster describes the unbridled dance of a young woman: "She danced away from our society and our life, back, back through the centuries till houses and fences fell and the earth lay wild to the sun" (Forster, *Collected Short Stories*, 82). Similarly, a youth possessed in *The Story of a Panic* (1902) cannot stand the claustrophobic oppression of his room: "'Not in my room,' he pleaded. 'It is so small'" (Forster, *Collected Short Stories*, 30). "The Machine Stops" (1909), the apt answer to one of H. G. Wells' "earlier heavens" (Forster, *Collected Short Stories*, 6), it is via recapturing the sense of space and touch that human beings die content. He further on elaborates this motif in all his novels, e.g. *Maurice*: "He was not afraid or ashamed any more. After all, the forests and the night were on his side, not theirs; ..." (Forster, *Maurice*, 190)

Forster repeatedly and vocally endows natural images with liberating properties and spiritual power. But the land he is referring to gets progressively deprived of its liberating potential, as he remarked on the subject in 1951: "We cannot escape any more to the sands or the waves and pretend they are our destiny. We have annihilated time and space, we have furrowed the desert and spanned the sea, only to find at the end of every vista our own unattractive features. What remains for us, whither shall we return?" (Forster, *Two Cheers*, 273).

Consequently, he embraces the approach already introduced in the short story "The Machine Stops"[29] and that is an inclination towards unattainable, uninhabited skies, stars and planets: "For some of us who are non-Christian there still remains the comfort of the non-human, the relief, when we look up at the stars, of realizing that they are uninhabitable. But not there for any of us lies our work or our home" (Forster, *Two Cheers*, 274). It is nevertheless the craving for the unspoilt, the unmarked, the "inviolate" which is "at the heart of Forster's religion, ... even at the expense of social justice, in a world being overrun" (Stone, "Forster, the Environmentalist", 179). However, Forster subverts his antisocial cravings for "unpeopled" spaces and an unobstructed view through his faith in what is good in people and that is "their insistence on creation, their belief in friendship and loyalty for their own sakes" (Forster, *Two Cheers*, 80), despite describing violence as the major factor in people's muddled relations:

> We don't know what we are like. We can't know what other people are like. How, then, can we put any trust in personal relationships, or cling to them in the gathering political storm? In theory we cannot. But in practice we can and do. Though A is not unchangeably A or B unchangeably B, there can still be love and loyalty between the two. For the purpose of living one has to assume that the personality is solid, and the "self" is an entity, and to ignore all contrary evidence. And since to ignore evidence is one of the characteristics of faith, I certainly can proclaim that I believe in personal relationships. (Forster, *Two Cheers*, 176)

Raymond Williams's *The Country and the City* emphasises the need to shake off the deeply rooted distinction between the country and the city and also their contrastive conceptions. According to Williams, the future

---

29 "For a moment they saw the nations of the dead, and, before they joined them, scraps of untainted sky" (Forster, *Collected Short Stories*, 146).

social and economic development depends on a necessary re-evaluation of the past and an ultimate refusal of the deeply rooted division of labour, whose roots he sees in the division of the rural and the urban. Only thus might its negative effects, such as the widening distance between rich and poor, the physical deterioration of the environment, overpopulated cities and deserted countryside, and the impending crisis caused by a growing population and diminishing resources, be overcome. Referring to Wordsworth, *The Country and the City* describes two major ways, in which to deal with the alienation and uncertainty peculiar to modern experience. In case we are unable to discern and classify the forces which move around us in incomprehensible forms, we may either withdraw into isolation of our subjectivity and observe and ruminate on the individual forces from a secure distance provided by a sheltered retreat, or to try to embrace the complexity of various social signs and messages, "to which, characteristically, we try to relate as individuals so as to discover, in some form, community" (Williams, 295).[30]

Similarly, the Schlegel sisters desperately and disparately strive for connection on the one hand and a view on the other hand. Since they try to unite such opposing tendencies, they tend to crush those who stand in their way with what they honestly believe to be good intentions. The ruined lives of both Leonard Bast and Henry Wilcox are shining examples of the Schlegels' successful attempts at communion and universal goodness. Charles's hermit trial also seems to be replete with good intentions and challenges that in the end turn out to be unattainable. Still, the conclusion, where Charles finally adheres to the dictum of his great idol, Shakespeare: "The world must be peopled" (*Much Ado about Nothing*, Act 2, Scene 3) proves to be highly instructive. In her monograph entitled *Human Relationships in the Novels of Iris Murdoch*, Milada Franková claims that the novel explores the rivalry and love between two figures incarnating two philosophical and aesthetic principles – the

---

30   In his *Pastoral*, written twenty years after Williams's *The Country and the City*, Terry Gifford cites Leo Marx's suggestion that the essence of pastoralism is "a dialectical mode of perception" (Marx qtd. in Gifford, 174). Gifford himself stresses the current lack of a clear separation between urban and rural existence. Unlike Williams, the author amplifies the necessity of reviving the experience of this division. Post-pastoral literature might be seen as an answer to these attempts, exploring simultaneously the impulse towards "retreat, renewal and return" on the one hand and the "notions of roots, neighbourhood and community" (Gifford, 174) on the other. The author calls these two contradictory impulses "the circle of postmodern mobility". With the paradox of retreat informing our sense of community, the post-pastoral, or "complex pastoral" might help us to ameliorate our relationship with our neighbours as well as imagine our self-sustained survival on the planet.

artist and the saint. The role of the artist is obviously assumed by the re-tired Shakespearean director Charles, who besides attempting to become a selfless person also tries to produce a piece of writing in an unspecific form: "Charles's wanting to be good after his London life of power and ego may have been inspired by James, his cousin and the saint-figure in the novel" (Franková, 37). Unlike Charles, James is capable of finally renouncing his life and stopping his heart from beating, by doing which he fulfils the Buddhist maxim that requires the ultimate destruction of ego, which corresponds with "achieving fulfilment in death" (Franková, 37). Charles is unfit for such a leap of faith but what he attains is by no means less valuable. He finally acknowledges the impossibility of attain-ing any finality in life, any conclusions or ultimate solutions. Life, unlike art, is where it is impossible to achieve shape and unity:

> ... life has an irritating way of bumping and limping on, undoing conver-sions, casting doubt on solutions, and generally illustrating the impos-sibility of living happily or virtuously ever after. ... Then I felt too that I might take this opportunity to tie up a few loose ends, only of course loose ends can never be properly tied, one is always producing new ones. Time, like the sea, unties all knots. (*TS*, 512)

The impossibility of reaching definite conclusions could also be seen as the summary of numerous novels written by Murdoch: "... there is no finality to Murdoch's endings, they dissolve into a vagueness sug-gestive of the ever recurring cycle of life, of human relationships being so similar and yet so different, of everything repeating itself but never quite in the same way" (Franková, 78). *The Sea, The Sea* represents thus yet another example of Murdoch's favourite quotation, reverberating through her novels. It comes "from the medieval woman mystic Julian of Norwich, and proclaims 'all shall be well and all shall be well and all manner of thing shall be well.'" (Sage, 72). Charles and his story both incarnate and voice the eternal question concerning the possibil-ity of changing oneself. Once again, his conclusion may be seen both as hypocritical self-delusion or honest revelation. A person cannot change and, if this is so, gone are the theatrical aspirations to a fundamental spiritual rebirth. The only attainable route is one where a person lives quietly, harming no one and 'doing little good things,' however, even those good things are not likely to occur frequently: "I cannot think of any good thing to do at the moment, but perhaps I shall think of one tomorrow" (*TS*, 537).

Similarly to the continuous rotation of one round motif around another, the circular orbits of the two novels, *The Sea, The Sea* and *Howards End*, meet, echo and at times intersect. They both treat the theme of attempting to attain an ideal, the outcome of which seems to be doomed to failure. A successful quest for authenticity appears to be conditioned by the activity of searching and coveting. Both Forster's work and Murdoch's novels also elaborate on certain elements of summer house fiction as explored in the works of authors ranging from John Galsworthy, Virginia Woolf, Vita Sackville-West, Evelyn Waugh and Albert Camus to Elizabeth Jane Howard, Don DeLillo, Sadie Jones, Alan Hollinghurst, Herman Koch, Emma Straub and Sue Miller, particularly temporality, cyclicality, enrapture and bedazzlement. All these elements are triggered by places whose exceptional properties set them apart from real sites as their access is both literally and metaphorically restricted, which emphasises their exclusivity, and they are able to transform the linear passing of time into a circular loop. This circular temporality is projected into the structure of the novels as well as their overall imagery, which accumulates a surprising number of individual motifs endowed with round disposition in both literal and metaphorical sense. Not only does the fleeting character of the season depicted in summer house fiction, whose definition both *Howards End* and *The Sea, The Sea* at least partly fulfil, accentuate the urgency of contemporary ecological and ethical issues, but it also mirrors the elusive nature of attaining of any sort of idealised state.

Howards End and *The Sea, The Sea* revolve around two middle-class country houses, one being an ancient, converted farmhouse and the other an ordinary seaside villa. The relation between the place and its inhabitants, as it is presented on the example of Howards End and Shruff End, challenges the stereotypical depiction of a country house situated in a seemingly idyllic, rural setting. The actual portrayals reveal a wide range of implications of such a type of often idealised living arrangement in connection with class as well as the extreme, people-exclusive interpretation of environmental preoccupation.

Though the houses are still depicted as being essential to the process of establishing, shaping and constructing the authentic existence of their inhabitants, it is, nevertheless, the desire for a view, both literal and metaphorical, which determines the narrative and the nature dwelling presented in both novels. The frequency of the view from or of the house considerably exceeds the presentation of the inside of the houses. The depiction of the house from the outside, quite an unexpected angle for its inhabitant, who you would expect *inside*, is especially prominent in *The Sea, The Sea*, where Charles spends the majority of his peaceful nights sleeping on the rocks rather than returning to the stifling atmosphere of Shruff End reminding him of a "doll's house" (*TS*, 389). This perspective emphasises the theatrical preoccupation of Charles as he continues in his life-long carer of a famed director and stages his retreat. Yet it echoes, in its own, twisted way, his major undertaking to become a real, authentic, good human being. Ironically, it is the house and the sea, which should have represented his new mind-set, which expel him so that he realises that what he wants to achieve cannot be rehearsed and performed in the secluded environment of Shruff End, but that it requires a life-long commitment and endeavour. What is more, it is not the countryside, but the city that is his natural habitat.

Howards End opens and closes with a view from the house, into the garden and the meadow. Although the red rust of civilization will likely find its way there and invade the Schlegel's sanctuary in the future, for the time being the Wilcoxes are defeated and the meadow is mown: "Tom's father was cutting the big meadow. He passed again and again amid whirring blades and sweet odours of grass, encompassing with narrowing circles the sacred centre of the field" (*HE*, 286). Margaret and Helen, the two heroic connectors, are looking into a future marked solely by seasonal change and domestic demands such as frozen pipes or a gale blowing down the wych-elm, with Helen thinking about "these little events becoming part of her, year after year" (*HE*, 286). Merging gradually with the house and its surroundings, it is their turn to encompass, with narrowing circles, the sacred centre of existence and thus to dwell.

The view presented in *The Sea, The Sea* and *Howards End* is never devoid of interruptions and obstacles: there are wild elements, lost wills, inquisitive visitors and a number of misconceptions, failed efforts and faulty judgements on the side of the main protagonists. The bourgeois, class-exclusive pastoral, which would omit all these inappropriate intrusions, is abandoned and replaced by, if highly ironical and far-reaching at times, meditation upon the nature of genuine dwelling.

4. Strangers' Children in the House: Post-millennial Echoes of the Post-war Poetics of the Country House

Beside it on his bookshelf in Tooting Graveney stood his small collection of related items, some with a very thin but magical thread of connection; the books that only mentioned Cecil in a footnote gave him the strongest sense of uncovering a mystery.
(*SC*, 397)

He spread a warm glaze over the place and time, as if they were much more distant than was the case.
(*SC*, 377)

The Stranger's Child, Alan Hollinghurst's fifth novel, is a densely layered, highly nuanced exploration of the shifting ideals of class, beauty, literary creation, sexuality and the perpetually fluctuating tide of English society. The author anchors the narration by the juxtaposition of two houses, two settings, two symbols of the tightly connected, if profoundly dissimilar, social classes as well as two diametrically different interpretations of domestic space and history: Corley Court, a ghastly Victorian monstrosity, the stately home of the Valances, and Two Acres, a sprightly suburban villa of the Sawle family. These houses, shining emblems of social diversity and financial superiority, become the field of negotiation of new identities. The motivation of the majority of characters' is not upward social mobility, but rather the emotional and intellectual fulfilment which comprises social acceptance. Unlike in Hollinghurst's previous novel, Booker-prize awarded and widely critically acclaimed *The Line of Beauty* (2004), the less socially privileged characters do not automatically strive to appropriate a new identity by means of lodging with the more privileged ones.[31] It is quite unexpectedly the less financially secure who

---

31 In her article "The Role of Dialogic Organisation in Reflexive Construals of Identity in Selected Fiction Texts", whose main focus is the constituents of personal/social identity as

inspire the creation of and often also the liberation from uptight conventions and expectations. The novel opens with an evocation of the last lustrous days of the summer of 1913. Cecil Valance, a mercurial aristocratic youth, an aspiring poet and lover of George Sawle, arrives for his first and last visit to Two Acres, the humble abode of the Sawles, taking quick and decisive control "of their garden and their house and the whole of the coming weekend".[32] Ironically, both the mediocre talent of Cecil, as well as the meagre charm of Two Acres fundamentally determine the course of events. At the end of his fatal visit, Cecil, a condescending satyr, becomes intoxicated by the conventional unconventionality of the Sawle family: his lover George over-compensating for the lack of worldliness of his background and himself, George's overzealous, precocious sister Daphne, alcoholic, self-professed opera admirer mother Freda, and

they are presented in communicative transactions performed by the protagonists of three selected novels, namely John Braine's *Room at the Top*, Stephen Fry's *The Stars' Tennis Balls* and Alan Hollinghurst's *The Line of Beauty*, Matuchová claims that: "... the driving force behind these characters is their upward social mobility. Thus, their identity is constructed and negotiated in the context of suppressing the original identity and appropriating the new desired identity. Rather logically, making them lodge with the more socially privileged is a narrative framework all three authors employ" (104). Accordingly, *The Line of Beauty*'s aptly named main character, Nick Guest, relishes staying in the Feddens' big white Notting Hill house, quickly embracing the idea of the house being almost his own or becoming his own in the future. Despite being a temporary lodger, he succumbs to the grandeur of the privileged living arrangement, unwilling to abandon its elitist and, from Nick's point of view, entirely pleasurable social implications:

"And Nick was in residence, and almost, he felt in possession. He loved coming home to Kensington Park Gardens in the early evening, when the wide treeless street was raked by the sun, and the two white terraces stared at each other with the glazed tolerance of rich neighbours. He loved letting himself in at the three-locked green front door, and locking it again behind him, and feeling the still security of the house as he looked into the red-walled dining room, or climbed the stairs to the double drawing room, and up again past the half-open doors of the white bedrooms. ... Like his hero Henry James, Nick felt that he could 'stand a great deal of gilt.'" (Hollinghurst, *The Line of Beauty*, 6)

The sense of mockery and superficiality typically associated with gilt, be it in its literal, physical sense of heavily embellished and decorated surroundings, or the metaphorical one of a gilded existence, is also reflected in the way Nick Guest tends to present to his unassuming hosts, rather than his own identity, a mock one, which he gradually embraces as his sole true, authentic identity. At this point, Matuchová employs the concept of presenting *alterity* instead of identity to achieve a desired semiotic effect on the recipients. Her understanding of alterity marks a slight departure from the original, based on Hastings and Manning's definition. From Matuchová's point of view "the degree of recipient awareness of mock identity negotiation is minimal, if not altogether absent. Moreover, the alter-identity is not constructed as mock in order to temporarily entertain but to realise a long-term desire" (105).

32 Hollinghurst, Alan. *The Stranger's Child*. London: Picador, 2011, p. 4. [Subsequent page references preceded *SC* are given in parentheses in the text]

closeted brother Hubert. Particularly captivated by Two Acres, a house with a tendency "to resolve itself into nooks" (*SC*, 8), he scribbles a poem in honour of its subversive pettiness. Shortly after, he leaves and is torn to pieces by a German grenade in the French trenches.

Ironically, it is Cecil's mildly prankish poetic creation which becomes a defining, memorable piece of literature feeding the starved imagination of a famished nation with images of a suburban idyll: "'He was a first-rate example of the second-rate poet who enters into common consciousness more deeply than many greater masters. 'All England trembles in the spray / Of dog-rose in the front of May'... "Two blessèd acres of English ground"' – he looked almost teasingly at them, as though he were a prep-school master himself" (*SC*, 527–8).

Besides the additional tang of a literary thriller, which arrestingly develops the theme of the biographical and critical interpretation of a literary work, the novel masterly depicts the troubled history of the involvement of sexual mores and literary renown and their mutual conditioning. Therefore, *The Stranger's Child* engages in a wide-ranging, far-reaching dialogue with both its literary predecessors and contemporaries. The deep-rooted intertextuality of the novel reverberates throughout the majority of its poetic constituents and thus becomes another of a number of subtle layers of its stylistic complexity. The direct literary references[33] are mingled with a number of indirect allusions, spun into an intricate network. These "thin but magical thread[s] of connection" (*SC*, 397) echo the thematic preoccupation of the novel with the question of the mutual influence of personal and literary history, as well as playfully observing the degree of involvement of both the literary canon and counter-canon in shaping national identity.

The Stranger's Child uses and juxtaposes motifs, thematic and poetic elements that have been employed by the preceding canonical works of English literature. In view of the number of these influences, the novel verges on a playful pastiche. It is the identification of the members of the dialogue between *The Stranger's Child* and other works which accentuates the pleasure gained from reading. The novel cites Alfred Lord Tennyson's 1832 poem "The Lady of Shallot" while owing its title, *The Stranger's Child*, to his 1849 "In Memoriam A. H. H.": "And year by year the landscape grow//Familiar to the stranger's child". It also bears the mark of Evelyn Waugh's *Brideshead Revisited*, *The Sacred and Profane Memories*

---

33 "And there, at the end of the table, in a sober brown jacket with the title in red and yellow, was *The Letters of Evelyn Waugh*, a book with an aura, it seemed to Paul, and fat with confidence of its own interest." (*SC*, 433)

of Captain Charles Ryder (1945) and of *A Handful of Dust* (1934), and it features references to E. M. Forster's work, most explicitly *Maurice* (1913, published 1971),[34] *Howards End* (1910), and *A Room with a View* (1908), as well as his short stories. Further on, the idyllic atmosphere present-ed in *The Stranger's Child*, one of an Edwardian Garden of Eden on the brink of collapse and destruction, reflects the works of Virginia Woolf or Ford Maddox Ford tetralogy *Parade's End* (1924–8). The looming "Ger-man war" is marked by a close resemblance between Cecil's poem "Two Acres" to Rupert Brooke's "The Soldier" . Theo Tait also mentions echoes of Lytton Stratchey's letters in his review of the novel for *The Guardian*. All these references clearly evoke Hollinghurst's lifelong commitment to English literature, but there are allusions where the author's devotion becomes passionate. In his interview with the novelist, Stephen Moss emphasises Hollinghurst's enduring love of Henry James, who became his role-model of an artist utterly committed to writing perfect fiction. This is evidenced in *The Stranger's Child* which displays traces of *The As-pern Papers* (1888), and possibly also of *What Maisie Knew* (1897). Glimps-es of Hollinghurst's academic career, which involved his MA thesis on Ronald Firbank, E. M. Forster and L. P. Hartley, three gay writers, are to be caught in the two most notable of Forster's works and L. P. Hart-ley's famous coming-of-age novel *The Go-Between* (1953). The imprint of the author's editing work is to be found in reflections of *Shropshire Lad* (1896), whose author's, A. E. Housman's, poetry collection Alan Hol-linghurst edited in 2001.[35]

4.1 Hollinghurst's Subversive Sonata

The story of *The Stranger's Child* opens in the garden of a compara-tively small, middle-class suburban villa belonging to the Sawle fam-ily on a particularly luscious summer day. George Sawle brings in the anxiously awaited guests, his aristocrat of a friend, a fellow-member of The Apostles, a fellow Cambridge student residing at King's College,[36]

---

34 Forster famously completed the novel in 1913, but he had deliberately had it published only after his death, in 1971.

35 A. E. Housman, Oscar Wilde, the idiosyncratic creation of a literary canon and the peculiar workings of memory are at the centre of Tom Stoppard's 1997 highly-acclaimed drama *The Invention of Love*, which adopts a similar approach to the degree of dramatic irony involved in the revelation of truth about the characters, with the reader/spectator knowing or assuming knowing more than the characters, as *The Stranger's Child*.

36 Forster resided at King's College during his studies at Cambridge University.

Cecil Valance. Within the span of a weekend, the mercurial Cecil, a "keen worshipper of dawn", wrecks his room, violently kisses George's sixteen-year-old sister Daphne, secretly makes love to George in the shrubbery and manages to write a poem, the faulty interpretation of which changes the history of English poetry. The rest of the novel revolves around the attempts at more or less truthful insight into the events of that weekend, which either nourishes the legend or refutes it completely.

"The stranger's child", an allusive, highly flexible metaphor, firstly refers to Cecil Valance, who embodies a mysterious, mildly exotic individual, whose slight arrogance prevents the members of the Sawle family, George included, from establishing any truly cordial relationship with him. The situational pattern is also quite unexpected and unfamiliar. Reversing the expectation and the traditional pattern of the outsider being a young man of a modest background, such as in the case of Evelyn Waugh's Charles Ryder from *Brideshead Revisited*, in *The Stranger's Child* it is the aristocrat who plays the part of an outsider, of a strange guest coming to visit a middlebrow house of a modest size situated in the suburbs. The stranger in question being Cecil Valance, the child might be interpreted as referring to the poem, "Two Acres". Through this poem, he celebrates the unknown terrain of the English middle-class suburb, which he is more likely to mock and despise later, similarly to strangers mocking and denigrating their bastard children. The variation on a theme of an outsider provides the novel with a number of its different aspects and surprising reversal of expectations. The author twists and turns the majority of the motifs typical for country house fiction and shows a different point of view by putting them into a different perspective.

The seat of the Sawle family, Corley Court, is contrasted with Two Acres, which involves a great number of paradoxical implications. It is Corley Court, which is treated as a forbidding house, that provokes a stifling feeling and the overcrowded shabby Two Acres that relaxes its guests with its plain air: "The front door stood open, in the summer way, into the shadowy hall. Beyond it, the garden door too stood open, the afternoon light glinting softly on polished oak, a china bowl – one could pass right through the house, like a breeze" (*SC*, 86). The size of Two Acres acquires a paradoxical dimension comparable to the grotesque shrinking and growing of Alice in Wonderland or that of Lemuel Gulliver. In time, it ultimately overshadows Corley Court from the viewpoint of its historical significance, despite its miniscule proportion of literally two acres compared to three thousand acres of the former. As Dudley, Cecil's brother comments: "'I can't help feeling slightly mortified that my brother Cecil, heir to a baronetcy and three thousand acres, not to mention one of the ugliest houses in the south of England, should be best remembered for his ode to a suburban garden'" (*SC*, 124). The same air of unexpectedness applies to Cecil's creation, the majority of which had been inspired by Corley Court, but whose single poem on Two Acres secured his and its immortal popularity. For Daphne, however, two acres mean a considerable piece of land, compared to the properties of her peers: "To her the 'Two' in her house's name had always been reassuring, a quietly emphatic boast to school friends who lived in a town or a terrace, the proof of a generous over-provision" (*SC*, 42). In the middle sequence of the novel, on the occasion of Paul's excursion into the abandoned, ramshackle property, an accidental encounter with a lady walking her dog foreshadows the future development of the real-estate market, marked by the contemporary astronomic prices of land in London and its outskirts: "'I mean, two acres is quite big, you realize'" (*SC*, 383). The fact that the opening and the closing of the novel are set in the realm of suburbs, with the major events taking place in "the faint glimmer of the suburban night" (*SC*, 96), directs general interest towards this previously neglected part of the city and confirms its dominance in contemporary settlement. It also highlights the tendency of contemporary fiction to focus on this fruitful, subversive area.[37]

By means of dramatic irony, the readers know more than characters assume or do. Whereas some of them, usually only later in the story, realise that "[t]he habit, so familiar to many of us after the War, of thinking of our earlier selves as foreign beings, Arcadian innocents, proved refreshingly a merely partial truth" (*SC*, 436), others tend to cement their rigid approach by trying to divert attention away from their own story elsewhere: "'I think if people ever do get to learn the real details of what went on among the Bloomsbury Group,' Sawle said, 'they'll be pretty astonished'" (*SC*, 320). The author does not present a moralising tale, nor does he glorify the past: "'There have been big Victorian country houses in my last three novels. I had to be careful this book wasn't marketed as a Downton Abbey-type thing, and I hope it doesn't trade in easy nostalgia and fantasy about the past; rather the opposite'" (Moss).

Daphne Sawle is the first, and basically only, female to become a main character of Hollinghurst's novel. The traditionalist tendency would be to place her at the heart of Cecil's story, as a youthful muse inspiring his creation and later marrying his handsome brother and becoming Lady

---

37 See Chapter 2.3 *The Evolution of Country House Fiction in Historical and Literary (Con)texts.*

Sawle, the mistress of Corley. Instead, she is constantly victimised by her own wrong assumptions. Both her romantic counterparts, be it Cecil, the man who is supposed to have loved her, or Revel, the man she falls in love with and for whose sake she abandons her husband, are gay. Seemingly the centre of the story, she fails to play a role of anything else besides an intellectual, highly sensitive loner, unable to establish any feasible ties with the outside world.

Cecil and George, the doomed lovers, swept away by war and prejudice, are the true, if not misjudged and forlorn, romantic couple of *The Stranger's Child*. The lustrous weekend and their affair close with the mentions of the German war and Daphne's ominous remark: "'I mean, George is all right, but we won't see Cecil for ages, perhaps never again!'" (*SC*, 87). The short-lived pastoral opening, which sharply contrasts with the majority of the further development of the plot, occupies a prominent place in the poetics of country house fiction. The Arcadian beauty of the moment, the heat and the balmy smell of the evening air contribute to various lapses of judgement and the general relaxation of morality. This applies to the opening passage of Forster's *Howards End*, where Helen Schlegel has fallen head over heels in love with Paul Wilcox, as well as McEwan's evocation of Cecilia falling prey to the heat and confusion in *Atonement*: "this was the kind of summer's evening one dreamed of all year, and now here it was at last with its heavy fragrance, its burden of pleasures, and she was too distracted by demands and minor distress to respond" (McEwan, 101). The peculiar splendour of a summer's day equally utterly intoxicates Charles Ryder in *Brideshead Revisited*:

> I had been there before; first with Sebastian more than twenty years ago on a cloudless day in June, when the ditches were white with fool's-parsley and meadowsweet and the air heavy with all the scents of summer; it was a day of peculiar splendour, such as our climate affords once or twice a year, when leaf and flower and bird and sun-lit stone and shadow seem all to proclaim the glory of God; and though I had been there so often, in so many moods, it was to that first that my heart returned on this, my latest. (Waugh, *Brideshead Revisited*, 23)

Likewise, it enchants one of the Cazalet's guests in Jane Howard's *The Light Years*: "As she opened the front door and stepped into what had been the old cottage garden she was assailed by the heat, by the sound of bees and the motor mower, by honeysuckle and lavender and the nameless old-fashioned climbing rose of ivory peach colour that was thickly wreathed round the porch" (Howard, 73). These sensuous odes to the marvels of the atmospheric weather amplify the rapture and bedazzlement of the short-lived English summer.[38]

The enchanting delicacy of summer is further intensified by the dichotomy between the inside and the outside. The garden of Two Acres, the forest behind the house and the darkness of the suburban night witness the most provocative and decisive moments of the whole iconic weekend of Cecil's visit to the Sawles' house. It is in the garden that Daphne reads, dreaming and where she meets Cecil and George. Later she sees Cecil and George in the forest, to their great unease. Then, it is back in their garden, where she is tricked and, in order to distract her from Cecil and George's intimacies, Cecil kisses her. The contrast between the unabashed, unconstrained outside and the strait-laced, well-lit inside is transposed onto the conflict between sensitivity, emotionality and false propriety, and human needs and conventions, in a way which reverberates with the echoes of poetics of Forster's work. In *Maurice*, he tells a story of the incurable "illness" of Maurice Hall, which coincides with his friendship with a fellow student, Clive Durham, and their reading and translating of mostly ancient Greek texts. With Clive miraculously cured by the prospect of an advantageous marriage, which might save the crumbling ancestral property, Penge, Maurice attempts desperately at the definite solution of his "condition". Failing to supress his natural needs, he finally leaves with Alec Scudder, an under-gamekeeper at Penge. Despite the accentuated lack of verbosity or zeal, Maurice's ruminations about the outside are the source of intensive, heartfelt, and passionate outbursts of authentic feelings, comprising both joy and fear: "Oh those jolly scents, those bushes where you could hide, that sky as black as the bushes! They were turning away from him. Indoors was his place and there he'd moulder, a respectable pillar of society who has never had the chance to misbehave" (Forster, *Maurice*, 166). Yearning for the outside is the purest expression of Maurice's authentic emotions. The authenticity of E. M. Forster's, Alan Hollinghurst's and Sadie Jones's characters' longing for the outside should by no means be reduced to longing for a place which, freed from minute social surveillance, physically provides for an undisturbed space for sexual encounters. Such crude underestimation would corrode the complexity of Forster's conception of the outside and lush country landscapes in particular, as a space able to translate its physical vivacity into the mental and emotional qualities

---

38   See chapter 3.1 *"Days of Peculiar Splendour": Summer in the Country House.*

of its inhabitants. Its beneficial, liberating properties are evidenced by the intensity and truthfulness of people, for whom to be locked alone in a room does not equal the sheer ecstasy of being outside.[39]

> ... and Penge, instead of numbing, seemed more stimulating than most places. How vivid, if complex, were its impressions, how the tangle of flowers and fruit wreathed his brain! Objects he had never seen, such as rain water baled from a boat, he could see tonight, though curtained in tightly. Ah to get out to them. Ah for darkness – not the darkness of the house which coops up a man among furniture, but the darkness where he can be free! Vain wish! He had paid a doctor two guineas to draw the curtains tighter, and presently, in the brown cube of such a room, Miss Tonks would lie prisoned beside him. (Forster, *Maurice*, 169)

Although Hollinghurst defies the classification of his novel as a work of gay fiction, it unobtrusively develops the topic via discussion of the long history of its tabooization and its social and cultural implications. Those, who try to excavate the hidden truth, the mystery behind the seemingly inconspicuous "Two Acres" face the appropriation of the story by hordes of ignorant "stranger's children". Their fictionalised version of the generally acceptable, heterosexual-romance background of the poem tramples severely on the truth about its origin and its author's life. As Mr Lasker Jones remarks in Forster's *Maurice*: "'England has always been disinclined to accept human nature'" (188). Cecil Valance is supposed to embody the ultimate incarnation of a heterosexual patriot, a romantic poet laying down his young life for his country. In reality, he happily, and quite prominently, uses double-entendres concerning his and George's "paganism" (*SC*, 41) or he homiletically speaks about love not always coming by the front door (*SC*, 66). These both are the source of the comic potential of the novel as well as its conception of history consisting of misheard misunderstandings and misinterpretations.

Where Hollinghurst attributes the appreciation of Victorian architecture to sensitive characters, Forster ascribes sensitivity and authenticity to the appreciation of, and a sense of belonging to, the outside. In *A Room with a View*, Lucy Honeychurch intuitively associates the image of her would-be husband, a clearly closeted aesthete Cecil Vyse, with

---

39 "'I have a feeling it's changed,' he says. 'I spent 20 years politely answering the question, 'How do you feel when people categorise you as a gay writer?' and I'm not going to do it this time round. It's no longer relevant'" (Moss).

a room.[40] Notwithstanding his superficial yet humorous attempts, which are more likely by-products of his aestheticism than of any serious effort, it is impossible to associate the supercilious Cecil with anything else than a room with no view: "The outdoor world was not very familiar to him, and occasionally he went wrong in a question of fact. Mrs Honeychurch's mouth twitched when he spoke of the perpetual green of the larch" (Forster, *A Room with a View*, 93). His existence is stifled by his intellectualism, by his repressed desires and by his inability to connect, since the only relationship Cecil was capable of was feudal: "that of protector and protected" (Forster, *A Room with a View*, 143).

Except for a few stolen moments, the characters in *The Stranger's Child* rarely achieve the joyous exhilaration of *A Room with a View's* Freddy, George and Mr. Beebe bathing in the Sacred Lake, despite the obvious similarity between the two scenes in the wood. Neither do they aspire to the exorbitant sense of liberation of Maurice Hall, whose final spiritual enlightenment is mirrored in a relationship of the inside and the outside, which blossoms into intricate, opulent symbolism. Thus Maurice declares that with nature being on his side, with the forest and the night on his side, he feels that "they, not he, were inside a ring fence" (Forster, *Maurice*, 190). "A ring fence" both literally and metaphorically points to all sorts of obstructions and to the social, religious, cultural and political forces which bind people. However, the forces also bring him and Alec closer together as they continue to sever the ties with society and to live outside, or better to say beyond it. Forster concluded his work by "Terminal note" which he added to the manuscript in 1960. There, he laments over the state of England's wild nature, which is practically absent. According to him, the effects of the two world wars made it practically extinct. The outlaws, people whose claim on wilderness is justifiable and lawful, have no place to go: "There is no forest or fell to escape today, no cave in which to curl up, no deserted valley for those who wish neither to reform nor corrupt society but to be left alone. People do still escape,

---

40 "I had got an idea – I dare say wrongly – that you feel more at home with me in a room."
"A room?" she echoed, hopelessly bewildered.
"Yes. Or, at the most, in a garden, or on a road. Never in the real country like this."
"... Do you know that you're right? I do. I must be a poetess after all. When I think of you it's always as in a room. How funny!"
To her surprise, he seemed annoyed.
"A drawing room, pray? With no view?"
"Yes, with no view, I fancy. Why not?"
"I'd rather," he said reproachfully, "that you connected me with the open air." (Forster, *A Room with a View*, 99)

one can see them any night at it in the films. But they are gangsters not outlaws, they can dodge civilization because they are part of it" (Forster, *Maurice*, 224).

In terms of the perception of homosexuality, whose authenticity Forster inextricably ties with the authenticity of nature, he notices a shift of public opinion from ignorance and terror to familiarity and contempt. The only path towards universal acceptance lies in the concept being slipped into the minds of people without them knowing it. Since, according to his experience and observations, knowledge does not bring understanding: "what the public really loathes in homosexuality is not the thing itself but having to think about it" (Forster, *Maurice*, 224). From this point of view, Hollinghurst's refutation of both the label of an idealising period drama and his rejection of the categorization of *The Stranger's Child* as a work of gay fiction contribute to its deft challenge of the institution of English country, unobtrusively laying its foundations on gay pastoral and shifting the focus from the country to the suburbs.

The arrival of guests typically operates as a plot device in country house fiction. A guest tends to play the role of a grateful alien, an observer, who unlocks the secrets of the house and its inhabitants and whose role gives the whole story a plausible context. The invited guests predominate over the uninvited, although sometimes these two groups mingle. This mingling provides a hint of unpredictability as well as a touch of determinism, since by doing so, the unfinished business of the past is finally settled. Agatha Christie's detective stories often operate under this principle, with Waugh's *A Handful of Dust* and *Brideshead Revisited*, Elizabeth Jane Howard's *The Light Years*, Ian McEwan's *Atonement*, Jones's *The Uninvited Guests*, or Waters' *The Little Stranger* developing variations on the theme. Hollinghurst's *The Stranger's Child* captures the essence of the anxious awaiting of guests with Daphne's simulation of nonchalant reading in the garden, his focus is, however, directed elsewhere than the inevitable ritual dining. It is *The Uninvited Guests* in particular,[41] which elevates the process of the preparation of lavish meals, their fantastic ar-

---

41 Although Elizabeth Jane Howard does not match the sumptuous rhapsody of Sadie Jones, her detailed observation of the contents of the larder reveals the quality and quantity of food and the toil involved in its preparation:

"The larder was cool and rather dark with a window covered with fine zinc mesh, in front of which hung two heavily infested fly papers. Food in every stage of its life lay on the long marble slab, the remains of a joint under a cage made of muslin, pieces of rice puddings and blancmange on kitchen plates, junket setting in a cut-glass bowl, old, crazed, discoloured jugs filled with gravy and stock, stewed prunes in a pudding basin and, in the coldest place beneath the window, the huge, silvery salmon, its eye torpid from recent

rangement onto dishes and their subsequent consumption, into a truly sensual reading feast:

> Florence and Myrtle had toiled long and hard with fantastic and imaginative results. As well as the emerald-green roses and glossy chocolate cake, on a high crystal stand, there were bowls of cream; before that, gherkins, as well as various gratins and slabs of pork, forced or minced, with mace, capers, thyme. The rind of bacon soldered leaner components together. There were lemons, sharpening the edges of fat, and chervil.[42]

As a consequence the role of some characters, servants and cooks in particular, is reduced to that of strategists of a demanding, enslaving operation with a cacophony of ingredients and possible dishes being harmonised into a symphony (*UG*, 32). A similar amount of attention is given to the house, whose cleanliness should persuade the visitor about the enchanting potential of the place, which proudly evokes the qualities of its owners.[43] The freshly-starched sheets, radiant barristers, polished oaked panelling, shiny marble floors and rooms overflowing with the scent of fresh flowers spilling from their vases together with extravagant types and amounts of food erupting from their bowls and platters induce the pomp and grandeur of the place and the occasion. At the same time all this places overzealous demands on servants burdened by the sheer unfeasibility. Overloaded with tasks, they cause accidents and make mistakes.

What accentuates the gruelling nature of servants', and particularly cooks' toil, is that they are forced to prepare dishes whose quantity, verging on conspicuous waste, and character are in compliance with the expectations and demands on aristocratic cuisine. Therefore, intricate soups and spectacular roasts are prepared in a blistering heat of the kitchen on some of the hottest summer's days: "The labour in the kitchen had been long and hard all day in the heat, and the residue was

---

poaching, lay like a grounded zeppelin. The fruit basket was on the slate floor, the paper that lined it red and magenta with juice." (Howard, 73)

42 Jones, Sadie. *The Uninvited Guests*. 2012. London: Vintage Books, 2013, p. 57. [Subsequent page references preceded *UG* are given in parentheses in the text]

43 "The house shone about itself proudly. China bowls and glass vases held small collections of flowers from the garden: hyacinths, lily of the valley and narcissi. The smell of them, miraculous, with wax furniture polish and blue wood-smoke, went all though the rooms and in the air of the halls and stairs, too. A person might walk from a cool corridor full of the scent of lit fires into a bedroom to find the smell of damp flowers from a pot of wild violets and hot starch from the fresh sheets and flat-creased pillow cases." (*UG*, 57)

everywhere: the flagstone floor was slick with the spilt grease of roasted meat and trodden-in peel; sodden tea towels, tributes to heroic forgotten labours, drooped above the range like decaying regimental banners in church" (McEwan, 104). Although the majority of guests try to keep up appearances, they are not resistant to the heat and their appetites diminished severely, they do not appreciate the fruits of the incredible labour which went into the production of meals. McEwan aptly points to the slavish adherence to the rules of correct execution of social rituals through the example of drinks, which are served in the sweltering heat of a hot summer evening. Instead of water, which they would prefer, the guests are served warm desert wine, which further diminishes their appetites and makes the serving of their roast dinner nauseating. A glassful of cool water would definitely have been a much more sensible choice, but with water available only to children, the adult guests are forced to drink a dessert wine at room temperature (McEwan, 125).

The sumptuous manner in which the authors describe the processes involved in the preparation of country house feasts truthfully incarnates the spirit of the actual practice. In his *A Country House Companion*, Mark Girouard claims that the quality and especially quantity of food and drink consumed by hosts and guests symbolised power, wealth and also hospitality: "[f]rom the Middle Ages onwards the hecatombs that vanished down the throats of guests of feasts and funerals were carefully recorded" (Girouard, 63). To be served more than one course and one type of food was considered to be a sign of status for an individual. Ben Jonson's famous 1616 country house poem "To Penshurst" involves a description of the hospitality of the lord, which presents a sense of the unconstrained plenty of food the guests are invited to share:

> Where comes no guest but is allowed to eat,
> Without his fear, and of thy lord's own meat;
> Where the same beer and bread, and selfsame wine,
> This is his lordship's shall also be mine,
> And I not fain to sit (as some this day
> At great men's tables), and yet dine away.
> Here no man tells my cups; nor standing by,
> A waiter doth my gluttony envy,
> But gives me what I call, and lets me eat;
> He knows bellow he shall find plenty of meat. (Ben Jonson)

Serving up the individual meals also developed into a ritual. The kitchen was usually situated as far from the dining room as possible, so that the smells and danger of fire were reduced. This also called for a carefully choreographed procession of bringing the individual courses, which was regarded as another part of ritualised feasting. All these assiduous components of the ritual of eating were performed at the obvious expense of its key components, taste and temperature. It was not until the nineteenth century when the noble eaters realised that all these ritual components prevented the food from being served hot. What is more, "[a]ppearance was perhaps more important than taste; certainly, care was lavished on the visual conceits which diversified great feasts, and where the predecessors of the fancy wedding cakes of today" (Girouard, 64).

In view of the presentation of food in the majority of contemporary country house novels, its symbolism seems to acknowledge the desperate clinging to the past on the side of the hosts. They, in spite of dire climatic or economic conditions, unabashedly force their often defiant staff to perform a highly orchestrated routine, to which they grew unaccustomed due to the diminishing number of occasions. The failing patriarchal order leaves a nauseous aftertaste of a huge portion of roast meat on a stuffy July evening.

The absence of dominant male figures from the narratives, fathers in particular, or their marked suppression, mockery, or undermining of their traditional roles augurs the gradual corrosion of the traditionally patriarchal, male-dominated context of a country house. The absent father from Henry James's famous novella *The Turn of the Screw* (1898) is equally absent in Frances Hodgson Burnett's *The Secret Garden* (1911). At the same time, this treatment of typically central characters opens ways for the less dominant voices, typically children. With their fathers absent and their mothers and older siblings occupied with agendas of their own, the abandoned, unattended children provide distraction of their own and often colour the plot with a zealous involvement in a variety of unexpected activities. Thus two "Great Undertakings" of two little girls, Briony Tallis from *Atonement* and Imogen "Smudge" Torrington from *The Uninvited Guests* determine and enrich the plot. Whereas the results of Briony's dramatic efforts fail to impress due to bad staging, her subsequent fabrication completely and tragically alters the course of events. Smudge's intention is to get her pony, Lady, inside of her room, which, significantly, happens to be the most remote one of the whole new part of the house: "The Great Undertaking was within her grasp. This May Day eve was the day that the pony Lady would be immortalised in charcoal. She only had to achieve the sitting of the pony, and it would be done" (*UG*, 129). However, Lady's hooves were not meant for neither climbing up nor descending the stairs. With "The Great Undertaking" unfinished, as the pony failed to imprint its charcoaled side on the wall of Smudge's bedroom, the endeavour put into rescuing the pony from the steep flight of stairs unites the whole family and directs rightful attention to the abandoned Smudge.

The surprising lack of motherly attention and involvement of Freda Sawle, an aging alcoholic widow in The Stranger's Child, provides the right circumstances for the creation of the iconic "Two Acres", as well as Daphne's unimpressed involvement in the process, which is almost immediately mythicized, following the death of a young aristocrat Cecil Valance. The abandonment of children by their parents might have a catastrophic impact on the fellow characters, such as in the case of Atonement, but might also grow into a conflicted relationship, such as in the case of Sebastian Flyte. Sebastian's frustration grows into a complete estrangement from his family and his ominous remark on their arrival at Brideshead foreshadows the tragic development of the novel: "'It's where my family live." And even then, rapt in the vision, I felt, momentarily, like a wind stirring the tapestry, an ominous chill at the words he used – not "That is my home," but "It's where my family live'" (Waugh, *Brideshead Revisited*, 39).

Another brilliant observation of the treatment of male dominance and the patriarchal order *The Stranger's Child* elaborates on is the question of interior design. Dudley Valance invites a daring incarnation of the 1930s modern woman, Eva Riley, an Amazon with a penchant for fast cars, cigarettes and daring clothes which expose her boyish body to refurbish his family residence, a ghastly Victorian eye-sore, Corley Court. In view of her accentuated, nearly predatory, sexuality and her profession, Eva might be seen as a distant relative to Jenny, Princess Abdul Akbar, who is invited to Hetton in order to distract Tony Last's attention from his wife's affair with London socialite John Beaver in *A Handful of Dust*. Nevertheless, to Daphne's surprise, she is more likely to be sexually attracted to Eva than to her handsome husband Dudley, Lord Valance.

In spite of the undisputable aesthetic value of new interiors, their openness and practicality, Daphne, the young lady Valance, does not identify with their cool, modern appearance. She feels overly exposed and unable to find a soothing nook or a corner with which the old design abounded. Eva's "ruthless hand" (*SC*, 151) and sanitising designs strip Corley's rooms off their medieval gloom and quirky charm, and fill them with light and shine. This transformation is the result of the employment of light colours, gleaming surfaces and the avoidance of heavy velvet curtains, in particular. Aesthetically, Eva Riley's interiors match her clothes and accessories, which in turn compliment her narrow-hipped, boyish, angular frame. Daphne considers Eva's rooms unwelcoming, her clothing daring, and her self-confident attitude and personality in general purely obnoxious.

> She thought she'd never seen anything so short, for evening wear, as Eva Riley's dress, only just on the knee when she sat, or indeed anything so long as her slithering red necklace, doubtless also of her own design. Well, her odd flat body was made for fashion, or at least for these fashions; and her sharp little face, not pretty, really but made up as if it were, in red, white and black like a Chinese doll. Designers, it seemed, were never off duty. Curled across the corner of a sofa, her red necklace slinking over the grey cushions, Mrs. Riley was a sort of advertisement for her room; or perhaps the room was an advertisement for her. (*SC*, 123)

The Stranger's Child is a many-faceted commentary touching on sensitive topics such as the construction of individual, national, cultural, historical and even sexual identity. The fervour with which Cecil Valance wrecks the composure of the Sawles, how much the public adores his poem "Two Acres", how Dudley hates Corley House, how Daphne loves her gay lover Revel and the way Eva Riley wears her self-designed dresses might be all perceived as subversive statements. These elements simultaneously question, contest, address and parade a multitude of formative parts of English culture, mirroring the author's preoccupation with the authenticity of his statement.

4.2 Architectural Visions of the Country House

4.2.1 Fe/male Architects vs. Interior Designers

Eva Riley reflects the qualities of her rooms which aspire to the then-contemporary aesthetic of Modernist architecture. The sharp lines of her body echo the clear, razor-cut lines of uncompromising buildings. Despite the fact that the Modern movement postulated a break with the past as its defining quality, it, nevertheless, retained classical, centuries-old ideas of order and proportions, and firmly restricted the emotional and sensual from the design process. Some of its theoreticians, such as Loos or Le Corbusier, vocally promoted the division of architectural properties into male and female. According to Le Corbusier, who developed the notion established already by Vitruvius' *Ten Books on Architecture* in the first century BC and further elaborated by Leonardo da Vinci or Andrea Paladio's sixteenth-century *The Four Books on Architecture*, "[g]eometry is male, order is male, both are divine" (Moore, 151).

Moreover, Mrs. Riley, in spite of being a "mere" interior decorator, implies the self-centred, self-confident, egoistic comportment of the characters of architects as they are presented in fiction. The Architect is a cultural construct, the idealised epitome of virility, conflating his creation with his heterosexual manliness. With minor differences between their actual agendas, architects' fictional counterparts design either soaring monuments or robust reminders of their masculinity. The former, monumental, Babylonian theme of a man building a tower, which literally and metaphorically exceeds his possibilities, is developed in numerous works such as in Henrik Ibsen's emblematic drama *The Master Builder* which, first performed in 1892, focuses on Master Halvard Solness and his lethal ambitions. Dorothy L. Sayers's interpretation of the character of William of Sens, a real-life builder of Canterbury Cathedral, from her 1937 drama *The Zeal of Thy House* was further elaborated by William Golding in his 1964 novel *The Spire*, which revolves around the construction of Salisbury Cathedral and the tragic destiny of Roger Mason, its builder. The obscure practitioner of the rituals of black magic, Nicholas Dyer, from Peter Ackroyd's 1985 tour de force *Hawksmoor*, might be also classified as a fictional architect. Inspired by his real-life counterparts, in this case Nicholas Hawksmoor, the lesser known English Baroque architect, collaborator of Christopher Wren or John Vanbrugh, Dyer was surpassed by the sheer grandiosity of his schemes. The latter, less grandiose topic, is prominently developed in the first volume of John Galsworthy's *The Forsyte Saga*, the 1906 *The Man of Property* through the example of mercurial Philip Bosinney, in Ayn Rand's homage to Frank Lloyd Wright, the character of Howard Roark, whom she presented in her 1943 novel *The Fountainhead*, or the reminiscing Matthew Halland in Penelope Lively's 1991 novel, *City of the Mind*, as well as the uncompromising incarnation of Ludwig Mies van der Rohe, Rainer von Abt, from Simon Mawer's 2009 *The Glass Room*.

Accordingly, the architect is typically presented and perceived as the epitome of masculinity, his work often conflated with his manhood which corresponds with the conception of architecture as "an occupation of men and for men" (Sanders, 3). On the other hand, interior design has "since its inception, been viewed as a practice, if not always of women, then certainly for women" (Ibid). At this point, the character of Eva Riley with all her virile aggressiveness and square body clearly bridges the two poles of architecture and interior design, embodying a perfect example of the conflicted role of a modernist interior designer:

> Perhaps the best evidence of the porous boundaries between architecture and decoration can be found in the work of those most responsible for erecting the borders in the first place – the first generation of modernist architects. As the literal separation between inside and outside breaks down with the development of the transparent curtain wall, so too does the boundary between architect and interior decorator. (Sanders)

In his 2002 essay, "Curtain Wars", Joel Sanders interprets the significance of curtains in the determination of status of an architect and an interior designer and also in the contestation of the professionally conditioned gender bias. The two rival, if self-proclaimed as incompatible, overlapping professions, reflect deeper and broader cultural conflicts triggered by profound social angst concerning gender and sexuality. Sanders dates the beginnings of this profound conflict back to the end of the nineteenth century, when the professional decorator emerged, often recruited from the affluent upper-class bourgeois females. Interior design was regarded as a pass-time and marked the interior as a female domain. However, historically, domestic households which included furnishings were associated with patriarchy, since the estates as well as their contents were passed from generation to generation of male heirs. The decline of aristocracy at the end of the nineteenth century contributed to the rise of the bourgeois housewife as a major consumer. She now ran the household and bought and provided commodities her husband no longer inherited from his ancestors. The inferior understanding of interior design mirrors this historical development.

However, the origin of "Curtain Wars" is associated with the interpretation and treatment of fabric in domestic spaces in general, and is concerned with windows in particular. The soft fabric used to veil views, to modify sunlight and to facilitate domestic privacy, is often repudiated by architects, since it alters or completely eclipses the precious geometry of the architectural forms. The most vocal denigrators of curtains were Modernist architects, primarily because the key element of their aesthetic was a glass wall, called ironically a "curtain wall", which was achieved at the expense of incredible intellectual and technical effort. For good reason, they rejected to compromise and cover such an achievement with a piece of cloth. Coincidentally, it was also the first generation of Modernist architects which muddled the clear outlines of the boundary between architect and interior designer. With built-in furniture, architects aimed at designing the whole way of life of their clients, including furniture, tableware and the design of upholstery. Likewise, Rainer von Abt from Mawer's novel *The Glass Room* promises his clients not to design a house only, but a whole world, a whole life. He stresses that he wants to work "from the foundations to the interior, the windows, the doorways, the furnishings, the fabric of the place as well as the structure" (Mawer, 28). However, these dominant, macho male figures cooperated with talented female designers, whose considerable contribution to the resulting unified aesthetic cannot be denied. As far as fiction is concerned, the female contribution is rarely acknowledged.

The roots of division of the spheres, with the domestic interior being traditionally perceived as a female realm and the overall construction being identified as a male domain, spread further back into cultural history than the nineteenth-century rise of the status and spending power of a bourgeois housewife. Curtains and fabrics in general embody softness and the curves of their folds are typically associated with femininity. They obviously cannot significantly affect the physical qualities of a building, whereas genuine materials, such as stone or glass, typically associated with manliness, can. Perception of an ornament as an emblem of female "artifice" has been present in the Western architectural tradition over two thousand years. This understanding is the result of Vitruvius' reasoning behind the origins of Doric and Ionic columns: "[i]n the invention of two types of columns, they borrowed manly beauty, naked and unadorned for the one, and for the delicacy, adornment, and proportions characteristic of women" (Vitruvius, qtd. in Sanders). For classical architects, ornamentation was acceptable in case it was subdued to the structural logic of a building, reflecting the similar relation of men to women. The status of ornamentation deteriorated drastically with the advent of architectural Modernism where it was compared to overdressed women and the lack of their cultural and cognitive progress. According to Adolph Loos: "The evolution of culture is synonymous with the removal of ornament from utilitarian objects. ... The stragglers slow down the cultural evolution of the nations and of the mankind; not only is ornament produced by criminals but also a crime is committed through the fact that ornament inflicts serious injury on people's health, on the national budget and hence on cultural evolution" (Loos 20–21, emphasis in original). This attitude further enhanced the sharp division between architecture and interior design and affirmed the identification of interior design with womanliness and architecture with manliness. Fictional portrayals of architects in literature and films reinforced the cultural construction of macho male architects both by their suggestive poetics: "He was short, dark, bouncing in that boxing manner of his" (Mawer, 21) and also by the introduction of a gay decorator as a response to the womanliness typically associated with the profession of an interior designer. At this point, Eva Riley can be seen as an incarnation of a virile woman, with her physical appearance and voracious sexuality as well as her sanitising design showcasing this quality.

The minor importance typically ascribed to interior decorating, which is conducted by either effeminate gay men or women, endangers the status as well as the self-esteem of architects who are forced to professionally swing between the two borders. In view of its historical implications and the findings of gender and psychoanalytic criticism, it may threaten the vulnerability "which lies at the core of manhood. Whether seen from the vantage of psychoanalytic theory of cultural history, masculinity, while seemingly invincible, is fragile. The biological penis can never live up to the mystique of the cultural phallus" (Sanders). This inability might serve as one of many possible interpretations of Henrik Ibsen's drama, *The Master Builder.* The tragic downfall, both metaphorical and literal, of the main character, Halvard Solness, as he falls from the tower he built at the end of the play, might be understood as his inability, or at least his fear that he "cannot climb as high as he builds" (Ibsen, 117). Similarly, an architect asked to perform some inevitable decorating activities such as fabric picking, might comprehend it as a challenge to his manliness. Whereas a certain subset of architects might share this impression, the other group might secretly revel in such authorisation. Since, according to Sanders "for some practitioners the architectural profession represents a strange sort of closet, a refuge that allows them (albeit with some discomfort) to engage in practices otherwise unacceptable for 'real' men" (Sanders).

Therefore, architects' frequent disavowal of interior design and their conspicuously frequent portrayals typically endowing them with machismo and arrogant manliness seem to be both proofs of culturally constructed phenomenon and overcompensation for masculine vulnerability. As Sanders concludes, it is the right time for the arrival of a new generation of designers who would develop "a hybrid design vocabulary"

(Sanders) that would allow a wide spectrum of human activities and identities to develop. Hollinghurst's Eva Riley aptly demonstrates gender hybridity and puts an ironic twist on the stereotypical treatment of both architects and interior designers and their manliness and femininity, being simultaneously a woman architect and a virile interior designer. Similarly, the realm of architecture echoes the contemporary fluidity of gender identities, able to overcome the stereotypical division into masculine and feminine elements and freely merge logic and intuition, reason and emotions.

4.2.2 Victorian Eyesores vs. Modernist Sanatoriums

The results of Eva Riley's transformation of the interior of Corley Court echo the best of Modernist tradition, with their clean lines, crisp simplicity, dazzling light, and the palette of off-white colours enhancing the overall sanitising effect of the redecoration. The modernised, refurbished rooms offer clarity and light at the expense of the nooks and corners necessary for the proper functioning of human imagination and creativity. Daphne, the young, sensitive Lady Valance, feels exposed in the dazzling shine and unable to curl in her favourite spot in the refuge provided by the old drawing room.

> The off-white dazzle of it, on a bright April morning, was undeniable effective. It was like a room in some extremely expensive sanatorium. Comfortable modern chairs in grey loose covers had replaced the old clutter of cane and chintz and heavy-fringed velvet. The dark dadoed walls and the coffered ceiling, with its twelve inset panels depicting the months, had been smoothly boxed in, and on the new walls a few of the original pictures were hung beside very different work. There was Sir Eustace, and his young wife Geraldine, to-full length portraits designed to glance tenderly at each other, but now divided by a large almost 'abstract' painting of a factory perhaps or a prison. … In the old drawing-room, where the curtains, even when roped back, had been so bulky that they kept out much of the light, Daphne had loved to sit and almost, in a way, to hide; but no such refuge was offered by the new one, … (*SC*, 113–114)

Daphne's stance on Modernist redecoration of the interior mirrors and her identification with the ormolu of Victoriana reverberates with her desire to, both literally and metaphorically, withdraw into a corner, to possess a space of her own, where she would be allowed to dream and think. Thirdly, and from the point of view of this subchapter perhaps most importantly, it refers to the general attitude towards Modernist architecture from the perspective of the history of architecture and also its reflection in British fiction. [44]

The appreciation of Victorian architecture is conceived as a mark of sensitivity in *The Stranger's Child*. The efforts to supress the voluptuousness of the interior of Corley Court by boxing it in off-white sheen of the sanitising designs of Mrs Riley resonate with the futility of attempts at supressing the authentic sexuality of individuals by means of enforced, legitimised measures taken by the state. Daphne's unease at the new interior marks a universal challenge imposed by the majority of cool, impeccably proportioned modernist designs: the absence of nooks and corners, of semi-secluded spaces, which would allow hiding, retreating to one's own solitude, to one's own self. According to Bachelard, a nook or a corner is of capital importance in the space of the house, since it "is a symbol of solitude for the imagination; that is to say, it is the germ of a room, or of a house" (Bachelard, 136). To withdraw into one's corner does not necessarily imply any grand schemes, the process, nevertheless, evokes a number of images, some of them ancient and "psychologically primitive" (Bachelard, 137). This simplicity of images enhances their universality and urgency: "At times, the simpler the image, the vaster the dream" (Bachelard, 137). The corner is an emblematic refuge, whose primitiveness is anchored in its universal sense understood by all living creatures in general: "Physically, the creature endowed with a sense of refuge, huddles up to itself, takes to the corner, hides away, lies snug, concealed" (Bachelard, 91). The image of the corner bears resemblance to the primal images of nests and shells, which, according to Bachelard, revive primitive, archetypal daydreams.

The approach to Gothic Revival architecture varies considerably in the emphasis put on either its vulgar sumptuousness and impracticality, or its exaggerated emotionality and awe-inspiring richness of its decors. Historically, Gothic Revival architecture, whose beginnings are associated with mid-eighteenth century England, meant a return to traditional, idealising aestheticism, which accentuated emotionality in general, as well as the idealised medieval ethos. Its enormous popularity lasted for

---

44   Parts of this chapter's text appeared in "*The Glass Room*: Architecture as a Poetic Emotion." *Prague Journal of English Studies* 2, no. 1, 2013, pp. 65–79 and "On the Analogy between the Language of Architecture and Language of Literary Work: The Role of Conception of Architecture in Generating the Poetics of *The Glass Room*." *Filologické studie*. Univerzita Karlova v Praze: Karolinum, 2013, pp. 15–31.

over one and half centuries and was strengthened by the swift, vast development of industrial involvement in building technology. It contributed to the number of pseudo-Gothic buildings largely surpassing the number of the authentically Gothic ones. The Gothic Revival soon became interchangeable with Victorian architecture. Despite the intended evocation of traditionalism and the suppression of any sort of innovative approach, Victorian architecture unprecedentedly involved technological progress into all spheres of human life. All in all, it faithfully reflected the contradictory character of the period, which witnessed both the astronomic rise of wealth and the catastrophic spread of poverty and slums, with workers living in cellars and back-to-back houses, where only the most fortunate ones had access to a window. Life expectancy in industrial cities such as Manchester was lower than it had been 500 years before. At the same time, the ingenuity of contemporary engineering provided for a number of practically applicable inventions, such as an intricate sewage system and plate glass. The latter transformed shopping into a new leisure.

It became almost impossible to match the pride of the successful Victorian businessman, whose achievements, Dimbleby observes, could be measured only with regards to the merchants of fifteenth century Italy: "The deliberately built in a style that recalled those past glories. ... If you look carefully you can see a mixture of styles: one storey Italian, the next French and the one above with a touch of English Elizabethan" (Dimbleby, 192). It is true that Britain was the richest and the most powerful nation in the world. This progress considerably contributed to the swift development of a new class, a middle class. Its representatives, such as shopkeepers, tradesmen and clerks desperately strived for a book of wisdom, which would facilitate their orientation while moving upwards through the social hierarchy, was met by the 1861 publication of Mrs Beeton's *Book of Household Management*.

Terrace houses and diminutive villas of these Victorians prevail in most English towns and cities. They are built of brick, with walls just thick enough to muffle the sounds from the neighbouring house with a carefully and tastefully designed front room oriented towards the street. Mostly unused by the family, these rooms embody a quintessential Victorian quality, which is the presentation of a good face to the outside world. It was exactly this kind of speculation which lead to the separation of slums and the poor from the ways of other, more respectable citizens, whose residence in the assigned part of the cities and towns almost prevented any kind of contact.

The emphasis on keeping appearances and the aesthetic pretence might be at the root of the deep distaste for "Victorian monstrosities" of some of the contemporary literary characters as well as the general public. Difficult to admire, because of the lack of any universally recognisable and observable building style and the exuberant number of possible qualities ranging from gloomy and dark to flamboyant and quirky, many Victorian buildings were demolished in the course of time.

However, what cannot be denied is the Victorian partiality for the irrational, prevalently emotional, at times even fantastic, effect of its buildings. The chief components of its aesthetics are awe and surprise. Both the perspective of Hollinghurst's *The Stranger's Child* and Waugh's *A Handful of Dust*, highlight its appreciation as a sign of sensitivity. This emphasis on the emotional aspect of architecture is reminiscent of the principle of the baroque, whose dramatic effect was the desired result generated by a consistent juxtaposition of contrasts. In Waugh's *Brideshead Revisited*, Charles Ryder, a future "architectural painter" (Waugh, *Brideshead*, 260) owes his aesthetic and the subsequent spiritual and emotional awakening to the house of Brideshead itself, for although supressed, his "sentiments at heart were insular and medieval" (Waugh, *Brideshead*, 93):

> This was my conversion to the baroque. Hereunder that high and insolent dome, under those tricky ceilings; here, as I passed through those arches and broken pediments to the pillared shade beyond and sat, hour by hour, before the fountain, probing its shadows, tracing its lingering echoes, rejoicing in all its clustered feats of daring and invention, I felt a whole new system of nerves alive within me, as though the water that spurted and bubbled among its stones was indeed a life-giving spring. (Waugh, *Brideshead Revisited*, 93–94)

Similarly to the baroque, "Victoriana" or Victorian architecture abandons horizontality, symmetry, proportions, form, interior and practicality for the sake of chaotic, haphazard verticality, ornaments, effect, exterior and impracticality. Therefore, in terms of literary depictions of the clashes between opposing approaches, a battle is fought between the more appreciative, sensuous, sensitive minds such as Daphne's and the practical, future-oriented ones, such as Dudley's, Cecil Valance's brother. Sensing that the house, Corley Court, chose her, irrespective of her will and "she would be sick at heart to lose it" (*SC*, 141), Daphne, and later Peter, a music teacher, are perfectly capable of admiring changing patterns of polychrome bricks, various peculiarities such as turrets and gables, as well as the rainbow effect of plate glass windows. Whereas for Dudley, a fortuitous inheritor of an exorbitantly ugly, large and impractical Victorian house, "[a] deepening distaste for all Victoriana became a kind of mission" (*SC*, 437). Covering up the ingenious remnants of the earlier age, such as "the ornate ceilings, the sombre panelling, the childish and clumsy outcrops of stone-carving and mosaic" (*SC*, 437), even Dudley ponders the question of the possible future appreciation of its quaint charm. Maybe that is the reason why, despite his taste for modern brightness and simplicity, he leaves the library, "in its original state of caliginous gloom" (*SC*, 438).

The primeval gloom, foolishly loved and admired by some is abhorred by others. Corley Court replete with monstrous furnishings, glassed-in arcades, a chapel, a great polished staircase with a banister in Elizabethan style (too wide to hold on properly), a coat of arms, crimson carpets, Gothic fireplaces designed in order to look like castles, complete with battlements and turrets with tiny functional windows, and finally endowed with a white marble tomb of the dead poet in the basement, inspires the feelings of entrapment and constant pressure in some of its inhabitants. However, these slightly amusing qualities, atypical of a distinguished, gracious notion of the country house, seem to be perfectly suitable for educational purposes: "In fact, the house was perfect for a boarding-school – secluded, labyrinthine, faintly menacing, with its own tree-lined park now mown and marked out in pitches. No one, it was felt, could want to live in such a place, but as an institution of learning it was pretty much ideal" (*SC*, 269). The in-between wars alternations are perceived as disappointment and Peter, his students as well as Paul revel in the sight of the chapel, library and the great oak surface unmarked by the hygienic elimination of all primeval-like pseudo-Gothic ormolu.

The hygienic elimination of Gothic bric-a-brac was performed on behalf of Dudley by "Mrs Riley's ruthless hand" (*SC*, 151). Her major contribution, despite her indisputable talent as an interior designer, lies in the procedure she employed in order to achieve the desired luminosity of the rooms. The process also included a superficial covering up of the ceilings, whose historical and especially aesthetic value waits for a more sensible time and more appreciative minds, than hers or Dudley's. The moment when Peter, a music teacher and a future famed art and cultural historian, shows the remains of the original ceiling to Paul Bryant, his lover and future rival over the topic of Cecil Valance's biography, at the beginning of the 1970s, is yet another highly symbolical episode of the novel.[45] The admiration they both display at the sight of the formerly despised "jelly-dome vaulting", marks the shift in Paul's individual as well as the social attitude towards sexuality which marked this period.[46]

> But Peter got Paul climb up too, the planks jumping and yielding under their joint weight, and gripped his arm with insouciant firmness as they raised their heads and peered into the shadowy space between one ceiling and another. ... Then he got it going and as he swept his arm in a slow arc they saw festive gleams and quickly swallowing shadows flow in and out of the little gilded domelets overheard. Between these there was shallow coffering, painted crimson and gold, and where the water had come through, bare laths and hanging fragments of horse-hair plaster. It seemed far from the architecture of everyday life, it was like finding a ruined pleasure palace, or burial chamber long since pillaged. (*SC*, 345)

Corley Court is saved and, by a strange twist of fate in the form of Mrs Riley, preserved for the future generations. These are to either mock its Gothic glamour, or to admire it, much in the spirit of John Betjeman[47]as a pristine phantasm.

Daphne's reluctance to revel in modernist design illustrates, besides its possible sexual and phenomenological connotations, the approach of the British towards it. The Modern movement in architecture heralded the break with the past, willing to sanitise all its impractical, irrational, ornamental embellishments. Nevertheless, this revolutionary approach, despite having its roots in England, did not find fertile soil for its growth there. British historical development in the first forty years of the twentieth century differed from that of its continental neighbours. Britain was neither invaded, nor did it have to face political or social upheaval on the same scale as countries such as France or Germany. The aesthetic urge which mirrored the ethos of the period remained traditional even after

---

45   At the same time, this moment echoes the aesthetic preoccupation of the opening part of the novel, whose luscious suburban pastoral remains unparalleled by the rest of the novel as well as, with a few exceptions, the history of the English novel.

46   At this point the novel refers to Leo Abse's bill partly decriminalizing male homosexual behaviour, which was passed as the 1967 Sexual Offences Act homosexual behaviour: "'Mm, I was thinking,' said Peter, 'that of this Bill goes through next week it could open the way for a lot more frankness.' Paul, who hadn't been able to discuss the Bill with anybody, felt the grip of crisis again, but less upsettingly than in the drive with Jenny" (*SC*, 320).

47   John Betjeman (1906–1984) was a Poet Laureate, a founding member of Victorian society and an avid supporter and keen defender of Victorian architecture.

the end of the First World War, which otherwise meant swift severing of ties in the countries on the Continent. Where Germany, France, Swiss, Spain, Italy, Austria or the Czechoslovak Republic witnessed experimentation and abstracting tendencies of architecture and design of both public and domestic buildings, the British preferred, with a few exemplary exceptions, classical building in both the public and private domain. Therefore, the houses which were built in the period of transformation of the Home Counties owed to age-old ideas about design.

The robust London expansion into the countryside, known as Metroland, culminating in the 1920s and 1930s, was fuelled by romanticising nostalgia for the merits of both the past and the countryside. The Metropolitan Railway, which ran direct lines from the city centre towards the west of London, took advantage of the massive demand for new houses and invested in the house building development. By providing houses of dubious quality as far as the quality and the quantity of the living space is concerned, it contributed to the definition of a new style of living: the suburb.[48]

In his monograph on the nature and identity of English art, *The Englishness of English Art*, Nikolaus Pevsner, an acclaimed art critic, the author of the forty-six-volume series *The Buildings of England* and a founding member and a chairman of The Victorian Society, identified the aesthetic of nostalgic, traditionalist buildings with the Picturesque. He also tied its development with the disastrous impacts of the absence of proper urban planning during the boom of Industrial Revolution which Britain had undergone earlier than other European countries. The rapid, uncontrolled growth of industrial zones caused by "faith in tolerance on the one hand, in private enterprise on the other" (Pevsner, *The Englishness*, 185) as well as the urban population, the majority of which lived in appalling conditions in slums, cellars and back-to-back houses completely altered the appearance of towns. The response to its disastrous effects emerged around 1870, again sooner than on the Continent, and took the aesthetic of the Picturesque, not so much its philosophical principles, as its model. The result which Pevsner thinks the British should be proud of was the garden suburb and the garden city. This type of housing development successfully blended small-size buildings with nature. What it lacked, however, was a truly urban quality.

---

48   See 2.3 *The Evolution of Country House Fiction in Historical and Literary (Con)texts.*

While discussing the English contribution to the development of the new style, whose beginnings he situated between 1900 and 1910, Pevsner firstly separates architecture and design and underlines the leading position of Britain in the development of building technology, unlike in so-called Fine Arts. Modern architecture harmonises the English tradition with Perpendicular style and the simplicity and the suppression of ornament of Neo-Palladian style. Besides these factors, he states William Morris, Philip Webb, Charles Voysey, and other late-nineteenth-century architect-designers as its pioneers. Nevertheless, the new style was not created in England, but in France, Germany and America and its acceptance in England was remarkably slow. According to Pevsner, the reason is simple: "England dislikes and distrusts revolutions. That is a forte in political development, but a weakness in art" (Pevsner, *The Englishness*, 194).

In *The Sources of Modern Architecture and Design* (1956), Pevsner determines two principal aspects which have shaped the qualities of modern architecture, chiefly The International Style of the 1930s, and the 20th century major preoccupations: mass and speed:

> The twentieth century is the century of the masses: mass education, mass entertainment, mass transport, universities with twenty thousand students, comprehensive schools for two thousand children, hospitals with two thousand beds, stadia with a hundred thousand seats. That is one aspect; the other is speed of locomotion, every citizen being an express-train driver on his own, and some pilots travelling faster than sound. Both are only expressions of the technological fanaticism of the age, and technology is only an application of science. (Pevsner, *The Englishness*, 195)

Mass production, mass education, mass health care, but also mass production addressing the needs of mass consumption means the predominance of architecture over beaux-arts, of the emblematic city over the country, and especially "it means the concentration on architecture and design for the masses and on what new materials and new techniques can do for them" (Pevsner, *The Sources*, 9).

Besides its preoccupation with technology as an effective, logical response to the needs of the masses, architectural Modernism also emphasised certain aesthetics. The major attributes of these aesthetics, such as rationality and minimalist simplicity, have continued to shape our ideas about high-quality design even nowadays. There are brilliant, if isolated, examples of modernist domestic architecture, such as the three modernist houses on Ruislip and the spectacular Homewood in Esher by young architect Patrick Gwynne. Echoes of Modernism may be observed in high-rise tower blocks, pre-fabricated housing or contemporary High-Tech architecture, whose major proponents, Sir Norman Foster and Sir Richard Rogers, have designed their pioneering buildings for English companies, such as the Lloyd's building, housing its insurance institution in London. England's leading role in both the conception and inception of Modernism is indisputable despite the lack of actual buildings.

Literary response to this influential architectural development might be characterised as relatively meagre and might be seen as a projection of the scarcity of manifestations in England. Architectural Modernism had, until the publication of Simon Mawer's 2009 novel, *The Glass Room*, occupied only a minor place in the works of British fiction with the notable exception of J. G. Ballard's *High-Rise* (1975), an evocative study of failed attempts at collective co-living. Mawer's portrayal of this unique aesthetic might be regarded as an excursion into the cultural, social and political history of a young, delicate Czechoslovak Republic.[49] Despite the situation of the novel in central Europe, it reverberates with themes not unfamiliar to English country house fiction. *The Glass* Room shares several qualities with country house fiction, for example, centring the novel in one place threatened by a chaotic, often violent historical development, the juxtaposition of several temporal layers, and the accentuated, at points even exaggerated, aesthetic properties of the place and their key role in the overall aesthetic conception of the novel. Further on, it develops the idea of the level of impact the aesthetic properties have on individual characters. Similarly to *The Stranger's Child*, character's response to the aesthetic marks their qualities, and especially sensitivity. Further on, the house's, and especially the central room's peculiar ability to be simultaneously in time and thus witnessing the passage of time, becoming a relic of the olden days, as well as being unmarked by time and its inextricable implications, quite unexpectedly reflects some of the constitutive elements of an English country house.

The Glass Room is primarily a textual commentary on the nature of Modernist architecture. It presents a modernist villa, especially its capital room, the eponymous Glass Room, as the main character of a novel fictionalizing the history of the actual building of Villa Tugendhat and the overall historical development of the Czech Republic in the

---

49   Thomas Harding, the author of critically acclaimed *Hanns and Rudolf* (2013), builds upon a similar premise in *The House by the Lake* (2015), a novel which reveals the history of the twentieth century Germany through the inhabitants of a small house by a lake, which belonged to the family of Harding's grandmother.

twentieth century. The latter viewpoint was favoured by Anna Grmelová, who understood the novel primarily as a brilliant evocation of the
spirit of interwar Czechoslovakia and also: " ... a rhapsody on the Glass
Room of the Landauer Villa and ... a rhapsody on the ideals of interwar
Czechoslovakia, of the First Czechoslovak Republic" (Higgins). The
Glass Room functions as an extended metaphor of the period and the
incarnation of modernist aesthetic principles. The house and the room
in particular, frame the history of Viktor and Liesel, a newly-wed couple,
both descendants of upper-class, industrialist, German-speaking families
from Brno. They want to express their split with the past by constructing
an exceptional house: "... this clinging to the past. This is everything our
new house will not be!" (Mawer, 9) Their house should become the incarnation of their belief in progress, in the future, and in the emergence
of a modern society, which would be ruled by reason and democratic
values:

> The whole essence of the Glass Room is reason. That is what Viktor thinks,
> anyway. For him, it embodies the pure rationality of a Greek classical
> temple, the austere beauty of a perfect composition, the grace and the bal-
> ance of a painting of Mondrian. ... There is nothing convolute, involute,
> awkward or complex. Here everything can be understood as a matter of
> proportion and dimension. (Mawer, 137)

The house is situated in the fictional city of "Město", which bears
a striking resemblance to the Czech town Brno.[50] It sits on a hilltop and,
with a view of an enormous garden surrounding it and the Spilas fortress
situated on the hilltop it faces. Although it is set in the city, and most
probably on its outskirts, its elevated position together with the repeatedly accentuated view of the city extracts it from the urban environment.
The peculiarity of its placement invites the reader to closely examine the

---

50 Lukáš Novák, the author of the critically acclaimed Czech translation, found the universal
designation of the Czech word "Město" disturbing and misleading as far as Czech readers
were concerned and for the purposes of translation replaced it with "Brno". This decision has
certainly strengthened if not helped to establish the firm bond between Villa Tugendhat and
the Landauer House from the novel. On the occasion of the book signing held on 17th May
2010 the author, Simon Mawer, expressed his disagreement with this choice of the translator
and underlined that he would have favoured the maintenance of the formal distance and
universality which the toponym "Město" brings to the novel. According to him, what the
novel is mostly preoccupied with is the initial optimistic vision of the liberal and open society
of the First Czechoslovak Republic, which should have been reflected in the unspecified
denomination of the city.

set of spatial relations which house the story and provide the subject matter of the novel – a unique piece of architecture in the tide of the colourful history of the twentieth century Czechoslovak Republic. The aesthetic preoccupation of the novel with modernist architecture and its positioning in central Europe underline the idiosyncratic nature of the novel. Despite the uniqueness of its subject matter, it echoes motifs and elements typical of English country house fiction. The novel is placed into the heart of an immensely turbulent historical period. The house itself symbolises a new, hopeful, unspoiled and unthreatened direction in the social, cultural, political and economic development of the young country. Albeit its airiness and openness, it anchors the founding principles of a new society. It serves as the family seat of the Landauers and also, with regards to its cost and conception as a work of art, as a family heirloom, which can be passed from generation to generation. The Landauers, whose conception bears a slight resemblance to the mighty and noble patrons and lords from a seventeenth-century country house poem, conceive of the house as a work of art, struggle for it and, tragically, are destined to leave it. What is more, its roots, namely the aesthetic ones, are to be found in the classical, traditional, harmonic, well-proportioned, proper order. These links tie it inextricably with the past, despite its claim of serving as a break from tradition. Besides developing the dichotomy of inside and outside, the house encapsulates the past and survives as a relic of the golden past, physically marked by time and metaphysically placed outside time. Its heightened aesthetic properties reflect the degree of sensitivity of characters, whose appreciation serves as its mark. Mawer's creation could be viewed as paying homage to the irreplaceable role England played in the development of modern, and in this case chiefly Modernist, architecture and The International Style in particular and also paving the way for introduction of the "ultimate opulence of pure abstraction" (Mawer, 114) of Modernist architecture in English fiction.

4.2.3 "As a Ship in the Night": On the Productivity of the House-Ship Analogy

Viktor stands in the Glass Room looking out at the view that was once a wild hilltop panorama and now is something framed and therefore tamed, in the way that the ocean appears tamed when viewed from the bridge of a ship. He has always liked the ship analogy. Despite being a citizen of a country that has no shoreline, he feels an affinity with the sea. The Glass Room is a bridge and the floor above a promenade deck, with cabins for the passengers. The sound of the wind in the trees is a sea sound and the house itself is a ship pitching out into the choppy waters of the city with the wind beating about the stanchions and bulkheads. And ahead is the storm.

(Mawer, 167)

Besides its decisive role in the development of modern architecture, the ship as a frequent physical metaphor of a house has considerably inspired 20th century philosophy and literary theory dealing with space and its structure. The field of British 20th and 21st century fiction has also been influenced with this highly versatile trope, suggestive of a great variety of more or less expected meanings. [51]

From the point of view of this treatise, four works vocally develop the analogy between the house and the ship, often irrespective of the situationality of the plot. Although Iris Murdoch placed her mock pastoral *The Sea, The Sea* into a weathered seaside villa, Hollinghurst's *The Stranger's Child* is by no means involved with the sea and neither is Sadie Jones's *The Uninvited Guests*. *The Glass Room* repeatedly employs the analogy of the house and a ship.[52] By that Mawer elicits further study of the

51   Parts of this chapter's text were presented as a conference paper "'As a Ship in the Night: On the Productivity of the Metaphor of a Ship in Modern British Fiction." The 10th Brno Conference of English, American and Canadian Studies, 6 February 2015, Brno, Czech Republic.

52   The possibilities of access to the Glass Room are constricted to two flights of stairs, one leading from the garden outside and the other leading to the entrance hall. The stairway descending from the entrance hall is curved: "Twelve steps to the curve, and then round and down nine more … " (Mawer, 3) and sealed in milk-white glass panes which enhances the feeling of the gradual complete isolation from the outside world. The aim is to transform visitors and inhabitants into participants of the spectacular artistic potency of the building and to dissolute their engagement in the timely domain outside the walls of the Landauer House.

Anette Fierro observes a similar effect in the building of the National Library of France in Paris: "The city distantly viewed and acoustically muted from across the vast surface, becomes an oceanic mirage. The nautical allusion is as transportive as transformative" (Fierro, 254). Fierro compares its nautical impression with the experimental project of Cité de Refuge, "whose primary physical metaphor is also that of a ship" (Fierro, 254) commissioned by the Salvation Army and designed by Le Corbusier. The building thus became the herald of hope, a beacon of charity. Extensive and previously unseen employment of glass in this project underlined its pivotal intention – to serve as an instrument of salvation by means of transforming nonconformist, dislocated individuals into fully-fledged members of society. The resulting glass container was meant as an instrument of discipline and the normative functioning of the building surpassed all other interpretations. As such, the stifling building of Cité de Refuge developed principles of Le Corbusier's first commission for the Salvation Army, renovation of "Ile Flottante" or Floating Island, which was literally a ship housing the liminal inhabitants of Paris.

nature of the relationship between space, place and time, in *The Glass Room* as well as other analysed works.

In order to approach the trope in its complexity, it is necessary to broaden the scope of study, and, besides fiction and literary theory, also include the fields of architecture and philosophy. Never has such kind of interdisciplinary approach been more appropriate since today's perspective is highly inclusive as far as different fields of study are concerned. From the viewpoint of history of architecture, the preoccupation with ships as a source of inspiration has played a decisive role in the development of Modernist architecture. Its pioneers, such as Walter Gropius, and later also Le Corbusier or Ludwig Mies van der Rohe marvelled at the efficiency and beauty of ships, as well as other technological products, whose aesthetics stemmed from their function: "Every modern man has the mechanical sense. The feeling for mechanics exists and is justified by our daily activities. This feeling in regard to machinery is one of respect, gratitude and esteem" (Le Corbusier, 119). Similarly, Streamline Moderne, a late development of Art Deco, which reached its peak around 1937, copied materials and methods from contemporary methods of ship and aircraft production. However, Streamline Moderne's preoccupation with technology was purely aesthetic, its actual functioning of such technology was not really considered. Embracing the structural aesthetic of technology, Streamline Moderne focused especially on the visual properties which suggest movement. Therefore, compared to Modernism in general and the International Style in particular, Streamline Moderne may be viewed more as a "mannerist" branch of architectural development.

Nine years after the publication of Bachelard's *The Poetics of Space*, Michel Foucault coined "heterotopia" in his 1967 lecture entitled "Des Espaces Autres" or "Of Other Spaces". Unlike utopia, which is a site without a real place, heterotopia is an existing place deeply rooted in society. Heterotopias are defined on the basis of their peculiar relationships with other places since they simultaneously "represent, contest and invert" (Foucault, "Of Other Spaces", 24) real sites and thus they condition the existence of culture. Their distinctive position takes the form of either separation or exclusion regardless their location in reality. There are various types of heterotopias according to their position and functioning in spatial relationships and according to the meaning culture ascribes to them. All of their aspects are combined in "the boat" which is a perfect example of heterotopia, a place which does not have any specific place. What is more, it is a wooden construction, a "floating piece of space", whose major occupation is to move relentlessly and travel into exotic, faraway lands. Boats as almost inexhaustible stocks of the imagination have inspired numberless dreams, visions and artistic endeavours. Their absence in certain culture or their bans and controls impose a serious threat since: "[i]n civilizations without boats, dreams dry up, espionage takes the place of adventure, and the police take the place of pirates" (Foucault, "Of Other Spaces", 28).

Although *The Stranger's Child* does not feature any spatial affinity with the area of the sea or sea shore, it still successfully employs a simile of a ship: "For a moment she pictured the lit house behind them as a ship in the night" (*SC*, 35). The passage is to be found in the opening section of the novel. In terms of the plot, it corresponds with the pastoral summer evening at Two Acres. Children are left alone in the garden, Daphne, the youngest one, is moved by listening to a record of Senta's Ballad from Richard Wagner's *Flying Dutchman* sung by Emmy Destinn, which thematically accentuates the intricate analogy of the house and a ship in all its liberating aspects.

The Uninvited Guest presents the unexpected, nautical view on an entirely different occasion. The situation emerges when Smudge Torrington, again, the youngest, unattended child, looks into an ancient, uninhabited part of Sterne, the so-called Old House. This section is where the Torringtons lodge the uninvited guests, the ghosts of the victims of the railroad disaster nearby, finally showing, after some struggle, an adequate amount of hospitability and sympathy: "through the hole the enormous old place opened up like the wide underwater world seen through the porthole of a ship from a snug cabin; the long gallery banister, the rows and rows of bed, the chalky passengers far below, staring up at her, the leaping shadows thrown up by the fire; this really was the most rare of adventures" (*UG*, 322). Both Smudge and the rest of her family might be satisfied with the turn of events. Smudge having a fair share of adventure under her belt and other Torringtons assuming their traditional roles of generous hosts. Somewhere in between the Plato's cave and the cabin of a streamliner, the arrival of guests, their contented breathing and the joint effort of the family, revive the Old House, forlorn and forgotten, and thus, metaphorically, even the best of traditional country house hospitality.

Charles Arrowby, the main protagonist of *The Sea, The Sea*, witnesses his house rattle and screech, stretch and twitch, jerk and creak "like a wooden ship" despite the fact that there is no storm outside, just a light rain falling. The window frames shift, the bead curtain clinks and the front door rattles. Charles is "also startled by a sound coming from outside, from across the sea, a prolonged repeated booming, not unlike a ship's foghorn" (*TS*, 472).

The peculiarity of the Charles's residence, Shruff End, vividly evokes a haunted house. Although it does not exactly shield him from the storm, and if so, it is the emotional one, not a climatic one, it clearly displays animate properties. Those, together with the ability to shield inhabitants from the storm outside illustrate the constitutive elements of the spatial poetics of the secluded space of the house as stipulated by Bachelard. Coining Parisian blocks of flats as "superimposed boxes" (Bachelard, 26), he points towards the lack of houses in the proper sense of the word. What is more, he claims that the horizontal character of flats has considerably impoverished the experience of a house since one of its chief aspects is the "dual vertical polarity" (Bachelard, 18) between the subterranean, irrational forces of the cellar and the rational, logical and defining properties of the roof, which provides a house with protection against the rain and sun. Both the notion of centrality, of house being a centralised and centralising entity, and the notion of its verticality, channel a set of mental activities conditioned by the experience of a house. This basic, formative sensation is disturbed by the impossibility of achieving such form of dwelling in an urban environment, where the majority of people are concentrated in flats, surrounded by the hum of traffic. To lessen the impact of the hostility of the urban environment, Bachelard replaces its sounds and the impression of isolation with images of the ocean and the feelings of a lone sailor:

> I dream an abstract-concrete daydream. My bed is a small boat lost at sea; that sudden whistling is the wind in the sails. On every side the air is filled with the sound of furious klaxoning. I talk to myself to give myself cheer: there now, your skiff is holding its own, you are safe in your stone boat. Sleep, in spite of the storm. Sleep in the storm. Sleep in your own courage, happy to be a man who is assailed by wind and wave. (Bachelard, 28)

The theme of the city-ocean is obviously an attempt to naturalise the urban wasteland, but besides this it also consolidates another aspect of Bachelard's concept of a house, namely, seeing its dialectical relation to the outside world. A house can never be viewed as an inert box reduced to simplifying lines of inert geometrical forms. Quite the opposite, the way it shelters human existence transposes its properties to human virtues and "invites mankind to heroism of cosmic proportions" (Bachelard, 46).

The analogy between a ship and a house is as productive in the field of fiction as it is firmly rooted in the context of 20th and 21st architectural theory and practice and also within the context of literary theory and philosophy. Seen through their lens, the ship analogy implies various types of spatial and also temporal arrangements. This process entails the mutual conditioning of this type of space and mental activity labelled as "daydreaming", which may be described as the accumulation and chaining of associations connected with spatial memory. Besides this it is a process which integrates the already existing images of the house with the forthcoming. Consequently, the various temporal axes do not interfere with or disrupt one another, quite the opposite, they mingle and form a platform which absorbs different elements regardless of the strictures imposed by temporal existence. The particular employment of the trope of a ship replacing or describing a house in *The Glass Room*, *The Sea, The Sea*, *The Uninvited Guests*, and *The Stranger's Child* is connected with the fact that all of these novels are set in houses lost either physically or metaphorically in the tide of passing time, suburbs or false morals. The fictional houses in question tend to display numerous contradictory aspects. They function as anchors in the tide, either existential or historical, but at the same time there is an element of temporariness of such a living arrangement. They seclude their inhabitants, shelter them against the environment, while displaying openness and permeability of movement. From this point of view, their resemblance to ships is indisputable. The houses in question function as incredibly versatile, nuanced and evocative settings, symbols and motifs. It is this richness of meanings and number of possible employments which also elucidates their relatively frequent substitution or comparison to a ship. Similarly to the house, the productivity of the ship as the primary metaphor employed in whichever field of artistic rendering of space resides primarily in its archetypical nature. And it is exactly this concentration of widely-acknowledged transformative and transportive potential, which makes its employment productive while remaining apposite.

4.3 Barbarians at the Gates: Country House and the Poetics of the Imminent Decline

Houses have their own ways of dying, falling as variously as the generations of men, some with a tragic roar, some quietly but to an afterlife in the city of ghosts, while from others – and thus was the death of Wickham Place – the spirit slips before the body perishes. It had decayed in the spring, disintegrating the girls more

than they knew, and causing either to accost unfamiliar regions. By September it
was a corpse, void of emotion, and scarcely hallowed by the memories of thirty years
of happiness.
(*HE*, 219)

Both the First and the Second World Wars ultimately shattered the social and political arrangements the country house symbolised. With their former dignity, grandeur and legitimate owners vanishing quickly from view, some of the literary portrayals of the country house tend to display identical traits and accentuate the decline of the original status quo. However, the moral, social, economic, political, cultural and physical erosion cannot be solely attributed to the unfortunate historic development. It is often the general inability of the owners to tend properly to their property,[53] which is, due to its size and demanding nature, extremely prone to the harmful effects of neglect and maltreatment.

The degradation of the former position forces the owners to economise, to restructure and transform their economic functioning according to the demands of the contemporary economic situation. That often entails letting or selling the land at first. Later the sale might involve the house itself and its subsequent transformation into something more viable, given its enormous, superfluous spaces, such as a hotel, a school, a country or a golf club. These processes obviously often entail reluctance[54], resistance and an eagerness to save the property by any means, often irrational verging on abhorrence from the side of the owners. Evelyn Waugh foreshadows this grim development in his earlier satirical novel *A Handful of Dust*:

---

53 In *Persuasion* (1818), Jane Austen, as a keen observer of early nineteenth-century society, describes how Anne Elliot's father, Sir Walter, has to let his house, Kellynch Hall, due to his sheer economic incompetency. What makes the whole situation even more undesirable and more likely to produce unexpected plot twist is the fact that the house is rented by recently retired Admiral Croft, who happens to be husband of Sophia, sister of Captain Frederick Wentworth, a young man whose marriage proposal Anne turned down seven years before.

"The undesirableness of any other house in the same neighbourhood for Sir Walter was certainly much strengthened by one part, and a very material part of the scheme, which had been happily engrafted on the beginning. He was not only to quit his home, but to see it in the hands of others: a trial of fortitude which stronger heads than Sir Walter's have found too much. Kellynch Hall was to be let. This, however, was a profound secret, not to be breathed beyond their own circle." (Austen, *Persuasion*, 13)

54 "Clovis Torrington balanced the pearl-handled butter knife on his middle finger and narrowed his eyes at his mother. His eyes were dramatic, and he very often narrowed them at people to great effect. 'We can't leave Sterne,' he stated" (*UG*, 2).

"But I don't happen to want to go anywhere else except Hetton."
"There's a lot in what these Labour fellows say, you know. Big houses are
a thing of the past in England. ... I daresay you'll find it quite easy to sell
to a school or something like that. I remember the agent said when I was
trying to get rid of Brakeleigh that it was a pity it wasn't Gothic, because
schools and convents always go for Gothic. I daresay you'll get a very
comfortable price and find yourself better off in end than you are now."
(Waugh, *A Handful of Dust*, 151)

Later he added a nostalgia-infused love-letter to the "days of peculiar
splendour" of 1930s Oxford and great country house days, *Brideshead
Revisited* (1945). English authors of the first two decades of the twenty-
first century have demonstrated a remarkable interest in the topic of
the decline of the country house. It is projected in works such as: Ian
McEwan's densely layered *Atonement* (2001); Will Self's flirtation with
Oscar Wilde's *The Picture of Dorian Gray*, *Dorian, an Imitation* (2002);
Sarah Waters' luscious hymn to decadence and Gothic novel, *The Little
Stranger*; Alan Hollinghurst's *The Stranger's Child*, a satire on the nature of
Englishness, paying a stylistically brilliant homage to E. M. Forster and
Evelyn Waugh; or Sadie Jones's *Uninvited Guests*, a colourful variation
on Edwardian comedy of manners mingled with a surrealist ghost story
and mediation upon the nature of class and childhood. The thematic
connection between the individual works is further enhanced by their
prominent intertextuality.

In *The Little Stranger*, the Ayres family's fight to manage the ruin of
their formerly grand self-sustaining property and save it from bankrupt-
cy and disgraceful parcelling out ultimately corrodes their psyche. However, the Torringtons' Sterne in *The Uninvited Guests* is mysteriously saved
by Edward Swift, their one-handed step-father whose departure marks
the beginning of the story: "Edward, seeing Sterne slip through his fingers, turned away from the prospect of a sensible, smaller house nearer
the city and a broken-hearted wife and resolved to save it" (*UG*, 13), and
whose return marks its end, together with a miraculous sum of sixty
thousand pounds bequeathed to Imogen by a mysterious, unknown
aunt. The Valances from *The Stranger's Child* are less fortunate and Dudley Valance, Cecil's brother, leaves their country seat, Corley Court, and
sells it to become a preparatory school soon after the departure of the
militia at the end of war.

Besides the struggle over the destiny and future ownership and function of the properties, there is yet another challenge they face and that is

modernisation. If means allow, country houses are reconstructed, electrified, refurbished, modernised, or added on to.[55] Nevertheless, many of the buildings featured in the novels are highly insensitive replacements themselves. Owing their existence to the destruction of houses of historical value, these substitutes are typically Victorian buildings, whose ugliness is treated as the major component of their aesthetic: "Morning sunlight, or any light, could not conceal the ugliness of the Tallis home – barely forty years old, bright orange brick squat, leadpanned baronial Gothic, to be condemned one day in an article by Pevsner, or one of his team, as a tragedy of wasted chances, and by a younger writer of the modern school as "charmless to a fault" (McEwan, 19). The smothering effect of the house reflects the sinister, tense, hushed atmosphere of the household and is what unnerves Cecilia Tallis, contributing to her resolution to leave it. Regardless of her more or less sincere effort, Cecilia remains where she is and it is only later that the accumulation of unresolved frustrations explodes in a theatrical fashion and provides her with an incentive powerful enough to produce the definite severing of ties with the ugly place. Even sixty years later, Briony remains untouched by rosy retrospective, utterly unmoved by the sight of the house, now transformed into a hotel. She even acknowledges the suitability of the house for its new purpose, further emphasising her unwavering lack of seeing the house as a proud possession or tender memory "as the drive cleared a last stand of beeches, the main house came into view. There was no need to be nostalgic – it was always an ugly place" (McEwan, 363).

Some of the protagonists employ the exaggerated repulsiveness and sheer vulgarity of these buildings as an excuse entitling them to leave or sell the places, whereas others have them destroyed and rebuilt, or completely refurbished: "'You know a lot of the best people nowadays are getting rid of these Victorian absurdities. You should run over and see what the Witherses have done at Badly-Madly, Mamma. They've pulled down the bell-tower, and put an Olympic swimming-pool in its place'" (*SC*, 129). Both Corley Court, from *The Stranger's Child* and *A Handful of Dust's* Hetton Abbey are, similarly to the Tallis' home, Victorian replacements of earlier, historical and from the narrator's perspective definitely more graceful ancestral houses. What further strengthens the thematic link between these two novels is the treatment of attempts at the houses' modernisation. Both places are to be brightened, clarified of their

---

medieval gloom, and deprived of their quirky charm. Hetton's redecoration is performed under the supervision and at the request of Brenda Last. Her ruthlessness and lack of morality are projected onto the building process, which is superficial and heartless, as it stamps on everything Tony Last cherishes. It involves mainly the aesthetic side of the building without any substantial structural changes which might improve the quality of living there. Instead, most of the rooms are modernised with the pseudo-purist plastering and chrome plating. Chrome plating and smoothing refer to the pitiful character of the redecoration as well as the true nature of the Lasts' marriage: "Hetton, the house Tony loves, is itself no ancestral mansion, but a Victorian pile rebuilt in 1864, and he is no aristocrat, though his wife Brenda is. Hetton and everything Tony associates with it – Victorian architecture, Victorian marriage, the Victorian nursery – have no value in the age of chrome plating and easy adultery, and are fated to be lost" (Bradbury, *The Modern British Novel*, 245). Although the shallow focus on aesthetic properties echoes Brenda's immorality they nonetheless give a hint of the true nature of some of the modernist approaches to building and design. Speaking strictly from an architectural point of view it has to be noted that despite the effort modernist architecture made to amplify the structural simplicity and sincerity of buildings, the technology and quality of contemporary materials did not entirely allow for the intended purity. It is a well-known secret that Ludwig Mies van der Rohe, a keen promoter of a visible, crisp clean, razor-cut steel frame of his buildings was forced to cover the steel columns with cement to provide insulation. Only later some form of metal plating was added to provide the illusion that the steel columns were the fundamental, raw metal parts of the frame structure.[56]

The questionable veracity of modernist interventions ironically works in favour of *The Stranger's Child*'s Corley Court, in whose case the brightening of the place consists of covering up the intricate ornamentation and ornate ceilings in particular. Thus they are spared, unharmed by neither the army nor the school which make use of the house before it becomes a museum: "Cecil's brother, of course, had stayed on here for thirty years more, till the military took over. It was surely good luck in the end that all the Victorian work was boxed in – there was nothing for the army to ruin. Dudley Valance's hatred for the house was what had preserved it" (*SC*, 362).

---

56 Contemporary minimalism with its insistence on minimal appearance and maximally complex technology can be seen as an extension of this twisted sense of transparency pioneered by modernist designs.

Whereas Corley Court marks a typical mode of survival of a country house, becoming a boarding school and later a museum, the portrayal of its more graceful Georgian counterpart, Hundreds, from *The Little Stranger*, offers a bleaker if more luscious meditation upon the nature of decline. The novel, Sarah Waters' first spine-tingling venture into the realm of country house fiction, is a decadent hymn to both the literal and metaphorical decay of a building and all it symbolises. Reviving the tradition of Gothic fiction, it picks up the threads of Ann Radcliffe's *The Mysteries of Udolpho* (1794), Edgar Alan Poe's *The Fall of the House of Usher* (1839), Charlotte Brontë's *Jane Eyre* (1847), Henry James's *The Turn of the Screw* (1898) and Daphne du Maurier's *Rebecca* (1938), to name a few of its inspirations. The story is set in rural Warwickshire in the gloomy post-war years and revolves around the troubled history of the Ayres family and their formerly grand home, Hundreds Hall. The narrator is Dr Faraday, whose first name, as well as his true intentions and role in the tragic events surrounding the family's gradual descent into madness and death, remain unknown. It need not be stressed that his account of the events grows acutely unreliable. He assumes the role of the kind-hearted, sympathetic confidant and saviour, who is nonetheless fully aware of the gaping precipice of his social status and that of his "protégés". Tempted and smitten by the lustre and grandeur of the house, Dr Faraday is less concerned about the well-being of its owners, Mrs Ayres and her two children, Caroline and Roderick. Especially the latter's name and personal history of madness and arson refer to Roderick Usher from Poe's 1839 novella.

Dr Faraday first sees Hundreds as a small boy and even then its beauty inspires abusive behaviour, an act of vandalism when he cuts a piece of a decorative plaster border and cuts away a stucco acorn, motivated by the urgent need of possession of a part of the house. As his mother works there as a servant, he is lead inside by the side door (*LS*, 2), which is repeated years later when he arrives as a doctor to see one of the maids who took to bed. Charles Ryder in Evelyn Waugh's *Brideshead Revisited* is lead through a similar passage on his first arrival to Brideshead, which he enters "through the fortress-like, stone flagged, stone-vaulted passages of the servants' quarters – "(Waugh, *Brideshead*, 39). The way both Dr Faraday and Charles Ryder access the house traditionally marks their seemingly minor importance since they are both of incomparably lower social standing than their acquaintances. They nevertheless manage to sneak into the heart of events. This sort of entrance to the house signifies another factor and that is that the main entrance door is rarely used even by the legitimate inhabitants. It is often pompously grand and painfully impractical as Will Self remarks in his short, yet hard-hitting account of a country house in *Dorian*, where the guests also gain "admission to the central hallway of the house via an inconspicuous side door (the main ones, fully two storeys high, had not been opened since the visit of the last King Emperor)" (Self, 222). The absence of the opening and closing of the main entrance door, of approaching the country house in the way it was designed implies both the impracticality of the door, whose representative function and therefore gigantic size is at the expense of practicality and functionality. Its abandonment might be also interpreted as a sign of the waning of the grip of social convention. In both cases it involves relaxation of rigid conventions or even their subversion.

The Little Stranger is set in the aftermath of the Second World War, therefore roughly in the same period as Evelyn Waugh's *Brideshead Revisited*. Both novels share the gloomy, depressing atmosphere which evokes the post-war years connected with the war destruction of the country house. These former centres of power, wealth and beauty, often devastated by their employment by the military, have to face harsh historical development. After years of growth and prosperity, "in sudden frost, came the age of Hooper, the place was desolate and the work all brought to nothing; *Quomodo sedet sola civitas*. Vanity of vanities, all is vanity" (Waugh, *Brideshead*, 402). Although *Brideshead Revisited, The Sacred and Profane Memories of Captain Charles Ryder* was not Waugh's first excursion into the field of country house fiction, it lacks its predecessors' comical nature frequently suffused with black humour, such as *Decline and Fall* (1928) or *A Handful of Dust* (1934). According to Waugh progress is impossible and "in the light of eternity, history is a folly, the idea of progress absurd, the barbarian always at the gates" (Bradbury, *The Modern British Novel*, 287). The memory of the splendid interwar years becomes smothered by the chaos and madness of war. *Brideshead Revisited* was partly written while Waugh served in Yugoslavia and evokes a ravenous appetite for the lush beauty of English countryside on "days of peculiar splendour" (Waugh, *Brideshead*, 23). Brideshead, the consummate incarnation of a stately home, is at the heart of a story that is filled with nostalgic longing. As Waugh demonstrates throughout the novel, the best has already come to England and no reform or revolution of any kind may improve its perfection. However, this admiration is not reserved to the question of aristocracy as the ruling elite or the country house as an institution. Brideshead embodies Arcadia itself, the land of plenty, with its lustrous beauty, pastoral atmosphere and generous, accepting nature. The house, the needs, endeavours and wishes of the owners of the house, Lord and Lady Marchmain, as well as those of Charles Ryder, are dispersed in the chaotic war years. But, with a retreating army camp situated in the house and a lunatic asylum at its gates, Charles sees a tiny flicker of hope to be found in the small chapel adjoining the main building and that is the Christian belief which he compares to "the flame which the old knights saw from their tombs, which they saw put out; that flame burns again for other soldiers, far from home, farther, in heart, than Acre or Jerusalem. It could not have been lit for the builders and the tragedians, and there I found it this morning, burning anew among the old stones" (Waugh, *Brideshead*, 402).

Hundreds Hall, which is at the centre of *The Little Stranger*, is a postwar, derelict shadow of its former self. Despite this, it does not fail to enchant Dr Faraday whenever he visits. Comparing the house to an oyster and himself to a speck of grit being layered by its charming veneer, he enjoys Hundreds' cultivating effect upon him. However, from the point of view of the Ayreses, its claim on them becomes increasingly pressing and intolerable: "'Hundreds is lovely. It is a sort of lovely monster! It needs to be fed all the time, with money and hard work".[57] The pronoun *it* soon becomes the deictic tool for indiscernible pointing to either the house, or the mysterious, malicious, malevolent, manipulating presence *in* the house. Besides these two uses, it soon incarnates a third meaning and that is an insidious infection: "'I thought I could keep this thing at bay, stop the infection. But I'm too weak. The infection's been too long inside me. It's changing me. It's making me like it. I thought I was keeping it away from me. It's making me like it'" (*LS*, 225). *It* is identified as the reason of Roderick's slide into madness. Since *it* is greedy, it sucks and gobbles up the energy of all concerned except for Dr Faraday, who considers himself to be "a pretty indigestible fellow" (*LS* 148, emphasis in original), willing to take his chances with the house as well as the infection.

After an accident, which involves Caroline's beloved dog Gyp severely biting a little girl of new, snobbish neighbours and Gyp's disposal performed by Dr Faraday, Roderick's dangerous delusions put his room on fire. He leaves the house to be admitted to a mental clinic and similarly to Gyp before, vanishes without a trace, as though he "had never been master of the house at all" (*LS*, 233). *It* seems to be gradually tightening its grip, with the scribbles on the walls, the phantom ring on the

---

57   Waters, Sarah. *The Little Stranger*. 2009. London: Virago Press, 2010, p. 69. [Subsequent page references preceded *LS* are given in parentheses in the text].

call-bells and the paranormal activity witnessed by old Mrs Ayres in the nurseries. She interprets this vision as punishment from her first child, an infant daughter whose death she has not accepted and continued to walk behind her coffin every day of her life (*LS*, 425). Despite Mrs Ayers' subsequent suicide which is followed by the mysterious death of her daughter, Caroline, Dr Faraday is still persuaded about the purely rational explanation of all the events, though he falters for a short time, feeling the sickness of the place, "a sort of lingering infection in its floors and walls" (*LS*, 476).

The decline of the family is mirrored and foreshadowed by the physical decline of Hundreds, the formerly splendid residence of the Ayres family. Peter Baker-Hyde, a bossy representative of the newly stratified and modified upper class taking hold of the countryside, calls it a "scrapheap" (*LS*, 107). Like their house the Ayreses themselves are considered to be out of date, impractical, and unable to adapt or to keep pace with the modern world full of rapid changes and inevitable compromises. That is why Dr Faraday, in unison with his colleague, Seeley, declares that they were destined to be destroyed and defeated by history "unable to advance with the times, simply opted for retreat – for suicide, and madness" (*LS*, 498), alongside the other aristocratic families across the England. This ossification, demonstrated on many occasions, becomes evident when, while discussing the new housing project within the gates of Hundreds' park, Caroline Ayres wonders at the existence and popularity of "a fitted kitchen". Efficient, handy arrangement of kitchen utensils and furniture which saves space and material and rules out the possibility of odd nooks, corners and gaps are all impracticalities which, according to Caroline, provide the place with character: "'What's wrong with gaps and odd corners? Who'd want a life without any of those?'" (*LS*, 249) Dr Faraday insists on the necessity of the hospitalisation of yet another family member, old Mrs Ayres, another victim of the mysterious *it*. Because of this, Caroline comes to emphasise the exceptionality of the Ayreses and the necessity of justification of their privileged position by acknowledging that they were never allowed to yield to suffering as ordinary people do: "'She said, if we couldn't be better and braver than ordinary people, then what was the point of us? The shame of your taking my brother was bad enough. If you try and take her, too – I don't think she'll let you'" (*LS*, 398).

The Ayreses act as if the eyes of the whole country were still fixed on them. Burdened and tormented by excessive responsibility and the scarcity of any privilege underlined by the measures taken by the Labour government, they all feel stifled and smothered, frozen in a dance, unable to act while being weighed down by such an enormous pressure. Roderick, before he loses his mind completely, makes a plea for the nation to be ashamed of the abominable treatment of its former ruling elites, labelling himself and those in the similar situation as "'the ordinary hard-working Englishmen who since the war has had to watch his property and income vanishing like so much smoke?'" (*LS*, 152). The Ayres children, both in their respective ways do not seem to be able to toss away the mask of dignified aristocrats. Caroline does not comprehend the modern demand for efficiency, nor does she tolerate any public sign of weakness of her family members, whose superior qualities entitle their privileged existence. While Roderick battles for the respectable survival of his heritage, unable to get rid of his dignified posture even during the milking of the cows in the rotting cow-shed. The ritual impracticality, stiffness and rigidity of the past represented by the Ayreses clash with the insistence on practicality, efficiency, flexibility and openness of contemporary period. The combination of the historical circumstances with those two contrastive approaches proves to be an insurmountable obstacle, which leads to the growing irrationality of all the affected towards the building, the county and finally even the country: "'I need to get out. Get right away. England's no good any more for someone like me. It doesn't want me. ... But this house doesn't want me. I don't want it. I hate this house!'" (*LS*, 448) Although Caroline seems to babble and jumps from England to the house, her statement is perfectly coherent and directly corresponds with the conception of the country house as a concentration of the national spirit and a carrier of its grandness.

The outcomes of both the world wars as well as the measures introduced by a Labour government put the enthralling image of the country house to the test. The literal and metaphorical crumbling of its power and integrity is manifested in the example of Roderick's gradual selling of the land, first the farming areas, then a part of the park surrounding the house itself. Dr Faraday watches with dismay how the rubble of the wall surrounding the park around the house is being used for the foundations of new houses with Caroline remarking: "'It's somehow horrible, isn't it? Of course people must have homes, and all that. But it's as if they are chewing up Hundreds up – just so they can spit it all out again in nasty little lumps.'" (*LS*, 245–6). Both the reaction of Caroline and the one of Dr Faraday, which is surprising given his working-class background, are quite hostile, especially in view of the possibility of future trespassing of the children into the park.

In the meantime, Caroline's attitude towards the house begins to change. Abandoned by her brother and mother, while confronted with the odd squeaking, tapping sounds in the hallways, she initially attempts at bravado, calling them "parlour games" (*LS*, 304). She continues in this disparaging approach, but she quickly becomes increasingly pensive. At first, she relatively light-heartedly acknowledges that the house likes to catch the Ayreses out, testing their weaknesses, nevertheless, the playful nature of the house gets far from kind and pleasing, on the contrary, it becomes malicious and atrocious. Her growing gloominess gradually slips into a frantic observation of the house, which switches from a sinister stillness to lifelessness, from sulking, or even defiant opposition, to obedience (*LS*, 384). With Caroline no longer immune to the treacherous manipulation, she succumbs to *it*, this time meaning the house's, trials, persuaded about being its ally against her will: "'The house is still at last. Whatever it was that was here, it has taken everything it wanted. And do you know what the wort thing is? The thing I shan't forgive it for? It made me help it'" (*LS*, 416).

Despite her severe suffering, Dr Faraday insists on marrying and staying in Hundreds. Although Caroline is clearly indifferent to his advances and gradually abhors the place and he is unable to provide or secure any substantial financial support, Dr Farraday's. identification with the place is cemented. Unlike the Ayreses, he does not believe in the house being haunted. On the contrary, he continually shows his pity and respect for it and compares it to a mourning creature. Full of character, the house "appeared to be gazing, sightless with grief, across the hushed white landscape" (*LS*, 417). When he discusses the poor state of the family with another surgeon, Seeley, the torturing, testing, tantalising *it* or *something* acquires yet another dimension. This time *it* is not the house or any sort of poltergeist, but the Labour Government:

> I shook my head. "This is a weirder thing even than hysteria. It's as if – well, as if something's slowly sucking the life out of the whole family."
> "Something is," he said, with another bark of laughter. "It's called a Labour Government. The Ayreses' problem – don't you think is that they can't, or won't, adapt. Don't get me wrong. I've a lot of sympathy for them. But what's left for an old family like that in England nowadays? Class-wise, they've had their chips. Nerve-wise, perhaps they've run their course." (*LS*, 378)

In view of the current political situation, as well as the absolute absence of any vitality or viability of the Ayreses, their decline and the ultimate destruction become inevitable. Hundreds' exaggerated aestheticism and its identification with the mysterious force tormenting and consuming the family contributes to their failure while oozing scrumptiously decadent poetics filled with "nothing but wear and waste and neglect" (*LS*, 341). The invincible house and its enthralling splendour open and close the novel, with the family shaken off, "like springing turf throwing off a footprint" (*LS*, 498).

Once again, the house at the heart of the novel functions as an anchor, a fixed point of reference around which history revolves. Dr Faraday accentuates the idiosyncratic passing of time on several occasions. Not only that it does not seem to follow the ordinary course and life within Hundreds' walls thus acquires a mystical dimension, so "that ordinary life had fractionally tilted, and that I had slipped into some other, odder, rather rarer realm" (*LS*, 75),[58] but there is also its mythical, inexorable, inevitable side which binds its protagonists into repetitive patterns of fatality. Dr Faraday thus remembers the time, thirty years before, when he attended the funeral of the Ayreses' daughter: "I thought of the time, nearly thirty years before, when I had stood beside my parents in my College blazer to watch another Ayres funeral, its coffin half the size of this one; I thought it with an almost a giddy feeling, as if my life were twisting round its head to snap at its own tail" (*LS*, 424). From this point of view, it needs to be noted that the story closes in the same place and with the same impression with which it opened: Dr Faraday is captivated

---

58 Later in the story, this perception of the place as a phantasy, fairy-tale place is even instigated by winter weather and the snow covering the surrounding area. Bachelard studied this peculiar atmospheric state in the chapter entitled "House and Universe" in *The Poetics of Space*. There he claims that the perception of the house in winter differs from other seasons and that snow further accentuates the intimacy of spaces of the house since the snow muffles the sounds and diminishes the importance of the outside world. The effect on the narration in *The Little Stranger* is the intensification of a dream-like effect of the house both on the readers, its inhabitants and admirers:

"Breaking free of the snowy drive, I never got my first glimpse of the house without a thrill of awe and pleasure, for against the white, white ground it looked marvellous, the red of its brick and the green of its ivy more vivid, and all its imperfections softened by lace-work of ice. There would be no hum from the generator, no snarl of machinery from the farm, no clash of building-work: the building-work had been suspended because of the snow. Only my own quiet footsteps would disturb the silence, and I would move on, almost abashed, trying to muffle them further, as if the place were enchanted – as if it were the castle of the *Belle au bois dormant* I remember Caroline envisaging a few weeks before – and I feared to break the spell." (*LS*, 387)

by the beauty of the place, unable to fully embrace all its implications, reduced to causing damage by cutting off stucco acorns. His vandalising action foreshadows his role in the destruction of the family[59]. Although he does not cause any considerable harm directly, it was nonetheless on his insistence that the Baker-Hydes stayed longer than intended and their daughter was badly bitten by the unknowing Gyp. It was him who put Gyp to sleep and had Roderick transported to a mental institution. Again, it was Mr Faraday who insisted on Mr Ayres' and Caroline's staying in the house, persuading them of its beneficial effects. It was him who tried to make Caroline marry him and stay at Hundreds. If anything, his love affair with the house, together with a perverted social ambition, combines to present the stifling, smothering effect of a benefactor saving the wretched. The Ayreses, unable to resist his graceful behaviour and good intentions, maybe due to their inborn sense of importance and their being used to being waited on, are not able to see through to his true motivation. From this perspective his dubious role in the Ayres tragedy resembles that of the unnamed Governess from Henry James's novella *The Turn of the Screw*. Whether she acts as a saviour or a tool of

---

59   Female characters in Waters' novels heroically, and often pathetically, struggle to prevent destruction, both material and spiritual. If destruction occurs, they are seen restoring the ruins back to their former glory. Caroline's obstinate effort to salvage the wreck of Hundreds runs parallel to those of 2006 *The Night Watch*'s Julia working in the Damage Assistance Department in London during World War II, helping her father to make a survey of bomb-damaged buildings:

"It's a filthy business, not at all as exciting as it sounds: the rooms all smashed, the carpets wrecked, the mirrors in splinters. The water-pipes might have had it: the water runs and turns soot to sludge. I went into places last month and found things frozen: sofas and tablecloths and things like that. Or, things get burned. An incendiary will land on a roof: it might burn right through, quite neatly, from one floor to the next; you can stand in the basement and look at the sky ... I find damage like that more miserable, somehow, than if a house has been blasted to bits: it's like a life with a cancer in it." (Waters, *The Night Watch*, 225)

Waters depicts a similarly determined character trying to save a house, although a less ostentatious one, from the wreckage in *The Paying Guest* (2014). Frances Wray plots the letting of the part of the house to the Barbers, a young couple she has been observing with a growing unease since the day of their arrival. They: "were not quiet the couple she remembered, who were younger, and brasher, were going to bring them, and set them out, and make their own home, brashly, among them. ... What on earth had she done? She felt as though she was opening up the house to thieves and invaders" (Waters, *The Paying Guests*, 6). Uncomfortable with their presence in the house, Francis is nevertheless resigned to the necessity having lodgers to allow her to maintain the house in the suburbs of London. She later embarks on a love affair with Lilian Barber with a tragic and eventually unexpectedly liberating conclusion.

doom, whether she is the only sane one and unaffected by the evil scheming or the hysterical evil schemer, has remained equally unresolved.

The house and its various appearances throughout the year in which the story takes place are the central images of the novel. Nevertheless, the house itself also presents a central image, which accentuates its centrality, since a house is typically perceived as a concentrated being, appealing "to our consciousness of centrality" (Bachelard, 17). The pivotal image in this case is "a great translucent disk" (*LS*, 81), a circular, glassed segment of the roof above the main staircase and the entrance hall the glass dome in the roof. It fills the place with a brilliant, ethereal glow. From the cascading, joyous summer light to the hushed, murky one propelled through the snowy glaze in winter or the ghastly blue light of the full moon illuminating the fall of Caroline through the stairwell, it serves as one of the major atmospheric vehicles. Its functioning changes as well as the types of light it lets in. It alternately accentuates the lightness and airiness and the stifling, crippling atmosphere of a bell glass propelled and propelling the voracious *it*. The house replicates this dichotomy and swings between a fairy tale land and a nightmarish, outlandish wasteland in the same what that the majority of characters whose Janus-faced personalities swing between sanity and insanity, embracing alternately the purely rational and irrational approach.

4.4 The Country House and Time

Hundreds, the Warwickshire residence of the Ayreses, encapsulates many roles: the house is the subject of the story, the setting of the plot, a repeatedly employed motif and a powerful symbol of the class and its contemporary standing. Its distinctive position in *The Little Stranger* is amplified by both the oneiric quality of its narration and the accentuated fatality projected into the various circular aspects of the novel's plot. What is more, the long history of the house and its current dereliction emphasises the ossified nature of the tradition it embodies. Despite its beauty which should inspire some sort of higher aspirations or cultivated development, it instead petrifies its inhabitants. They are unable to neither adapt to a new social order nor comply with both the literal and metaphorical demands stipulated by the house. They live perpetually entrapped in the past, clumsily tottering through the present and hiding in the face of the future. The incapability of the Ayreses to move forward while burdened by the great house is projected onto a peculiar suspension of time within the walls of Hundreds: "There wasn't so much as the ticking of a clock. Life seemed held, arrested inside it" (*LS*, 416). It has to be noted that a house, in general, abounds with integrating properties, but in the case of a country house, these extend into the personal dimension. The past, the present and the future meet and intersect, giving "the house different dynamisms, which often interfere, at times opposing, at others stimulating one another" (Bachelard, 6). This anchoring of time provides an individual with the illusion of stability.

Novels focused on country houses have an exaggerated tendency to layer different time levels on each other. This proclivity is understandable, given the nature of the country house. However, what these novels tend to underline is the perils and pitfalls of the lack of separation of time: present, past and future. Especially in the case of the country house, the past looms over the heads of its inhabitants, who are frequently crushed by its weight. In *The Little Stranger*, this threat manifests itself in the form of obsession with the death of the Ayreses first child, Suzie, which heralds the downfall of the whole family. The compulsive idea of her return lies at the root of their destruction and further adds to their binding with history. Unable to cut the ties, they are consumed alive by the haunting shadows of the past. *The Stranger's Child* is built around the legacy of Cecil Valance, a young, aspiring poet torn to pieces in the trenches of the First World War. His unmarked, communal grave in France is supplemented by a spectacular marble tomb complete with an odd statue placed in Corley Court. His short life and particularly one evening during which he composed his mock-pastoral masterpiece, "Two Acres", trigger an enormous amount of public attention. That obviously inspires a soaring number of biographical works with each and every one of them projecting the frustrations of their authors into their account of Cecil's life. The plot revolves around a past event which, despite the effort and the more or less successful projection of the personal agenda of the researcher, can never be successfully interpreted and comprehended in all its complexity.

Paul Bryant, a former bank clerk turned into a would-be working-class biographer, systematically, maniacally and clumsily attempts to uncover the true circumstances of the composition of Cecil's fictitious iconic poem. His struggle comprises interviews with Cecil's contemporaries, but also a field trip to the home of the Sawle family, their suburban house Two Acres, which inspired the poem sixty years earlier. Paul is overflowing with excitement "[s]omehow he couldn't take the house in; but he would take photographs, so as to see it all later" (*SC*, 385). The realisation that the house is abandoned and uninhabited arouses contradictory feelings in him. The disappointment over its dereliction is countered by his eagerness to take hold of the house, literally and metaphorically: "It was empty, and therefore in a way his; he felt a lurching certainty that he could and should get into it" (*SC*, 385). Feeling authorised to perform these tasks, he assumes that the house will reveal its secrets to him, because it is more opened and inclined to his enquiry than human witnesses and definitely less judgemental concerning his social class, given its own social standing.

In view of its renown, Paul neither expects dereliction, nor is he prepared for ordinariness and expressionlessness. He expected the house to live up to its fame, wearing "its own mild frown of self-regard, a certain half-friendly awareness of being admired" (*SC*, 387). Yet, there is nothing to see, "the house condemned by its own urge for privacy" (*SC*, 385). Paul nevertheless feels inclined to mark his presence there as well as in literary history: "Taken by a sudden urge, territorial as much as physical, he turned his back on the house, put down his briefcase, and had a short fierce piss into the long grass" (*SC*, 385). Paul Bryant incarnates a blundering, fumbling biographer, whose intuition is failed by his practical skill, knowledge, class, and above all, time and its fleeting, slippery, practically irretrievable nature. Disappointed at its relentlessness and incapable of filling the void with fruits of his own invention, Paul is destined to leave fleeting, stinking, shadowy traces, with the bitter aftertaste of unfounded sensationalism (*SC*, 524, 525).

Two Acres failed to impress Paul; its "upstairs windows pondering blankly on the reflections of clouds" (*SC*, 387), failing to provide answers and commentary. The decline of the house and its gradual slide into a forgotten ruin does not correspond with Paul's intentions. Its changed appearance does not resonate with its literary image and therefore leaves him unmoved. This might be perceived as a sign of the ordinariness of the house and its incapacity to deliver any grand messages by its own means. It may be understood as yet another proof of Cecil's talent to transform a mediocre place into a national treasure. Paul's inability to perceive the place and accept its atmosphere serves as another explanation. Despite a number of different solutions for this dilemma and their possible combinations, Hollinghurst indisputably adds further satirical twist to the biographical theme and comments on the peculiar ways of time.

The theme of time and its passing represents a founding principle and one of the formative elements of country house literature. Both fictional and non-fictional accounts travel relentlessly back and forth in time. The narration rarely features a chronological ordering of individual time levels, most frequently the present is to a certain extent interspersed with the past. In non-fiction this is usually connected with an explanation of a particular phenomenon, such as the functioning of an individual room or the technique of vaulting. In fiction this tendency results in nostalgia, a hint of detective story or both. Aspects of detective stories is employed as a narrative twist and at the same time it entails a link with the past and history, as it logically provokes rumination and the desired excavation of its hidden secrets. From this point of view, *The Stranger's Child* embodies a literary thriller and *The Little Stranger* revives the tradition of Gothic fiction.

Besides being an Edwardian comedy of manners, *The Uninvited Guests* introduces a surrealist account of one tepid summer evening at Sterne, the family's country residence. The residence consists of two Houses, the Old, "a vast, illuminated cave" (*UG*, 305), and the New one, with the former employed as a shelter for the ghosts of dead passengers, who had fallen prey to a railroad accident nearby. *Atonement* galvanises its readers with its metafictional twists while it elaborates on the fatal events of one hot, midsummer night and consequently travels back and forth in time, while contemplating the novelistic cul-de-sac. The connection between the present, the past and the future, their mutual influencing, conditioning and interfering and their layering naturally reverberates through the theme of the country house. This idiosyncratic quality of temporality is accentuated by the richness of the intertextual references and allusions displayed in the novels, in *The Stranger's Child* and *The Little Stranger* in particular. Thus, the works analysed above display in various permutations how: Daphne du Maurier's *Rebecca* (1938) meets E. M. Forster's *Howards End* (1910) and *A Room with a View* (1908); Evelyn Waugh's *A Handful of Dust* (1934) and *Brideshead Revisited* (1945) encounter Henry James's *The Turn of the Screw* (1898); *The Mysteries of Udolpho* (1794) intersects with *Jane Eyre* (1847); and *Maurice* (1913, published 1971) is joined by Frances Hodgson Burnett's *The Secret Garden* (1911) and Wilde's *The Importance of Being Earnest* (1895). However, the exploration of time and its processes in connection with the country house has never been reserved for novels only. This fact is exemplified by T. S. Eliot's *Burnt Norton*, which intricately delves into the temporal layers with the country house, serving as an incentive for the powerful source of evocation of the nature of time.

Burnt Norton is the most overtly philosophical poem of *Four Quartets* (published collectively in 1943, written between 1935 and 1942). The first poem, *Burnt Norton* (published separately in 1936) was inspired by a visit to the ruins of a formerly grand country house in Gloustershire. Despite the fact that the background of *Four Quartets* involved Eliot's conversion to the Church of England, his naturalisation as a British subject, and the dramatic platform. Since parts of the poems were essentially taken from *Murder in the Cathedral* (1935),[60] *Four Quartets*, and *Burnt Norton* in particular, cannot be considered to be an example of devotional poetry. As Derek Traversi claims in his critical study *T. S. Eliot: The Longer Works* (1976), "[t]he impulse which went to their making is essentially *exploratory* and, at least initially, *tentative* in its nature" (Traversi 96, emphasis in original). Although the poems touch upon life in the present, they do not treat it philosophically, but instead, they pragmatically reflect the quality of the moment and thoughts by their structure, rhythm and the choice of words. According to Eliot himself, a poet cannot be identified with a philosopher, it is not his task to develop postulates, being persuaded about their universal applicability and ultimate truthfulness. A poet's major occupation is to trace and depict experiences which might lead to the development of such postulates, and which is poetically conditioned by the medium of image and rhythm, which are, if suitably synchronized, able to convey the experience in its full significance.

From this point of view, the five-part *Burnt Norton* is a meditation on the nature of time elaborating on the notion of simultaneity developed in the Eleventh Book of St. Augustine's *Confessions*. The repetitive and circular nature of the poem involves numerous variations and repetitions of:

> Time past and time future
> What might have been and what has been
> Point to one end, which is always present. (Eliot, 13)

Traversi further claims that its forceful, distinctive rhythm and the patterning of familiar and unfamiliar images facilitate the absorption and the comprehension of its basic premise. This premise is one concerning the nature of the present as an inter-stage between the no-longer-existing past and the future which has not yet come into being.

While the grim, ultimate reality is deictically embraced here: "Here is a place of disaffection" (Eliot, 17), Eliot develops an idea of *consciousness* whose experience was paralleled in works of Eliot's contemporaries such as Marcel Proust, Virginia Woolf, D. H. Lawrence or E. M. Forster.

---

60 *Murder in the Cathedral* (1935) is a versed drama Eliot composed on the subject of the murder of Thomas Beckett in Canterbury Cathedral in 1170.

Time past and time future
Allow but a little consciousness.
To be conscious is not to be in time
But only in time can the moment in the rose-garden,
The moment in the arbour where the rain beat,
The moment in the draughty church at smokefall
Be remembered; involved with past and future.
Only through time time is conquered. (Eliot, 15)

At this point Traversi again insists on the lack of any "mystical or specifically religious insight" (Traversi, 103). Instead, Eliot describes an experience which casts aside supernatural or extra-temporal implications of the reality outside one's self. It focuses rather on an increased consciousness which, under the right sort of stimulation, momentarily suspends the relentless, universal temporal laws of succession and allows for simultaneity. According to Traversi, it was Marcel Proust who excelled in this area and whose suggestive parallelism founds the whole design of his hepatology *In Search of Lost Time* (1913–1927). The full sense of the fugitive moments (the most iconic of which might be the transporting "madeleine" scene) is obscured by their role in the victorious fight with lost time. These moments are able to suspend time, make it elastic and thus to transport individuals in and against its current. The past, as well as in the case of Eliot's garden full of children's laughter, is successfully revived and relived, what has been irrevocably lost is found again. In terms of country house fiction, it is the house at the centre, whose function, given its forceful integrating properties, often parallel suggestively those transporting perceptions chiselled memorably by Proust.

The title of Evelyn Waugh's *A Handful of Dust* quotes T. S. Eliot's *Waste Land* (1922) and a fragment of this poem serves as the motto of the novel. Waugh's structural composition does not parallel that of T. S. Eliot's iconic poem, yet the individual motifs and the overall perspectives correspond. Waugh exhibits the decaying society in symmetrically arranged and titled chapters, which draw heavily on the work of Proust as yet another keen social observer. The first and the sixth chapters are entitled *Du Côté de chez Beaver* and *Du Côté de chez Todd*[61] and echo the first volume of *In Search of Lost Time*, *Du Côté de chez Swann* (*Swann's Way* published 1913). Also the title of the fifth chapter, *In Search of the City*, reflects the title of the hepatology itself. Waugh's stylistic perfection-

---

61   Originally Waugh employed a different, faulty preposition *À*.

ism flourishes in *A Handful of Dust*. Its composition, precise contextual framing and sharp satire outweigh the improbability of the plot and its palpable artificiality.

Tony Last, a significantly named proprietor of Hetton Abbey and a bourgeois husband of a morally slumped aristocrat Brenda Last, puts all his sincere effort into the salvation of the family's country seat, a formerly bourgeoning Hetton. The house was destroyed by his Victorian ancestor, who replaced it by yet another Victorian monstrosity, an example of late Gothic Revival, in whose footsteps follow both Corley Court from *The Stranger's Child* and the Tallis house in McEwan's *Atonement*.[62] Waugh presents the complex nature of English Gothic in three eponymous chapters, which delineate its three most significant meanings. The first one refers to Hetton, which is complete with polychrome glazed brick, red and gold ceilings, the dining hall "with its hammer-beam roof and pitch-pine minstrels' gallery; the bedrooms with their brass bedsteads, each with a frieze of Gothic text, each named from Malory, Yseult, Elaine, Mordred and Merlin, Gawaine and Bedivere, Lancelot, Perceval, Tristram, Galahada" (Waugh, *A Handful of Dust*, 17–18) a feeble imitation of Gothic architecture same as Tony is presented as a feeble shadow of chivalry of King Arthur, the embodiment of Gothic ideal. Owing to Tony's desperate efforts to save the place and his marriage, which falls apart after Brenda's infidelity and the death of their child in a riding accident, English Gothic acquires another meaning. In this case it corresponds with Tony's approach to life as well as the ethos of contemporary society especially in view of divorce proceedings, whose formality still emphasised the medieval concept of chivalry. The whole pitiful process of divorce was viewed, due to gender inequality, as slightly more respectable when it involved adultery committed by husband, not the wife. The last employment of English Gothic corresponds with Hetton again, occupied by Tony's successors and their breeding of silver foxes. Everything Tony fought for: the historical significance of the building, its religious heritage, and, by extension, English values seem to be irredeemably lost: "'I don't keep up this house to be a hostel for a lot of bores to come and gossip in. We've always lived here and I hope John will be able to keep it on after me. One has a duty towards one's employees, and towards the place too. It's a definite part of English life which would be a serious loss if…'" (Waugh, *A Handful of Dust*, 21).

---

62   See chapter 4.3. *Barbarians at the Gates: The Country House and the Poetics of Imminent Decline.*

Ironically and unexpectedly, Tony's life journey ends in the Amazon jungle, in the house of Mr Todd. The patriarchal behaviour of Mr Todd replicates the feudal system of the Middle Ages whose spirit and supposed truthfulness inspired the idealising Gothic Revival.[63] Because the authorities proclaim Tony dead after Mr Todd steals his watch and uses it as a proof of his death, Tony is enslaved and destined to remain trapped in the present. With his past stolen and his future dependant on his ability to please Mr Todd with his reading of Dickens's novels, Tony exemplifies both an extreme enslavement by the present moment and the powerlessness, resignation and reginal restriction of any subject, but feudal in particular.

Henry James's short story "The Great Good Place" (1909) elaborates on a different kind of imprisonment. It ponders the idea of retreat from the overstuffed, paradoxical existence of a successful man, George Dane. Overloaded with tasks and projects, he became a haunted intellectual unable to concentrate or relish in the quality of his own or others' production. Drowning in the endless stress and press, he seems "to have lost possession of [his] soul and to be surrounded only with the affairs of other people, smothered in irrelevant importunity" (James, "The Great Good Place").

His tortured existence is exquisitely captured within the painfully accurate details of the agony of his room. The scene suddenly changes and while what George experiences might be a fantasy, it is one that which brings salvation. Situated somewhere in between a golf club, a country club, a hotel, a spa and a convent, the great, good place and his companion there work wonders for George, who feels refreshed and utterly revived by his stay. What contributes to this transformation is the spirit of the place which is "a world without newspapers and letters, without telegrams and photographs, without the dreadful fatal too much. There, for a blessing, he COULD read and write; there above all he could do nothing--he could live" (James, "The Great Good Place"). The overwhelming sensation of peace and calmness does not entail the suppression of the time and its passing, but rather its expansion and a sort of joyous acceptance of its fluidity. The mystical great good place enthrals George Dane with its serenity and the emphasis on a holistic approach to matters, time included. Time is to be perceived as a smooth, gentle stream, not as disjointed clusters of tasks completed and missions to complete.

---

63 Tony's pitiful story was inspired by Waugh's own journey to British Guiana ends in the Amazon jungle. This was later successfully incorporated in Charles Ryder's expedition in *Brideshead Revisited*.

Despite the lack of specification of the place itself, it matches up with Malcolm Kelsall's conception of the country house. In his 1993 monograph *The Great Good Place: The Country House and English Literature*, he traces history of the real sites and he compares it with their direct and indirect influence on numerous literary works. Kelsall delineates the ways reading shapes our seeing of individual places. There he shows how the idea of the country house developed from the incarnation of an ideal, to a symbol of the good life, to today's abstract concept endangered by historical development. Since the beginning of the twentieth century, the country house became a thing of spirit and its image has accordingly approximated the level of abstraction and wholesomeness of the great good place from James's short story.

The twentieth and twenty-first centuries completed the developments whose seeds had already been sown in the nineteenth century. The great country houses, no longer tied to aristocracy, had been bought and sold, renewed and newly built by "strangers' children", prosperous capitalists and foreigners. Gradually, the stately houses became with a focal point of popular interest, with many of their owners declaring "an open house" to tourists. The gradual slipping of these places out of the hands of their owners was intensified both by their size and their cultural, political and social standing. Despite their abstract ability to converge temporal levels and revive some of the aspects of the past, these places are enormously prone to physical corruption. However, it is the level of impressiveness of their degradation which often unleashes their suggestive prowess. The realms of literature, poetry, fiction and non-fiction have nourished themselves by various degrees on the disintegration of the houses as well as the severing of ties between them and their owners.

The owners face a great challenge seeing their family possession slipping from their fingers. Either they try to fight to save the properties despite many issues, or they resign and relegate the house to its fate. Both of these options are amplified by the nature and standing of the country house in English culture. The quality of the contemporary fictional portrayals of the country houses suggests their abstraction from the sphere of idealised symbols. Their relevance is severely tested and the resulting portrayals are far from elegant and noble. Instead, they resemble ponderous prehistoric creatures trying to survive as stately homes declaring "open house" or museums, or otherwise blend in in the form of either a hotel or a boarding school. Their architectural quality and the extent of their modernisation conditions different modes of survival. Their immense integrating property enhanced by their cultural, historical and intellectual standing echoes their highly suggestive and transportive functioning as literary motifs, enabling various ruminations about the nature and quality of time.

The struggle of the country house mirrors the strife of humans in general, whose true centre of dwelling remains to be searched for and repeatedly found in diverse variations and translations only to be lost anew. Highly elusive, the centre remains hidden, revealing itself now and then by means of daydreaming, poems or existing places. When Martin Heidegger addressed a lecture hall full of architects whose main task was to find an impulse to continue the struggle of rebuilding Germany after the Second World War during his lecture "Building Dwelling Thinking", he asked them to reflect on the "plight of dwelling". This plight, as may be observed in *Howards End, The Sea, The Sea, The Glass Room, The Stranger's Child, The Little Stranger*, or *The Uninvited Guests*, does not reside in the housing shortage or corruption of any kind, but in the fact that humans have to incessantly learn to dwell, since the moment one's feels at home, the centre withdraws from his or her grasp. Human homelessness seems to be conditioned by the fact that they cannot dwell without being aware of their inability to do so and without even considering it as a task worth any effort. Nevertheless, the moment humans face and acknowledge their homelessness, its terror becomes eliminated and, what is more, "rightly considered and kept well in mind, it is the sole summons that calls mortals into their dwelling" (Heidegger, *Poetry, Language, Thought*, 159).

5. Conclusion: The Country House Revisited

I have always loved building, holding it to be not only the highest achievement of man but one in which, at the moment of consummation, things were mostly clearly taken out of his hands and perfected, without his intention, by other means, and I regarded men as something much less than the buildings they made and inhabited, as mere lodgers and short-term sub-lessees of small importance in the long, fruitful life of their homes.
(Waugh, *Brideshead Revisited*, 260)

The popularity of the country house, a phenomenon deeply rooted within the English tradition, has waxed and waned in the twentieth century. The depth of its involvement in English society is evident in the broad array of contexts of its possible interpretations explored in this monograph. Be it a stately home, a manor house, or an ancient farm, what is decisive in terms of the classification of the country house is its setting in the countryside. Otherwise, all its building blocks are prone to evolution and change, be it its size, its age or its connection with the aristocracy. With the process of diversification having been initiated in the nineteenth century, what is considered to be a country house nowadays might be an ancient converted farm, a Neo-Gothic Victorian eyesore, or the grand residence of a nouveau riche entrepreneur or celebrity. Its public image travels back and forth between being an admired incarnation of the contemporary or past national ethos to a rejection of and hostility toward its social and spatial exclusivity.

In terms of literature, the complexity of both the nature of and approaches towards the country house furnishes its representation with a diverse subject matter. What might nevertheless be regarded as their constitutive element is their embrace of certain aspects of a communal paradigm. A sense of community as regards the country house has always played a key role in its literary conception. From the earliest examples of country house poems, to the thematic variety covered by twentieth and twenty-first century portrayals, the country house has always involved a strong sense of social, cultural, geographic or historical belonging. Country house poems promoted an idealised form of community life. They celebrated a somewhat rigidly stipulated, nevertheless happily accepted social hierarchy, where each and every member understood his or her position and the importance of its maintenance for the functioning of the community of the country house. Echoes of the communal theme can be observed in country house fiction of the twentieth and twenty-first centuries, whether establishing, re-establishing, loosening or severing ties with community. From this point of view, *Howards End* might be interpreted as a story of outcasts, the Schlegels, struggling to connect. The establishment of ties with the wider contemporary society is the backbone of *The Uninvited Guests*. The Torringtons mysteriously solve all their troubles by providing those in need, the ghosts of the dead passengers who were the victims of a nearby railway accident, with food, comfort and heartfelt sympathy. Unsuccessful attempts to detach oneself from one's community, only to realise that it is impossible, as can be observed on the example of Charles Arrowby's trial in *The Sea, The Sea*, might be also viewed as a variation on the theme of belonging. What is more, seeing the individual fictional works from the perspective of their relation to other works and in terms of historical, cultural, political, economic, and physical circumstances, as well as architectural development, also emphasises their relationship to community.

Even the setting of the house in the countryside, or at least where the countryside used to be, which is obviously an important formative influence on country house literature, mirrors the communal perspective. The country is typically contrasted to the city and this dialectical experience is perceived differently by various architectural, ethical, and literary critical approaches, some of which are introduced in this work, their conclusions always highlighting the vital importance and value of a sense of community and belonging to a larger whole. This opinion echoes one of the major preoccupations of contemporary architecture. Karsten Harries identifies problems of dwelling as ethical problems, not architectural ones. A building makes a proposition about the future, which obviously never fully matches what happens. According to Rowan Moore, it has to combine decisiveness with an openness to all eventualities, "[f]or if buildings are obviously and literally built by their builders, by their contractors, architects, consultants, and clients who come together before they are there, they are also built by their users, in the way they inhabit them, and in the imaginations and experiences of the people who experience them, from owners and tenants to passers-by" (Moore, 380–1). The nature of residing therefore determines whether it truly embodies authentic existence. Nonetheless, the increasing reluctance of the population to commit themselves to something larger than their own selves imposes a threat to its traditional meaning. However, in order to live a meaningful life and face existential anxiety, and to dwell in this sense, Harries proposes that we "recognize ourselves as parts of a larger ongoing community. Such community in turns depends on certain shared values; and the inevitably precarious and changing authority of such humanly established values must be supported by our evolving and often warring desires and affects, as mediated and structured by society and reason" (Harries, 363). This understanding of Heidegger's conception of dwelling requires architecture which is built upon the premise of our incompleteness and our genuine need for concrete community as well as upon the universal demands of reason.

The first interpretative part of the book analyses poetic parallels between E. M. Forster's novel, *Howards End*, and Iris Murdoch's novel, *The Sea, The Sea,* in order to delineate the scale of the variation of the canonical form of English country house fiction as seen from physical, architectural, urbanist and ecological perspectives. The depiction of the country house in the novels is a far cry from the idealised, mythicising form it acquired in the country house poem, a distinctive, if minor, poetic genre of the seventeenth and eighteenth centuries, where it symbolised the existence and structuring of entirely orderly relations between the aristocracy and their tenants. Since the beginning of the twentieth century, the stately home has become a perishing, crumbling phenomenon, struggling to survive and ideally to find a fresh identity and meaning in a world in which its aristocratic roots alone cannot justify its existence or shield it from the continuous disintegration typical of emptied shells, pure relics from the past. This endeavour and the processes it entails triggered a widening of the spectrum of the types of settlement the country house might stand for and consequently inspired numerous literary portrayals. No longer confined to the realm of stately homes and manor houses, the concept of the country house has embraced all kinds of dwellings, ranging from old, converted, gentrified farms and cottages to mediocre, shabby sea-side villas.

Both Forster and Murdoch were keen observers of the processes involved in the formation, growth, definition and re-definition of identity, both national and individual. Their insights into the countryside and the country house and their implications regarding physical and spiritual belonging, cultural heritage and continuity, provide their novels with topicality and offer surprising observations of the social and intellectual significance of changing, diverse perceptions of the countryside. The thematic connection between *Howards End* and *The Sea, The Sea* is intensified by their post-pastoral qualities and their focus on the quest for authenticity, including compromises stemming from the inevitable failure of any idealised or definitive solution to the fundamental existential struggle. This endeavour is mirrored in the circular character permeating all aspects of the novels, from imagery and motifs to the overall arrangement of the plot and its philosophical interpretation. Besides echoing the major social, cultural and ecological concerns of their individual periods, these novels vigorously examine timeless issues such as the nature of dwelling, the extent of the influence of a social class on the treatment of environmental issues, unfulfilled desire for the pastoral and the fruitless search for eternal summer with its promise of spiritual and physical regeneration if not rebirth. Seen from the last mentioned perspective, these two works are marked as examples of "summer house fiction", whose constitutive elements, such as the house being perceived as a retreat, its cyclical character, class exclusivity and poetics stemming from the perception of summer as a short, limited period, they develop. The monograph stresses that both novels mirror the wide-ranging and longstanding debate that engages with diverse variables of the equation comprising technological progress, undisturbed nature and the intensity of human involvement.

The great variety of subject matter in both novels might easily have resulted in a melange of pompous moralising had they not featured two houses, namely Howards End and Shruff End, whose symbolism anchors the narration while adding to the thematic richness of both works. Operating on both metaphorical and literal levels, the houses in question provide a solid foundation for the analysis of the texts. *Howards End* emphasises the animate nature of the house, which is characteristic of Modernism, stressing its irreplaceable position in human life, whose attributes it partially adopts. Shruff End also displays some human qualities, malice in particular. Its overall character, nevertheless, approximates the Gothic, with supernatural elements and a blurred division between reality and nightmares. Some of the traits of these two houses, namely their seclusion, exclusivity, splendour, or at least broken promises of all these qualities, connect them with summer house fiction whose universal appeal means it is not limited to a particular geographical location, e.g.

such fictional houses are to be observed in works of American, Irish or French provenance.

There is one common feature in all of the studied novels, and that is the class of the owners of the fictional places. As the country house in the twentieth century is no longer necessarily a stately home, neither is the typical owner a budding capitalist or prosperous aristocrat. The privilege of ownership has been shifted into the hands of the middle classes. Forster sees the future of England in Howards End and its upper-middle-class liberal inhabitants; the house is to provide them with roots, establish their continuity with previous and following generations, secure authenticity and distil and transmit the essence of the English land. In the case of Murdoch's Shruff End, class does not play such a prominent part, though the characters and their aspirations are markedly middle-class.

These perspectives form the summit of the thematic connections between *Howards End* and *The Sea, The Sea*. Nevertheless, both novels are far from promoting a pre-ordered set of middle-class ideas. They rather focus on the search for authentic human existence and individual, social, national and intellectual identities, the fear of a loss of spirituality and its replacement by growing materialism or the introduction of populist, instantaneous solutions in the form of shallow attempts to attain spirituality via the cult of the land or ersatz Buddhism. This existential dimension is reflected in the lack of finality and definitiveness of the plot, echoed by the circular character of time which permeates the plot construction, as well as the prevalent circular imagery, which in both cases echoes the true nature of dwelling.

An enquiry into country house fiction at the beginning of the twenty-first century, revisiting its original residence, the stately home, is made in the second half of the interpretative part of the work, which is focused on affinities between Alan Hollinghurst's novel, *The Stranger's Child,* and its literary predecessors and contemporaries, such as Ian McEwan's metafictional pun, *Atonement,* Sarah Waters' variation on the Gothic novel, *The Little Stranger*, and Sadie Jones's surrealist adaptation of the Edwardian comedy of manners, *The Uninvited Guests*. As is illustrated in this section, all of these works explore the highly poetic, atmospheric universe of decaying country estates, which encapsulate the new historical role of their owners. Their desperate struggle to maintain their houses and their social position is reflective of the paradoxical nature of the former grandness of the places, which, both literally and metaphorically, becomes the chief obstruction to their successful survival.

The ramshackle character of buildings on the verge of extinction, the tragic dimension of this *götterdämmerung* and the growing pains of the newly established social order supply fertile soil for the distinctive poetics of various artistic explorations of the theme. The chosen literary portrayals appear to share a similar outset: the narrator tends to play the part of a grateful outsider who sympathetically observes the gradual dereliction of a formerly grand family and its equally grand and obscenely high-maintenance seat, frequently identifying with it more than its legitimate owners do. The failing patriarchal order is metaphorically translated into a ludicrous hysteria or a lack of certain rituals, as well as into indifferent, or otherwise incapable, absent, missing, crippled, dying or dead heirs. It is the death of the first child that marks and dictates the development of the story in *The Little Stranger* as well as in *The Stranger's Child,* which respectively become haunted with the spectres and shadows of the past, and obsessed with the unattainability of the past and having to face the inevitable blurring of its images. Accordingly, *The Little Stranger* is imbued with the spirit of the Gothic novel, and *The Uninvited Guests* is a twisted ghost story. *The Stranger's Child* transforms into a thrilling detective inquest into the circumstances and events surrounding the creation of a legendary poem and the deliciously romantic life of its prematurely dead author, Cecil Valance, with each of his biographers heavily projecting their own agendas and insecurities into their interpretations. Hence, all the works discussed might be perceived as depictions of attempts to structure chaos and find orientation and ways to reintegrate individual members, dead or alive, into their families, and their families into their residences and consequently into society. The disintegrating institution of the country house generates portrayals which might be labelled as post-pastoral meditations on the loss and replacement of the social hierarchy, such as is illustrated on the example of *The Stranger's Child*, or which verge on being sadistic depictions of the incapability of the former ruling classes to integrate within the new order, as in *The Little Stranger*.

Architecturally, the houses are often Georgian red-brick buildings or sandstone English Baroque, but most prominently they are faux-Gothic Victorian eyesores on the verge of collapse, sale or insensitive transformation into a visitor attraction, hotel or golf club. From the point of view of aesthetics, the novelists either sentimentally exaggerate the beauty and nobility of the places or, on the contrary, denigrate their prestige by acknowledging their thoroughgoing ugliness. An example of the denigration of prestige is Corley Court, the country house of the Valance family in *The Stranger's Child*, which occupies a comparatively short middle-section of the novel, with the story opening and closing with an evocation of summer and autumn in the suburbs. The two acres of the suburban villa of the Sawles also inspired Cecil Valance's iconic poem, his ode to Englishness, not Corley Court. The size of Two Acres is reminiscent of Forster's Howards End, and its location in the suburbs of London echoes and further develops the new conception of the country house and also reinforces the pre-eminence of the suburb in contemporary spatial poetics.

Given the architectural development during the period in which many examples of country house fiction were set, i.e. the first half of the twentieth century, it comes as a surprise that it avoids or neglects the contemporary dominating architectural force of the Modern movement. The absence of any considerable employment of this architectural style by the occupants of the country houses and its subsequent absence in the works of the country house chroniclers might be explained on the grounds of the relative scarcity of Modernist buildings in England. There is a multitude of reasons why England, despite its immense importance for the development of this style, did not fully embrace it. The first reason for this lack of popularity was the soaring cost of new building techniques and materials, whose employment was stipulated by the modernist architects. Secondly, Modernism's insistence on the severing of ties with the past and its traditions, its focus on the future and swift progress and its denigration of a nostalgic clinging to traditions did not appeal to a conservative general public or the tradition-focused owners of country houses.

Besides the parallels between the conceptions of spatial poetics in the novels in question, the thematic connection between them is enhanced by their prominent intertextuality, by means of which they establish a dialogue with both their literary predecessors and contemporaries. Textually and thematically, these novels develop a dense, intricate intertextual web of allusions, ranging from Shakespeare to Edgar Allan Poe, from Henry James to E. M. Forster or Evelyn Waugh. From the spatial and temporal points of view, the narrations are set in different time periods, be it the 1910s, 1930s, 1940s, 1970s, 2000 or the present time, often featuring multiple timelines within a single novel, with the houses often functioning like capsules, their situation in the countryside even enhancing the separation of their inhabitants from the outside world and the ordinary course of time, which is frequently projected into the theatrical nature of the narration (*The Uninvited Guests* is concluded with the word "CURTAIN" (*UG*, 354). Nevertheless, the contrast between the original conception of the place and its current dereliction inspires an inquiry into the realm of individual time levels and their harmonious coexistence or their replacing of one another with a systematic inexorability.

The country house, owing to its primary quality of being a house, is a highly powerful and evocative source of concentrating properties. Exuding these integrating qualities, the house constitutes "a body of images that give mankind proofs or illusions of stability" (Bachelard, 17) and successfully faces, and, occasionally, even defies temporal constraints. Accordingly, the literary point of view analysed in this volume amplifies this conception and provides a plethora of memorable portrayals of these properties in country house fiction. At the same time, a discussion of the depiction of the country house in twentieth and twenty-first century English literature necessarily involves an excursion into the realm of architecture as buildings are either designed and newly built, or the heritage of previous generations undergoes a slight or a thorough reconstruction, a sensitive or a mutilating renovation. The number and importance of such transformations, the owners' involvement and the striking presence or similarly conspicuous absence of a profound relationship to the house have transformed it into a versatile vehicle for commentary on global social, cultural, political and ecological matters. Its close connection with the land, soil, history and community therefore accentuates its universal existential dimension, which has established its position within the modern literary canon and anticipates a greater volume of enquiry into its complex nature in the future.

Works Cited

Ackroyd, Peter. *Hawksmoor*. London: Penguin Books, 2010.

Bachelard, Gaston. *The Poetics of Space*. Boston: Beacon Press, 1994.

Ballard, James Graham. *High-Rise*. London: 4th Estate, 2016.

Blaser, Werner. *Mies van der Rohe*. London: Thames and Hudson Ltd, 1972.

Bowen, Elizabeth. *Bowen Court &Seven Winters*. London: Vintage Books, 1999.

—.*The Hotel*. Harmondsworth: Penguin Books, 1943.

—. *The House in Paris*. New York: Knopf, 1936.

—. *The Last September*. London: Penguin Books, 1943.

Bradbury, Malcolm. *The Atlas of Literature*. London: De Agostini Editions Griffin House, 1996.

—. *The Modern British Novel*. London: Penguin Books, 1994.

Bryson, Bill. *At Home. A Short History of Private Life*. London: Random House, 2010.

Camus, Albert. *A Happy Death*. Translated by Richard Howard, New York: Vintage Books, 1973.

Case, Thomas. "Preface." In Francis Bacon. *The Advancement of Learning and The New Atlantis*. London: Oxford University Press, 1913.

Černá, Iveta, and Dagmar Černoušková. *Tugendhat – Ludwig Mies van der Rohe's Commission in Brno*. Brno: Brno City Museum, 2011.

Chalupský, Petr. "Like a Furnace Burning and Turning" – London in Peter Ackroyd's *The Great Fire of London*." *World Journal of English Language* 3, no. 1, 2013, pp. 11–22.

—. *The Postmodern City of Dreadful Night. The Image of the City in the Works of Martin Amis and Ian McEwan*. Saarbrücken: VDM Verlag Dr. Müller, 2009.

—. "The Urban Pastoral: Hybridisations in Jim Crace's Arcadia." Litteraria Pragensia 20, no. 40, 2010, pp. 38–54.

—. "Valuable and Vulnerable – The City in Ian McEwan's *Enduring Love* and *Saturday*." *Prague Journal of English Studies* 1, no. 1, 2010, pp. 25–41.

Cook, Olive. *The English Country House, an Art and a Way of Life*. London: Thames and Hudson, 1974.

Day, Christopher. *Spirit&Place. Healing Our Environment*. London: Routledge, 2002.

De Botton, Alain. *The Architecture of Happiness*. London: Penguin Books, 2007.

De Certeau, Michel. *The Practice of Everyday Life*. Berkeley: University of California Press, 1984.

DeLillo, Don. *The Body Artist*. London: Picador, 2011.

De Singly, François. "Have a Room of One's Own. On Relation between Space and Personal Identity." *Sociální studia* 4, 2009, pp. 13–22. Fakulta sociálních studií Masarykovy university.

Dimbleby, David. *How We Built Britain*. London: Bloomsbury Publishing, 2007.

Farrell, James Gordon. *Troubles*. London: Fontana Paperbacks, Flamingo, 1984.

Eliot, Thomas Stearns. *Four Quartets*. London: Faber and Faber, 1963.

Fierro, Annette. *The Glass State: The Technology of the Spectacle, Paris, 1918–1998*. Cambridge: The MIT Press, 2003.

Flueckiger, Urs Peter. *How Much House? Thoreau, Le Corbusier and the Sustainable Cabin*. Basel: Birkhaüser, 2016.

Ford, Maddox Ford. *Parade's End*. London: Campbell, 1992.

Forster, Edward Morgan. *Collected Short Stories*. London: Penguin Books, 1987.

—. *Howards End*. With an Introduction and Notes by David Lodge, London: Penguin Books, 2000.

—. *Maurice*. Edited by P. N. Furbank, with an Introduction and Notes by David Leavitt, London: Penguin Books, 2005.

—. *A Passage to India*. Edited by Oliver Stallybrass, with an Introduction by Pankaj Mishra, London: Penguin Books, 2005.

—. *A Room with a View*. With an Introduction and Notes by Malcolm Bradbury, London: Penguin Books, 2000.

—. *Two Cheers for Democracy*. 1951. London: Penguin Books, 1965.

—. *Where Angels Fear to Tread*. Edited with Notes by Oliver Stallybrass, with an Introduction by Ruth Padel, London, Penguin Books, 2007.

Foucault, Michel. *Discipline and Punish: the Birth of the Prison*. Translated by Alan Sheridan, New York: Random House, 1979.

—. "Of Other Spaces." *Diacritics* 16, no. 1, 1986, pp. 22–27.

Fowles, John. *The Collector*. 1963. London: Vintage, 2004.

Frampton, Kenneth. *Modern Architecture. A Critical History*. London: Thames and Hudson, 1994.

Franková, Milada. *Human Relationships in the Novels of Iris Murdoch*. Brno: Masarykova Univerzita, 1995.

Fransman, Karrie. *The House that Groaned*. London: Square Peg, 2012.

Galsworthy, John. *The Country House*. London: William Heinemann Ltd., 1934.

—. *The Forsyte Saga. Volume 1*. London: Penguin Books, 2001.

Gifford, Terry. *Pastoral*. London: Routledge, 1999.

Girouard, Mark. *A Country House Companion*. New Haven: Yale University Press, 1987.

Glendinning, Victoria. Introduction. *All Passion Spent*, by Vita Sackville-West, London: Virago Press, 1986, pp. vii–xxvii.

Grahame, Kenneth. *The Wind in the Willows*. New York: Heritage Press, 1940.

Harding, Thomas. *The House by the Lake*. London: Penguin Random House, 2015.

Harries, Karsten. *The Ethical Function of Architecture*. Cambridge: The MIT Press, 1997.

—. "Is Stone Today 'More Stone than it Used to Be'? *Matter, meaning and Mind in Architecture*." Edited by Pirkko Tuukkanen. *Matter and Mind in Architecture*. 15–17 August 1997, Jyväskylä, The Alvar Aalto Foundation, 2000, pp. 10–24.

Hart, Vaughan. *Sir John Vanbrugh: Storyteller in Stone*. New Haven: Yale University Press, 2008.

Hartley, Leslie Poles. *The Go-Between*. London: Penguin Books, 1999.

Head, Dominic. *Modern British Fiction, 1950–2000*. Cambridge: Cambridge University Press, 2002.

Heidegger, Martin. *Basic Writings*. London: Routledge, 2011.

—. *Poetry, Language, Thought*. New York: Perennial Classics, 2001.

Hilský, Martin. *Shakespeare a jeviště svět*. [Shakespare and the World as Stage.] Prague: Academia, 2010.

Hodrová, Daniela. *Poetika míst. Kapitoly z literární tematologie*. [The Poetics of Places, Chapters from Literary Thematology. *The Poetics of Places, Chapters from Literary Thematology*.] Prague: H&H, 1997.

—. "Příbytek." ["An Abode".] In *Citlivé město. Eseje z Mytopoetiky*. [Sensitive City: Essays from Mythopoetics.] Prague: Akropolis, 2006.

Holl, David. *Parallax*. Princeton: Princeton Architectural Press, 2000.

Hollinghurst, Alan. *The Line of Beauty*. London: Picador, 2005.

—. *The Stranger's Child*. London: Picador, 2011.

Howard, Elizabeth Jane. *The Light Years*. London: Pan Books, 1991.

Ibsen, Henrik. *The Master Builder*. Whitefish, Montana: Kessinger Publishing, 2010.

Ishiguro, Kazuo. *Never Let Me Go*. London: Faber and Faber, 2006.

—. *The Remains of the Day*. London: Faber and Faber, 1993.

James, Henry. *English Hours. A Portrait of a Country*. New York: Tauris Parke Paperack, 2011.

—. *The Portrait of a Lady*. 1881. Ware: Wordsworth Edition, 1996.

Jones, Sadie. *The Uninvited Guests*. London: Vintage, 2013.

Kelsall, Malcom. *The Great Good Place: The Country House and English Literature.* New York: Columbia University Press, 1993.

Klein, Zach. *Cabin Porn.* Penguin Books, 2016.

Koch, Hermann. *Summer House with Swimming Pool.* London: Hogarth, 2015.

Kreilkamp, Vera. *The Anglo-Irish Novel and the Big House.* New York: Syracuse University Press, 1998.

Lamprecht, Barbara. *Richard Neutra. Survival through Design.* Köln: Taschen, 2009.

Le Corbusier. *Towards a New Architecture.* London: The Architectural Press, 1976.

Lessing, Doris. "To Room Nineteen." In *The Norton Anthology of Short Fiction.* Edited by R. V. Cassill. New York: W. W. Norton &Company, 1981, pp. 875–903.

Liddell, Robert. "Galsworthy Contrasted with Henry James." *A Treatise on the Novel.* London: Jonathan Cape, 1955, pp. 125–6.

Lively, Penelope. *City of the Mind.* London: Penguin Books, 1992.

Lodge, David. Introduction. *Howards End*, by E. M. Forster, London: Penguin Books, 2000, pp. vii–xxviii.

Lomax, Eric. *The Railway Man : A POW's Searing Account of War, Brutality and Forgiveness.* New York: Norton, 1995.

Loos, Adolph. "Ornament and Crime." *Ornament and Crime.* Riverside, CA: Ariadne Press, 1997, pp. 19–24.

Lucas, John. "The Sunlight on the Garden." *Seeing Double, Revisioning Edwardian and Modernist Literature.* Edited by C. M. Kaplan, A. B. Simpson, London: Macmilan Press, 1996, pp. 59–75.

Máchalová, Jana. *Příběhy slavných italských vil.* [The Stories of Famous Italian Villas.] With an Introduction by Dalibor Veselý. Prague: KANT, 2010.

Mandler, Peter. *The Fall and Rise of the Stately Home.* New Haven & London: Yale University Press, 1997.

Matuchová, Klára. "The Role of Dialogic Organisation in Reflexive Construals of Identity in Selected Fiction Texts." *Prague Journal of English Studies* 2, no. 1, 2013, pp. 101–118.

Mawer, Simon. *The Glass Room.* London: Little, Brown, 2009.

McCormick, Frank. *Sir John Vanbrugh: The Playwright as Architect.* University Park: Pennsylvania State University Press, 1991.

McEwan, Ian. *Amsterdam.* 1998. London: Vintage Books, 1999.

—. *Atonement.* London: Vintage Books, 2002.

McKean, John. *Pioneering British High-Tech (Architecture 3s).* London: Phaidon Press, 1999.

Miller, Sue. *The Arsonist.* London: Vintage, 2014.

Moore, Rowan. *Why We Built.* London: Picador, 2012.

Montrose, Louis. "Renaissance Literary Studies and the Subject of History." *English Literary Renaissance* 16, no. 1, 1986, pp. 5–12.

Murdoch, Iris. *The Sea, The Sea*. London: Vintage, 1999.

Naipaul, Vidiadhar Surajprasad. *A House for Mr Biswas*. London: Penguin Books, 1992.

Pallasmaa, Juhani. *The Eyes of the Skin: Architecture and the Senses*. Chichester: Wiley, 2012.

Neumeyer, Fritz. *The Artless World: Mies van der Rohe on the Building Art*. The MIT Press, 1994.

Patočka, Jan. "Fifth Essay: Is technological Civilization Decadent, and Why?" *Heretical Essays in the Philosophy of History*. Translated by Erazim Kohák. Edited by James Dodd. Chicago and La Salle, Illinois: Open Court Publishing Company, 1996, pp. 95–118.

Pevsner, Nikolaus. *The Englishness of English Art*. London: Penguin Books, 1984.

—. *The Sources of Modern Architecture and Design*. London: Thames and Hudson, 1968.

Poe, Edgar Alan. *The Fall of the House of Usher and Other Stories*. London: Penguin Books, 2011.

Rand, Ayn. *The Fountainhead*. 1943. With an Introduction by the Author. New York: Signet, 2009.

Sackville-West, Vita. *All Passion Spent*. With an Introduction by Victoria Glendinning, London: Virago Press, 1986.

Sage, Lorna. *Women in the House of Fiction: Post-war Women Novelists*. London: Macmillan, 1992.

Saggini, Francesca, and Anna Enrichetta Soccio, editors. *The House of Fiction as the House of Life: Representations of the House from Richardson to Woolf*. Newcastle upon Tyne: Cambridge Scholars Publishing, 2012.

Shakespeare, William. *Much Ado about Nothing*. London: Methuen Drama, 2006.

—. *Shakespeare's Sonnets*. London : Thomson Learning, 2007.

Sharr, Adam. *Heidegger's Hut*. Cambridge, The MIT Press, 2006.

—. *Heidegger for Architects*. New York: Routeledge, 2007.

Spurr, David. *Architecture and Modern Literature*. Ann Arbor: The University of Michigan Press, 2012.

Steffens, Jo (ed.) *Unpacking my Library: Architects and Their Books (Unpacking Series)*. New Haven: Yale University Press, 2009.

Stone, Wilfred. "*Howards End*: Red-bloods and Mollycoddles." *The Cave and the Mountain, A Study of E. M. Foster*. Stanford: Stanford University Press, 1966, pp. 234–275.

—. "Forster, the Environmentalist." *Seeing Double, Revisioning Edwardian and Modernist Literature*. Editors C. M. Kaplan and A. B. Simpson, London: Macmilan Press, 1996, pp. 174–192.

Stoppard, Tom. *The Invention of Love*. London: Faber and Faber, 1998.

Straub, Emma. *The Vacationers*. New York: Riverhead Books, 2014.

Tichá, Jana (ed.) *Architektura: tělo nebo obraz?* [Architecture: A Body or an Image?] Prague: Zlatý řez, 2009.

Thoreau, Henry David. *Walden and Resistance to Civil Government: Authoritative Texts, Thoreau's Journal, Reviews and Essays in Criticism*. Edited by William Rossi, New York: Norton, 1991.

Topolovská, Tereza. "On the Analogy between the Language of Architecture and Language of Literary Work: The Role of Conception of Architecture in Generating the Poetics of *The Glass Room*." *Filologické studie*. Prague: Charles University in Prague, Karolinum, 2013, pp. 15–31.

—. "Days of Peculiar Splendour: *Howards End* and *The Sea, The Sea* in the Context of Summer House Fiction." *English Language and Literature Studies* 5, no. 3, Toronto: Canadian Center of Science and Education, 2015, pp. 1–12.

—. "*The Glass Room*: Architecture as a Poetic Emotion". *Prague Journal of English Studies* 2, no. 1, 2013, pp. 65–79.

—. "In Search of a House with a View: The Conception of Dwelling in E. M. Forster's *Howards End* and Iris Murdoch's *The Sea, The Sea*." *International Journal of Applied Linguistics and English Literature* 5, no. 4. Melbourne: Australian International Academic Centre, 2016, pp. 189–199.

Traversi, Derek. *T. S. Eliot: The Longer Poems*. New York: Hartcourt Brace Jovanovich, 1976.

Troy, Charlotte (ed.). *Home Sweet Home. 102. An Anthology*. London: C. T. Editions, 2004.

Veselý, Dalibor. "Vila mezi Snem a Utopií." ["A Villa between a Dream and Utopia."] Introduction. In *Příběhy slavných italských vil.* [The Stories of Famous Italian Villas.] Edited by Jana Máchalová, Ivan Chvatík, Prague: KANT, 2010, pp. 26–31.

Vidler, Anthony. *Warped Space. Art, Architecture, and Anxiety in Modern Culture*. Cambridge, MA – London: The MIT Press, 2001.

Walsh, Helen. *The Lemon Groove*. London: Tinder Press, 2014.

Walzer, Michael. "Liberalism and the Art of Separation." *Political Theory* 12, no. 3, August 1984, pp. 315–330.

Waters, Sarah. *The Little Stranger*. London: Virago Press, 2010.

—. *The Night Watch*. London: Virago Press, 2006.

—. *The Paying Guests*. London: Virago Press, 2015.

Waugh, Evelyn. *Brideshead Revisited*. New York: Back Bay Books, 2008.

—. *A Handful of Dust*. London: Penguin Books, 2000.

—. *Vile Bodies*. London: Penguin Books, 1938.

Wells, Herbert George. *Tono-Bungay*. London: Penguin Books, 2009.

White, Hayden. *Tropics of Discourse: Essays in Cultural Criticism*. Baltimore and London: John Hopkins University Press, 1978.

Williams, Raymond. *The Country and the City*. London: The Hoghart Press, 1993.

Wilk, Christopher (ed.). *Modernism. Designing a New World*. London: V&A Publishing, 2007.

Wodehouse, Pelham Grenville. *The Girl on the Boat*. LaVergne, TN: Aegypan, 2009.

—. *Young Men in Spats*. London: Herbert Jenkins, 1957.

Woolf, Virginia. *Contemporary Writers*. London : Hogarth Press, 1965.

—. *A Haunted House: The Complete Shorter Fiction*. Edited by Susan Dick, with an Introduction by Helen Simpson. London: Vintage Books, 2003.

—. *Orlando: A Biography*. London: Penguin Books, 2006.

—. *A Room of One's Own*. London: Penguin Books, 2000.

Zimmerman, Claire. *Mies van der Rohe. The Structure of Space*. Köln: Taschen, 2009.

Lectures and Conference Papers

Hammer – Tugendhat, Daniela. "Das Haus Tugendhat und Seine Bewohner." Guest lecture. Prager Gäsprache organized by Das Österreichische Kulturforum Prag, 1 October 2012, Veranstaltungssaal des Tschechischen Kulturministeriums, Prague, Czech Republic.

Mawer, Simon. Book Signing. 17th May 2010, The Luxor Book Palace, Prague, Czech Republic.

Topolovská, Tereza. "As a Ship in the Night: On the Productivity of the Metaphor of a Ship in Modern British fiction." Conference presentation. The 10th Brno Conference of English, American and Canadian Studies, 6 February 2015, Brno, Czech Republic.

Internet Sources

Brooke, Rupert. "The Soldier." 1914. *Poetryfoundation.org*. Poetry Foundation, www.poetryfoundation.org/poetrymagazine/poems/detail/13076. Accessed 12 December 2015.

Crown, Sarah. "A Life in Books – Simon Mawer." The Guardian, 3 October 2009, www.theguardian.com/culture/2009/oct/03/simon-mawer-life-in-books. Accessed 1 November 2010.

Day, Elizabeth. "Elizabeth Jane Howard: 'I'm 90. Writing is What Gets Me up in the Morning.'" *The Observer*, 7 April 2013. https://www.theguardian.com /books/2013/apr/07/elizabeth-jane-howard-novelist-cazalet. Accessed 29 July 2013.

Doward, Jamie. "England's Pastoral Symphony – A Celebration of the Country Garden." *The Guardian*, 10 January 2016. www.theguardian.com/lifeandstyle/2016/jan/10/year-of-english-garden-capability-brown-bake-off. Accessed 10 January 2016.

Elvy, Michelle. "Interview with Keri Hulme." *Flash Frontier*, 22 Nov. 2012. www.flash-frontier.com/2012/11/22/interview-with-keri-hulme/. Accessed 10 October 2014.

Higgins, Bernadette. "Czech History Through a Glass Darkly." Radio Prague. *Czech Books*, 22 Nov. 2009. www.radio.cz/en/section/books/czech-history-through-a-glass-darkly. Accessed 14 March 2010.

"Ian McEwan." *The Guardian*, 22 July 2008. www.theguardian.com/books/2008/jun/12/ian.mcewan. Accessed 11 August 2012.

James, Henry. "The Great Good Place." 1909. *State University of New York*, 2014. www2.newpaltz.edu/~hathawar/goodplace.html. Accessed 23 July 2014.

Jonson, Ben. "To Penshurst." 1616. *Poetryfoundation.org*, 2014. www.poetryfoundation.org/poems-and-poets/poems/detail/50674. Accessed 14 November 2014.

Kunzru, Hari. "*The Stranger's Child* by Alan Hollinghurst." The Observer, 25 June 2011. www.theguardian.com/books/2011/jun/17/strangers-child-alan-hollinghurst-review. Accessed 28 March 2012.

Mawer, Simon. "Science in Literature." 2005. Simonmawer.com. www.simonmawer.com/ScienceandLiterature.htm. Accessed 6 November 2012.

—. "Theo van Doesburg: Forgotten artist of the Avant Garde." *The Guardian*, 23 January 2010. www.theguardian.com/artanddesign/2010/jan/23/theo-van-doesburg-avant-garde-tate. Accessed 1 December 2010.

Monbiot, George. "I Love Nature. For this I am Called Bourgeois, Romantic – even Fascist." *The Guardian*. 8 July 2013. www.theguardian.com/commentisfree/2013/jul/08/philistinism-nature-scientific-ignorance-money. Accessed 16 July 2013.

Moss, Stephen. "Alan Hollinghurst's: Sex on the Brain." *The Guardian*. 18 June 2011. www.theguardian.com/books/2011/jun/18/alan-hollinghurst-interview. Accessed 28 March 2012.

Poole, Steven. "Is Our Love of Nature Writing Bourgeois Escapism?" *The Guardian*, 6 July 2013. www.theguardian.com/books/2013/jul/06/nature-writing-revival. Accessed 16 July 2013.

—. "I Belong in a Field." *Stevenpoole.net*. 6 July 2013. stevenpoole.net/articles/i-belong-in-a-field/. Accessed 11 October 2014.

Purdon, James. "The Glass Room by Simon Mawer." *The Observer*. 25 April 2010. www.theguardian.com/books/2010/apr/25/the-glass-room-simon-mawer. Accessed 4 October 2010.

Robbins, Martin. "Class and the Countryside." *The Guardian*. 9 July 2013. www.theguardian.com/global/the-lay-scientist/2013/jul/09/1. Accessed 21 July 2013.

Sanders, Joel. "Curtain Wars. Architects, Decorators, and the Twentieth-century Domestic Interior." *Harvard Design Magazine*, Harvard University Graduate

School of Design, no. 16, S/S 2002. www.harvarddesignmagazine.org/issues/16/curtain-wars. Accessed 22 February 2012.

Sansom, Ian. "Design for Living." *The Guardian*. 24 Jan. 2009. www.theguardian.com/books/2009/jan/24/simon-mawer-the-glass-room. Accessed 1 November 2010.

Spatial Perspectives Conference. 2012. spatialperspectives.wordpress.com/. Accessed 28 December 2014.

Tait, Theo. "*The Stranger's Child* by Alan Hollinghurst, Review." *The Guardian*. 17 June 2011. www.theguardian.com/books/2011/jun/17/strangers-child-alan-hollinghurst-review. Accessed 28 March 2012.

Tennyson, Alfred Lord. "In Memorian A. H. H." 1849. *Bartleby*. 2015. www.bartleby.com/73/1135.html. Accessed 13 December 2015.

The Oxford Companion to New Zealand Literature. Eds. R. Robinson and N. Wattie. "Keri Hulme." *New Zealand Book Council*. www.bookcouncil.org.nz/writers/profiles/hulme,%20keri. Accessed 10 October 2014.

Vine, Richard. "Downton Abbey Review: The Glorious Fantasy of Britain Comes to an End." *The Guardian*. 26 December 2015. www.theguardian.com/tv-and-radio/2015/dec/26/downton-abbey-christmas-special-review-glorious-fantasy-britain-comes-to-an-end. Accessed 28 December 2015.

Visit England. www.visitengland.com. Accessed 27 December 2015.

Weldon, Fay. "Weekend." 1978. *Teachingenglish.org*, 2013, www.teachingenglish.org.uk/sites/teacheng/files/weekend_text_0.pdf. Accessed 12 August 2013.

Index